GHOSTS OF PRESIDENTS PAST

A RECKONING

TABLE OF CONTENTS

PREFACE

"Nothing discloses real character like the use of power. If you wish to know what a man really is, give him power."

Robert G Ingersoll wrote the above passage in his 1884 essay on Abraham Lincoln. By the nature of their position, presidents of the United States possess enormous power. How they exercise it reveals character, a topic visited throughout this work of historical fiction.

On the eve of my birthday two years ago, while watching a syndicated news broadcaster conduct an interview with a political commentator, I had an epiphany. About time, you say!

I decided to interview myself. How many presidents have I voted for? Ten. How many were Republicans? Six. Following the math, that leaves four Democrats. Not telling you who 'cause that's none of your business.

Evidently, I don't believe in a straight ticket. Voters who pull one simple lever or punch one button exclude the most talented and capable person to serve his or her city, county, state, and country. No political party holds a monopoly on all the best suited candidates. For example, members of the Lincoln Project, mostly Republicans, support Joe Biden, the Democratic candidate running for president. In the interest of the nation, they are reaching across the aisle. But surely, they will vote for other Republicans who share their values.

Then, just to be ornery, the interviewer brought up the incumbent in a succession of U.S. presidents. He wanted to know: What would my parents, my wife's parents, our aunts and uncles make of him? They too always voted for the character of the man, regardless of political affiliation. I think I can hear their answers from the cosmos.

I can also make an educated guess how my earlier ancestors dating back to the Revolutionary War might respond. Our family has served the country in almost every major war, including those in the Middle East.

Next, the interviewer threw me a harder ball. He asked could I imagine a fictional president whose behavior resembles the incumbent? Then he asked what might past presidents say to such a president? I wasn't sure. So, beginning with George Washington, I set out on a year's journey to get reacquainted with many of them. The research took me to lots of places, some new, quite peculiar, and even bizarre.

The result is this book, a hybrid of political satire and historical fiction, in which a series of ghosts of past presidents deliver a haunting message for Daniel Johnson Hands. The fictional President serves as a metaphor and inhabits a parallel universe in which he responds to similar, but not always identical, people and events as the incumbent.

President Truman believed that ghosts of past presidents occupied the White House. He even claimed to hear them walking up and down the hallways. Winston Churchill, Franklin Roosevelt, and Eleanor Roosevelt supposedly spotted Abraham Lincoln's ghost. Others have reported sightings as well. If one were to accept that the White House is haunted by spirits, real or imagined, then no doubt some of them would be displeased about the disturbances President Hands creates.

Even though we lack the wherewithal to march up to these presidential ghosts and ask them their opinion of President

Hands, we can speculate about their thoughts of his time and deeds in office. It seems imponderable that anyone in the history could mess up his presidency as much as Daniel Hands. Or, perhaps one already has?

Beginning with George Washington, notable ghosts and phantoms from the nineteenth, twentieth, and twenty-first centuries warn President Hands of the consequences of his ways. Each one reflects on his own greatness, confesses some regrets, and reveal the price paid in the afterlife.

There is a tendency for current generations, in particular those no longer in the prime of their youth, to think these are the worst of times. Such a pattern has existed through the ages.

I recall that when I was a younger, some of my relatives thought the country was speeding toward ruin under the Nixon and Carter administrations. Others disagreed. Then along came Reagan, who lifted the spirits of the nation. Today we can laugh about it. Whatever trials and tribulations we face today as a nation will pass. From the foundation onward, controversy, scandal, civil rights issues, and outright incompetency have haunted our nation's capital.

Is the country more divided today than ever before, or does it just seem that way? For many, the nation seems irrevocably fractured along political, social and ideological lines. Republican versus Democrat. Liberal versus conservative. Red versus blue. White versus people of color. Poor versus rich. Rural versus metro. Right-to-lifers versus Planned Parenthood. Walls versus no walls. And so on.

Joseph M. Pierre, Clinical Professor of Psychiatry and Biobehavioral Sciences at UCLA School of Medicine, asks "Why Has America Become So Divided?" He says It's hard to argue that that the nation is more divided now than, say, during the Civil War, or the turbulent civil unrest of the 1960s. Pierre submits that "many of us who feel that the nation has never been so split have only been politically conscious for a few decades. Therefore, we have a narrow timeline from which to compare." In *Ghosts of Presidents Past*, the reader gets a glimpse of a broader timeline. As Shakespeare wrote, "What's past is prologue."

Whether one agrees with the dialogue in each chapter, the author hopes the narrative prompts the reader to contemplate the best qualities past presidents possessed to unite and inspire the nation. Along the way, think about POTUS's (President of the United States) conduct in the novel.

The reader is also invited to reflect on the essence of Prime Minster Winston Churchill's famous 1946 Iron Curtain speech. At the invitation of President Harry Truman, it was delivered on the Westminster College campus, in Fulton, Missouri.

Born of British and American parents, Churchill said: "Let us preach what we practice, let us practice what we preach. The people of any country have the right, and should have the power by constitutional action, by free unfettered elections, with secret ballot, to choose or change the character or form of government under which they dwell; that freedom of speech and thought should reign; that courts of justice, independent of the executive, unbiased by any party, should administer laws which have received the broad assent of large majorities or are consecrated by time and custom. Here are the title deeds of freedom which should lie in every home."

And lest we become too jaded, George H.W. Bush reminded us in the winter of his years: "Politics remains a noble calling. Don't be turned off by the latest scandal or press pronouncement. Serving something greater than one's self is worth doing."

SHOULD YOU READ THIS BOOK?

*"The price good men and women pay for
indifference to public affairs is to be ruled
by evil men." (Plato 428–348 BC)*

Y ou should read this book if you believe in bi-partisanship
and that solutions to the nation's problems and challenges
internally and externally necessitate cooperation on both
sides of the aisle. You should read this book if you are tired of
political gridlock and grandstanding. You should read this book
if you possess an open, inquisitive mind. Crustaceans, please
don't bother.

ACKNOWLEDGMENTS

First, a word about my unsung "coauthor" Casper Magi Spotswood. Casper was the friendly cartoon ghostwriter who whispered in my ear as I worked on this composition; he was the catalyst for completing the work. Magi were wise men who looked to the future and spread hope. And Spotswood was the lieutenant governor of the colony of Virginia who decided enough was enough. In 1718 he disposed of Blackbeard, the notorious seafaring pirate who was rumored to be in cahoots with the governor of the colony of South Carolina.

A special thank you to my patriotic family, who provided guidance, constructive criticism, and solace in my labor to give President Daniel Hands a character. Also, my gratitude for Matthew Arkin's challenge to stretch my level of comfort as a writer and for Meghan Pinson and Rhonda Erb's editing to help make this work more digestible. My five beta readers were essential in fine tuning the story. I cannot thank them enough. This is the third book that Tod Gilpin has illustrated for me. His talents remain indispensable. As always, I remain appreciative to Julia Holofcener for permission to use her late husband Lawrence Holofcener's artwork; in this case, the crab in *Should You Read This Book?*

I have been fueled by all the twenty-first-century political extremists on the right and left, here and abroad, who have provided so much raw material for this book. Factions within the United States Congress, the executive office, the judiciary, and the press on the right and left deserve a thank-you. Who would have thought they'd cast the twenty-first century back to the 1930s—a time when the world was full of autocrats, dictators, tribalists, narrow-minded partisans, isolationists, and harmful religious and cultural biases? Life is stranger and often scarier than fiction.

Charles Dickens's *A Christmas Carol told a story* about a particular moment in English history. Dickens first thought he'd write a pamphlet called "An Appeal to the People of England on Behalf of the Poor Man's Child." Upon further thought, he decided to incorporate his opposition into a story with a main character of despicable complexity. What might have been a mere political attack and lecture became a story that audiences found powerful, compelling entertaining, and relevant to the time…a force for change.

In Jon Meacham's book *Soul of America: The Battle for Our Better Angels,* he observed that "extremists on either side look at politics not as an opportunity to optimize solutions to the country's opportunities and challenges but rather as total war, where no compromise can be granted." He pointed to Jane Addams, social activist and cowinner of the 1932 Nobel Peace Prize, who wrote that "if we grow contemptuous of our fellows and consciously limit our intercourse to certain kinds of people whom we have previously decided to respect, we not only tremendously circumscribe our range of life, but limit the scope of our ethics."

First Lady Eleanor Roosevelt mirrored Jane Addams's thoughts when she "offered a prescription to guard against tribal self-certitude." Roosevelt said, "It is not only important but mentally invigorating to discuss political matters with people whose opinions differ radically from one's own."

Meacham stated, "If Mrs. Roosevelt were writing today, she might put it this way: Don't let any single cable network or Twitter feed tell you what to think." He added, "wisdom generally comes from a free exchange of ideas and there can be no free exchange of ideas if everyone on your side already agrees with one another."

One of the major challenges of this book was the question of when to stop researching and writing. The template for President Daniel Hands continues on a daily and weekly basis to provide unparalleled, outrageous, bizarre and raw historical material. The resources listed in the Bibliography proved invaluable in casting his character.

INTRODUCTION

President Daniel Hands and his vice president, Poppy Warbucks, have isolated America from the historical footprints of some of their predecessors. The narcissistic president and conniving vice president possess neither compassion for the lower- and middle-income classes nor comprehension of their plight.

In this parallel universe, populism, nationalism, isolationism, territorial aggression, intolerance, economic and social decay, trade barriers, walls, racism, and anti-Semitism threaten once again to disrupt and destabilize nations at home and abroad. A massive migration wave and unheralded virus fuel global tensions.

Known to his adversaries as President Little Big Hands because of his huge hands and small stature, POTUS (President of the United States) grows ever more out of touch with the populace. With slight forethought to consequences, he's impulsive, heavy-handed in response to perceived opposition, superbly confident, egotistical to an extreme and delighted to impose his perverse biases on the American public and its institutions. He had never served in public office before his election.

Like POTUS, VP Warbucks hails from Louisiana, and both can trace their roots to old-line plantation families in the Mississippi Delta. They were fraternity brothers at the University of Mississippi and went to the same Louisiana prep school, which was heavily financed by their parents to assure graduation.

When Warbucks successfully ran for governor of Louisiana and then the US Senate, he had the full financial support of the Hands family's connections and business enterprises. Rumor has it that he bought the governorship and then sold the influence of his US Senate seat—along with his soul—to the highest bidders. Having put seven previous governors behind bars, Louisiana is surpassed only by Illinois as the state with the distinction of most incarcerated governors. Warbucks soon earned the nickname Governor Morebucks. His enemies labeled him "the people's pickpocket." Why? Many of his transactions were quid pro quo, conducted under the table for his personal benefit and pleasure.

The twenty-three presidents that come to visit Little Big Hands over the course of several evenings served as Democrats and Republicans; theirs is a bipartisan endeavor to save the republic. History shows that no US president has avoided making mistakes and errors in judgment. Several were racists by today's standard. We must not think of them as mythical figures. They have on and off days, and biases in their upbringing just like the rest of us. The most articulate can split an infinitive, mispronounce a word, forget a name, or mess up a speech. Even at the peak of greatness, they are subject to human imperfections. They all sometimes falter and fall short of expectations, to the disappointment of their partisan base and fans' idol worship.

But some presidents are more flawed than others. As we soon discover, President Little Big Hands, an outlier in the history of the office, exhibits a low human quotient, and his political base has been numbed by repeated blunders. Under POTUS's administration, a standard of underperformance for the office has been accepted as the new norm.

The visiting presidents mention a few accomplishments, but it is the consequences of their failures that they wish to impress upon Little Big Hands—and the consequences of his failures, as well. Although the presidents remain skeptical, they persevere in the hope that just *maybe* they might penetrate the corrosive veneer that coats POTUS's soul. Their collective and cooperative efforts are a last-ditch attempt to restore the dignity and legacy of the United States as a bastion of democracy, a force for good and a beacon of global citizenship.

In recognition of a coming political train wreck, mainline conservatives in Congress have begun to distance themselves from President Little Big Hands. The Democrats attained the necessary votes to impeach him in the House but did not get the necessary votes in the Republican held Senate to remove him from office.

So, despite the noise emanating from the extreme left (disparagingly called the Free Ticket Wing) and the extreme right (disapprovingly called the Neti Pot Wing), traditional Republicans, Democrats, and independents have resolved to ride out POTUS's remaining first term and to neutralize him as much as possible.

The Free Ticket Wing and the Neti Pot Wing each view the world in black and white terms. They are uncompromising. They believe if they don't win, they'll lose everything sacred to them, and it's the end of democracy as they have come to understand it. Each would like to immolate the other.

Partisans have drifted apart both in geography and ideology. In conducting the government's affairs, they've forgotten how to be civil to one another. They are intolerant and antagonistic toward anyone with a contrary point of view. At the fringes, distrust has become so fanatical that right-wing activists in Texas and left-wing activists in California have revived talk of secession.

The Neti Pot Wing, an aberration of the Republican Tea Party, stonewalled the process of impeachment to remove the political infection. In response to the liberals' accusations, the Netis pride themselves on their slogan: "A group with a clear head and uncongested thinkers."

Each group demonizes the other. For instance, the Free Ticket Wing perceives that all members of the Neti Pot Wing hold the second amendment sacred and support ownership of assault weapons. They interpret the Bible literally and believe there is a global holy war underway. They are self-righteous and fanatic. They fear minority groups and the popular vote. They distrust science. And, they favor a strong military and a rigid police force.

For their part, the Netis perceive that the Free Ticketers advocate a wide range of social actions and entitlements that include free medical care, free transportation, free cell phones, free food, taxing the wealthy upwards of ninety percent, a four-day work week, salary caps, guaranteed income, advancement in government jobs by seniority rather than merit, free access to EZ TAG lanes, retirement benefits at age fifty-five, and free hearing aids for those who chose in their youth to boombox loud music from their open car windows. They favor liberalization of drugs. They advocate a popular vote. They blame others for their misfortunes. They are communists. And, they favor a smaller police force and military.

The Free Ticket and Neti Pot Wings find much wrong with the country but offer few viable solutions. They are incapable of listening to one another. Malcontented, they reside inside echo chambers and find nourishment there. The primary tool employed by both extremes is not objective fact or legal justification. Social scientists would say that Free Ticket and Neti Pot people have internalized their political beliefs to the point that it has become who they are...their personal identity and soul. A contrary view represents an affront, a personal attack, and a threat to existence.

Although sensitive to the dangers from the extremists in their parties, both mainstream Democrats and Republicans stonewall each other's legislative initiatives. Some believe this malaise traces to Republican Senator Mitch McConnell, who pompously declared on the Senate floor that his party's number-one priority, above all else, was to make sure newly elected President Barack Obama didn't get reelected. McConnell set in motion a cycle of ugly partisanship that crippled the government and disgusted the electorate.

Other people believe the real playbook for all the political acrimony began with Newt Gingrich several decades ago. As the Republican Speaker of the House, it is said he set the tone for "today's napalm politics." Ideologically, he paved the way for an outsider like POTUS to steal the presidency and eviscerate the party.

President Daniel Hands and the former speaker share many characteristics. Inflated egos. Savoring of conspiracy theories. Questionable ethics. Fomenting conflict. Normalization of character assassination. Contempt for custom. Baiting the media. Transforming political opponents into enemies. Harboring grudges. Resisting affirmative action. Distain for established institutions. And pandering to the far right.

But the vitriol was not one-sided. With equal bitterness, Republicans protested being left out of big legislative pushes like the Obama administration's Affordable Care Act and Dodd-Frank. Senator Harry Reid, the Democratic leader of that era, first deployed the so-called nuclear option to squelch filibusters of President Obama's nominees for various political appointments.

Now the sorry saga continues no matter which party wins election. The nation wearies of a dysfunctional, do-nothing Congress. The press and critics frequently compare Congress and Little Big Hands to Nero, who fiddled while Rome burned.

With few pieces of legislation passing, Congress has lost most of its institutional memory of how to approve a bill—let alone pass a bipartisan bill. Consequently, the thing it spends most of its time on and does best is dial for dollars to get reelected and fatten their wallets with congressional entitlements like huge pensions and excellent health care. Only a brave few congresspeople put the nation ahead of party affiliation.

Although white evangelical Christians provide the core political support that got Little Big Hands elected, they are beginning to feel conflicted. Most wholeheartedly approved of POTUS's Supreme Court nominees, his defense of religious liberty, his distrust of science, his stance on right-to-life, and his disengagement from world organizations believed to dictate America's behavior.

One brave evangelical leader recently declared that enough is enough. The revered editor of *Christianity Today* has drawn a line in the sand that he says President Daniel Hands has crossed. The editor proclaimed that POTUS's "moral deficiencies damage the institution of the presidency, the reputation of the country, and the spirit and future of its people." He has gone on record that the President's merits cannot begin to offset the risks the country faces "under a leader of such gross immoral character."

In a series of episodes that traverse time, each president has an admonition to deliver to the tone-deaf Little Big Hands. Just perhaps, they can save him from himself. See what you think.

Day One

THE WHITE HOUSE

President Daniel Little Big Hands stormed around the Oval Office and then on impulse kicked an oak wastepaper basket that scattered trashed documents, most unread, across the carpet. He ignored the pain in his twisted big toe and cursed everyone within sight for not doing more to whitewash his presidency. He steamed with unrepentant anger over the latest self-inflicted crisis. POTUS gave new definition to the traditional genteel phrase "political correctness." Wasn't it enough that fake news blamed him for the rapid and relentless spread of the Covid-19 across the country?

Sir Jamie Z. Baird, The U.K. Ambassador to the US had just called him inept, shallow, and ill-suited for office. He added that only two things seem to command the president's attention: women and sports. To make matters worse, just the day before, one of the president's own staffers anonymously commented on his mental instability, saying, "I have never met anyone crazier than President Hands." Somehow both remarks were leaked to the press. To POTUS's exasperation, it made front-page news on every continent and broadcast network. He planned to demand that the U.K. recall Sir James and then identify the leaker and rip the mole from office.

Hands was the offspring of fathers and grandfathers who in the 1890s founded what became a nationwide franchise of butcher shops, bars, restaurants and hotels. The president's grandfather, Andrey Handtrov, hailed from Russia. He opened up Mivkys, an infamous New Orleans institution that was at once a hotel, bar, back-room brothel, and restaurant.

The family fortune originated with Andrey, a shrewd businessman who catered to the ravenous appetites of the captains and crews of vessels abreast the Mississippi River and Gulf of Mexico as well as entrepreneurs in the cotton, rum, and railroad industries. A painting framed in purple garter lace over Mivkys' bar featured a curvaceous young brunette. She sported a lascivious smile and was fitted in a scarlet silk dress. The tight fabric, that barely covered her plump breasts, looked ready to burst. Underneath, a sign read "What goes on behind these doors stays here." Las Vegas would eventually capitalize on a variation of this slogan.

Trying to distance his family from the socialist revolution in Russia, Little Big Hands's father, Anthony F. Hands, changed the family name from Handtrov. Ever since, he swore on the Bible that the original family had immigrated from Sweden. Anthony had been bullied as a kid and cruelly nicknamed Red Russie because he had red hair and his father and mother were Russian. Andrey felt that joining the Ku Klux Klan would cleanse the family name and give him respectability among the southern aristocrats he so admired.

Although POTUS had never held political office, his instincts were exceptional, particularly in the vicious way he could humble and demean others. He was a force of nature who steamrolled opponents and broke them into small pieces. A little cock rooster, his bluster was full of promises. He crowed, preached and fancied that he was the only one who could overhaul the nation's infrastructure, fix health care, reduce the deficit, drain the swamp, rescue dying industries and make America great again.

This was a vaudeville act. He had little intent to honor his pledges and lacked a clue how to implement them. Little Big Hands didn't understand or care how government functioned or political statesmanship worked. Nor did he give much forethought to the selection of a skilled cabinet or an A-team of senior administrators. He had inherited from his father and grandfather the unique ability to capitalize on the fortune and misfortune of others and bend them for his purpose.

Little Big Hands ran an inflammatory, negative campaign that catered to a carefully profiled audience on the electoral college map. Some of his partisan voters, had they lived three hundred years ago, would have sworn the world was flat.

POTUS strategically and cynically concluded he could win the highest office in the land if he could correctly identify and deliver a message that resonated with cocoon-minded voters. These people feared many things including the future, invasions of their privacy, globalization, minority groups, and non-Christians. They denied scientific evidence of climate change. And they demanded less government (except for the military, the federal courts, and the justice department), fewer subsidies for the poor and disabled, and less separation of church and state.

POTUS framed his election as a clash of civilizations, claiming "They come for you, they hate you, they despise America." He understood and capitalized on a partisan electorate who professed a strong belief in individual rights and freedoms while they rejected the hypocrisy inherent in their eagerness to regulate a woman's freedom of reproductive choice. He pandered to the Neti Pot Wing and even flip-flopped on the abortion issue to win election. Secretly, he paid for several of his mistresses to have abortions and extracted promises that they never mention the affair.

His platform didn't have a leg to stand on, which made it all the more incomprehensible when he won the election. Even more confounding was that although he lost the popular vote by over three million, the minority of voters came to rule the majority. This victory will amuse, befuddle, and trouble future historians.

While POTUS would lead you to believe that he identified closely with the US armed forces, no one in his family had ever fought in any war or served in any branch of the military. In fact, POTUS kept it a secret that he had washed out of the University of Mississippi's ROTC program for conduct unbecoming a gentleman. While governor, Morebucks made sure that any record of his pal's lapse in character disappeared without a trace. Perhaps this favor lead to his vice presidency.

At age seventy-three, POTUS's appearance and demeanor invited striking comparisons to a shorter, squatter, more rotund version of financial adviser Bernie Madoff, America's most notorious white-collar criminal, as well as to Al Capone, the infamous gangster from the 1930's and 1940's. President Hands's cheeks appeared perpetually puffed out, like a chipmunk with a mouthful of acorns to cache underground for a winter day. Instilled with high energy, he made the same jerky movements as a chipmunk, ready to tunnel down a hole when cornered.

Considering his small stature, gargantuan hands were perhaps his most memorable feature. Genetically, they predisposed him to be a butcher. If it hadn't been for the extraordinary skills of his chief financial officer and his cadre of attorneys, he would have butchered the family restaurant and hotel chains that he had inherited. Truly, he was a lucky sperm who traded on the success of those before and around him.

Figuratively speaking, POTUS's hands skillfully cleaved and bullied all objectors. They loved women. Like brushes on the end of broomsticks, his meddlesome hands protruded from his shirtsleeves, ready to sweep criticism aside or deny allegations as fake news. All the while, he displayed an angelic facade.

POTUS had always been vain about his hair. He was very particular about how it should be trimmed, ordering, "Cut here, cut there, that's enough." He went to no end to conceal that his hair was thin and gray. Alphonse Robicheaux, his barber, strove to cover POTUS's bald spot and dyed his hair a medium brown every three weeks. Robicheaux swept back the hair on the sides and top to camouflage the shiny, rumpled pink flesh on the crown. From all angles POTUS's combed-back hair looked like a bird gliding in flight. His pointy, beaklike nose enhanced the image.

POTUS's aftershave lotion was distinctive, too. His aroma reminded some of a simmering batch of Cajun catfish, oysters, and crawfish. His secret lotion, customized by a French Creole perfumer, consisted of a special concoction of rosemary, chives, and Tabasco sauce. Men found it distinctive. Most women, unless they smoked cigars, detested it.

POTUS manipulated and projected his image by shopping at the best men's stores in New Orleans. His two favorites were Rubensteins, founded in 1924, and Goldberg M for Men and Boys. Both offered the conservative, classic designs he favored, and conveyed power and invincibility. When it came to suiting POTUS up or dressing him down, these haberdashers, by sleight of hand, performed magic.

Most of his adult life, POTUS chewed tobacco. Hooked on nicotine, he compounded the addiction as an inveterate chain-smoker until he weaned himself from cigarettes. His grandchildren frequently complained about the pungent, stale odor of smoke that emanated from his clothing and body, so he quit.

By the beginning of his first term in office, POTUS had developed tongue cancer from his pocket-tobacco habit. Although surgery and radiation treatments at MD Anderson were largely successful, they left him with a raspy voice and a lazy drool that seeped out of the left corner of his mouth. He always had a handkerchief pressed to his lips, which made him mumble. Perhaps that's why his favorite message of communication was sending out tweets in the middle of the night. Tweeting required no direct interaction and resembled proclamations from days of royalty.

At a young age, Daniel Hands had begun to perfect the art of deceit. Once he had killed a large rare blue bull frog. Placing it behind his back, he asked his distressed playmates if he could bring the frog back to life, would they give him all the marbles in their trousers? With the frog in the palm of his hand, he squeezed both sides of its cheeks. As the upper and lower jaws opened and closed from the applied pressure on the joints, Hands, like a ventriloquist, croaked like a frog, producing several ribbits that tricked his friends into giving him their possessions.

As he dealt with the press, lobbyists, Congress, other governments, and even his series of wives, he made sure the right hand never knew what the left hand was doing. His pattern was to tell them what they wanted to hear and believe.

After all, isn't that what other presidents did once they got into office—reverse themselves? As they squatted in the Oval Office, they claimed to see the world suddenly different than they had during their campaigns. Fool the public once, and then just keep it up.

Other than a temporary distraction with the U.K. Ambassador this morning, today Little Big Hands was determining how to retaliate against Canada and Mexico, who had pledged to finish the high-tech security barrier that he had begun along his country's northern and southern borders. They bragged that they would make him pay for it. This infuriated President Little Big Hands. Canada and Mexico wanted no more illegal U.S. immigrants trying to escape the decay of the country's crumbling institutions and infrastructure due to the ignorance of Hands's administration.

Furthermore, the construction of a wall around the nation's capital that Congress had approved at POTUS's insistence has stalled. Now the wall lies decaying in a state of half completion. Enemies, angry at POTUS's attempt to insulate the government from the voice of the people, suggested that his presidential monument had been prepaid; they wanted his epitaph written on the ugly wall collapsing around the capital.

The nation's cities were crippled. The auto industry remained under pressure to build vehicles that operate more like tractors to negotiate the buckling roads, broken pavement, flooded streets, and mudholes. The new tire requirements put less pressure per square inch on crumbling bridges, streets and highways.

POTUS asked himself why citizens couldn't understand that their low taxes generated little direct income for making America great again. Citizens were supposed to spend the nation back to prosperity. Instead, savings had gone up to hedge against recurring recessions, skyrocketing health care costs, and general uncertainty. Now that damn virus, which he had convinced himself would be over any day, had drained the federal coffers to subsidize the unemployed. National debt had soared to record heights. He intended to bill the Chinese.

Many corporations had used their tax breaks to buy back stock to add value to their shareholders, rather than invest in employment and innovation. Now many of them paid no taxes at all. The resulting deficit compromised essential government services and the ability of the country to borrow money and pay its debts. Servicing that debt would create complications for future administrations and spur inflation.

The rest of the world had built an economic trade barrier with the US as a result of President Little Big Hands's America First movement. His policies had backfired. Trade pacts in Asia,

Europe, Latin America, Africa, and the Middle East excluded the United States.

Along with the Russians, U.S. citizens have been banned from traveling to Europe due to his administration's inability to contain the virus.

Foreign tourists no longer felt welcome in the United States. The hospitality industry was in an uproar over revenue that declined year after year. The more energy and environmentally conscious tourists spent their vacation dollars elsewhere. They didn't like that POTUS favored coal and nuclear generated power to the detriment of solar and wind generation. It was also well known that many of the nation's nuclear sites were well past their prime. Many feared, perhaps unreasonably, a Chernobyl like event on American soil. They had heard rumors that POTUS was slashing budgets for regulation and that nuclear's high cost of operation was leading to bankruptcies. No state wanted to store the waste, so that was an additional headache.

Tourists' other significant reservations pertained to the rampant spread of the virus and gun violence, both one of the highest in the world among so called advanced nations. Because of generous campaign donations, the National Rifle Association continued to hold sway over Congress. Gangs who couldn't shoot straight possessed military-grade automatic weapons. Extremists and nutcases continued to massacre civilians. The FBI, CIA, FDA and Department of Justice had been vindictively hollowed out by POTUS with budget cuts for partisan political gain.

Asia was now beginning to look to the US to provide them low-cost goods and services . . . the kind of jobs that have a fluid and spurious future if another nation can do the same work at a lower cost. More of the blame for America's demise came to roost on the Senate and the executive office.

In an ill temper, President Daniel Hands felt the sudden urge to relieve himself. Afterwards he could not completely wash his hands. He lashed out at the nearest person, Henry Noxolo, who was assigned to service the White House bathrooms. Usually ignoring Noxolo's existence, POTUS screamed, "Again! Why are we out of soap and nearly out of towels? If this continues, you're fired!" Then, leaving his mess, like always, for someone else to clean up, he threw his spent paper towels on the floor and stalked out. Pushing the blame on others and threatening to fire people were two of Little Big Hands's specialties. Few wanted to work for or with him anymore.

Henry, who had a limp from a war wound earned in Afghanistan, cowered, not knowing how to tell the president that all bathroom supplies had been rationed. If the president weren't so wasteful or so compulsive about clean hands, there would be enough to last through the week. In the Zulu language, Noxolo means peace, but Henry never felt peaceful around President Little Big Hands.

But what Noxolo didn't tell the president was that he had been taking small quantities of soap home so that his seventeen-year-old son, Timothy, could keep an infected wound clean after a nasty fall on the Washington Mall's broken steps.

Scrambling to pay medical bills and make ends meet, Noxolo could not find time to better himself. But he dreamed that perhaps Timothy, at the head of his class in his public high school, might emigrate to South Africa or Nigeria for a college education and a bright career. Noxolo would do whatever it took to make this happen.

Timothy also suffered from asthma. The pollution from coal-fired plants nearby had poisoned the air and aggravated Timothy's condition, stunting his growth. His mother died prematurely from lung cancer. Such incidences had soared since President Little Big Hands's decision to reduce regulations on industrial air emissions.

Days Two and Three

BELLADONNA WINTER RETREAT
BACK SWAMP, LOUISIANA

To temporarily escape the fickleness of late winter in the Capital, the next day the president took Air Force One to Belladonna, his private estate in Back Swamp, Louisiana. It was situated on the edge of the Atchafalaya Basin, America's largest swamp. The Belladonna Golf Course was nearby. The course was privately owned by Daniel Hands and frequently used for the entertainment and persuasion of his guests.

Prior to his presidency, some years ago, Daniel Hands hosted a private golf outing and fundraiser for the friends of Poppy Warbucks's Senate campaign. Wives were not invited because Daniel had arranged for young women from a New Orleans strip joint to drive the golf carts topless.

None of these young ladies had ever driven a golf cart. And Hands, eager to get on with the fundraiser, provided them the briefest of instructions on the basics.

One accidentally drove her cart into a pond defending her honor against a wealthy, drunken middle-aged donor from Iowa. Both passenger and golfer had consumed too many Bloody Marys. The cart tipped over and spilled her, her randy passenger, and his clubs into the brackish water that fed off the swamp.

Although no one drowned, a hungry ten-foot alligator seized the opportunity to chomp off the donor's left thumb. The young lady, a Canadian, promptly fled back to her homeland to avoid potential lawsuits and bad press.

The *Lafayette Daily Advertiser* sent a young reporter to cover the mishap, but the story never made the paper or the local network stations, thanks to Hands and Warbucks. All the participants were sworn to secrecy and rewarded for their discretion.

And what about the donor from Iowa? He used his good right hand to write a large check to the campaign to keep the news from getting back to Iowa, and to his wife!

Little Big Hands's adversaries wondered if he knew the sinister implications behind the estate's name. *Atropa belladonna*, commonly called belladonna, is an herbaceous perennial plant in the nightshade family. Its foliage and berries are extremely toxic. Belladonna has a long history as a poison, medicine, and cosmetic. Ancient rumor has it that the wife of Emperor Augustus used it to murder rivals. Predecessors to the Romans used it to poison the tips of their arrows. During the Renaissance, women used the herb in eyedrops to dilate their pupils to look seductive.

POTUS was quite aware of the meaning behind the estate's name, and rather liked the implications. The Italian translation of belladonna means "beautiful woman." POTUS particularly liked that, and he used it to his advantage to lure attractive ladies to his estate and his bedroom. As a result of this and many other marital infractions, he and his wife, Angelica, a former Miss Universe who had trouble seeing her toes, separated.

It was not POTUS's first fractured marriage. As a young man, he married Blair, a Southern Baptist woman from a very conservative family in Baton Rouge, Louisiana, who quickly bore him two children, Jessica and Clyde. The young couple became close friends with a country minister and his wife. Their children went to the same school. The Handses frequently vacationed with the minister and his wife and kindly paid their way.

The sultry news got around that Little Big Hands couldn't keep his own hands off the minister's wife. They had been carrying on a lurid affair. Upon discovering her husband's infidelity, the first Mrs. Hands threw all Daniel's clothing and other personal possessions onto the front yard from a second-story bedroom window. Word has it that his precious collection of vintage *Playboy* and *Penthouse* magazines scattered to the winds. Many were quickly snatched up that Saturday morning by gleeful neighbors mowing their yards as their kids rode bicycles around the cul-de-sac wondering what was going on.

Years later in an interview, Blair offered advice to women with wandering husbands. Flashing her diamond earrings and necklace, she offered these words of wisdom… "Don't get mad, get everything!"

Jessica and Clyde were now adults. As a result of the circumstances of the divorce and resultant childhood trauma, they chose to become Buddhists. Jessica worked for Planned Parenthood and vehemently disagreed with her father's pandering to evangelicals. Clyde, a promising young attorney, worked for an African Missionary. The children saw their dad twice a year and refused to be held hostage by the promise of inheritance.

Little Big Hands spent more time on the links than any other president in history. During his campaign, he criticized his predecessor's enjoyment of the game. He lamented to his trusting constituency that, if elected, he might have to forsake his sacred golf for the pressing duties of the White House. That didn't happen.

Now at his private club, he enthusiastically gouged the turf like a feral pig rooting for grubs and acorns. Caddies and groundskeepers who followed immediately repaired the damaged fairways and greens before evidence of POTUS's ground-engaging swing could be photographed and sent to his enemies.

After several rounds spent indulging his senses on the golfing escape from Washington, Little Big Hands, exhausted from a hard day's work, fell asleep on Belladonna's screened veranda. A moderately cool late winter southern breeze whispered through the screen while he dozed under a blanket. A fog crept in from the nearby swamp. The porch overlooked ancient live oaks thickly draped in moss.

The president often ate dinner alone because few could tolerate his miserable company. After several beers, fried chicken, and a mound of French fries and onion rings, the president felt lethargic and groggy. The first sensation was not unusual. Many people noted his lack of alertness and attributed it to the tirades of tweets he impulsively posted throughout the night.

Although the porch felt lonely, it was not as solitary these days as his bedroom off the veranda. He rather enjoyed the creatures of the night who serenaded him: hooting owls, howling coyotes, fluttering bats, croaking bullfrogs, chirping crickets, clicking cicadas, drumming alligators, splashing fish, flickering lightning bugs, warbling nightingales, and chanting whip-poor-wills. The dissonant sounds gave the president a weird sense of peace.

For many years now, the First Lady had refused to share his bed. The frequent rumors of affairs and prostitutes slid off the president's conscience like water on a duck's feathers. His adversaries whispered behind his back that he was born with Teflon skin. Nothing seemed to stick. But any remnants of romance between the First Couple had turned frigid. Their marriage was a convenient shell—hollow and dead. And because of the bad press about his womanizing and sexist views, few ladies remained interested in his companionship. Some publicly said that a fling with Little Big Hands was unremarkable—and that his nickname wasn't all that was miniature.

Ghost #1: George Washington

THE TEMPLE OF VIRTUE

A little after nine p.m., POTUS stirred from his sleep. He was startled and confused by the rhythmic splash of oars dipping into the swamp waters not far from the elevated porch. With each stroke, the sound drew closer. Soon the bow of a Durham shallow draft boat rowed by six men came ashore. The wooden hull scraped over the debris, gravel, and broken shells on the beach. The sound penetrated the swamp and announced its arrival. Momentarily, the creatures in the swamp fell silent.

Brandishing a sword, a regal figure emerged from behind Spanish moss draped oak trees. He wore a tricorn hat, a cape, and an odd military uniform. Under the hat sprouted long gray hair tied back in a queue or ponytail. Or was it a wig? As the figure approached, Little Big Hands (who was a collector of military uniforms) recognized the eighteenth-century apparel. Although he didn't like to read about history, POTUS rather enjoyed military symbolism. As the figure came closer, a powerful scent of mold permeated the air.

In the blink of an eye, a musty apparition appeared beside Little Big Hands. He resembled the painting of President George Washington in the National Portrait Gallery.

Astonished, the president at first trembled, and then mumbled, "Who are you? What do you want?"

"Sir, let me present myself. I am George Washington. The weight of my years admonishes me. I have been summoned from the grave to once again preserve the nation which I helped birth." As George took a step closer, the creaking of brittle bones and snapping joints pierced the veranda. "Sorry about that," said George to no one in particular, using his sword like a cane. "One cannot shield himself from centuries of dormancy. It's been a long time since I've gone on an expedition. Too much inactivity!"

Little Big Hands questioned his senses as he nervously held his handkerchief to the corner of his mouth. Trembling, he mumbled in a barely audible sentence, "Ah, wha . . . why are you here? Are you an agent of the grim reaper?" Then he thought—for just a second—that he was talking to himself. He could hardly understand the man. He seemed to speak in some stilted 18th or 19th century dialect.

The reply that boomed back convinced POTUS that the ghostly presence was not inside his head. The roar abruptly silenced the creatures that had resumed their nightly rituals and routines in the swamp.

George pointed his rusty sword toward the heavens and said, "I have been summoned to rescue liberty and examine your soul . . . if we can find one. Come with me. I want you to make a discovery."

Before Little Big Hands could resist, he found himself inside the boat with a crew of ancients who strained on the oars as they rowed into the mist. Like a reversal of the film *Back to the Future*, in a flash of time he found himself in New Windsor, on the Hudson River north of New York City.

***

As the craft crunched to an abrupt stop on shore, George commanded, "Follow me." Together they stumbled along on uneven terrain known as the Hudson Highlands. George's ancient bones groaned every step of the way as they trudged up a hill through a blackened forest. He stabbed the sword into the frozen earth for balance and used it as a crutch on the slippery slopes. The trees and brush blocked out most of the starlight overhead and made the well concealed trail hard to see.

During the trek, Washington's trusty companion and ghost dog, Sweet Lips, an American Foxhound sniffed the trail ahead for intruders. She'd periodically turn her head and growl at Little Big Hands. Washington would tell her to hush, but privately agreed with her assessment of character. He was proud of the key role he'd played in inventing the breed.

As he staggered upward, fear and curiosity occupied POTUS's mind. On impulse, he blurted out: "President Washington, I've always wondered why you turned down an additional term in office. You could have served a lifetime in the office, perhaps even been crowned the first king of America. Really, I think that was dumb of you to just walk away from all that power, authority, and adulation. Think of the marketing opportunities afterwards. In my opinion, it was a flaw in your character. I wouldn't have made that mistake. This country could have been so much easier to rule—I mean run—if you had just taken that step."

"Well, sir, I trust that you will soon discover the answer on your own. Naming a town after me was satisfactory enough."

Other than that, Washington said little as they climbed. Instead, he ground his dentures, a combination of animal and human teeth, gold wire, lead, springs, and brass screws. The heavy and ill-fitting dentures made his gums sore and him irritable. He silently clutched the corner of his waistcoat. As was his habit when he wanted to conceal his emotions, George squeezed the garment hard and maintained a poker face.

Finally, an hour or so before sunlight, they arrived at a large log cabin. George said, "This is the Temple of Virtue. The building served as a chapel, office, commissary, court-martial site, meeting hall, and mountain sanctuary for the Continental Army under my leadership during the Revolutionary War. Perhaps the most important gathering ever in the United States occurred here on March fifteenth, 1783. I'm quite sure, with your lack of interest in learning anything from history applicable to your job, you've never heard of it!"

POTUS felt a little feistier now that he hadn't been deposited at the bottom of the Louisiana swamp with an anchor attached snuggly around his ankles or drowned in the Hudson River. He said, "You got that right, I live for the present. And I have no doubt this is all a bad dream. I have little to gain from my predecessors. Ever since childhood, I deplored dry, archaic history. Bored by it all. I'm a self-made man, and certainly not tied to the past."

Tired and convinced that this was just a perverse nightmare, Little Big Hands thought back to his college days. He thought, "Hmm, Temple of Virtue. What an odd name. Is this where those old revolutionaries shacked up with the willing ladies of the night who raised their skirts for them?"

George ground his teeth, tugged the lapel of his coat, and bellowed, "It's not what you are thinking, you wicked man! You cannot shield your thoughts from me." George grabbed Little Big Hands with an iron fist, lifted him in the air, and tossed him into a heap on the long house earthen floor. "I have just violated the first rule of ghosthood: Bring no physical harm to earthlings. In your case, I feel justified, and am not going to appeal for forgiveness.

"This is a mostly forgotten, sacred place for the United States, not unlike a treasured spring, valley, mountain, canyon, or bluff where North American Indians reached out to the great spirits. We call it the Temple of Virtue because in the chronicles of the Revolutionary War, men and women put their God, the concept of a republic, honor, and duty above their own lives."

Bruised but not broken, POTUS slowly opened his eyes, hoping that he had simply fallen off the couch on the veranda. The large room was dark, cold, and damp from the inclement late winter transition to early spring. A chilling draft penetrated the room. He saw a group of army officers bundled in winter coats and blankets, listening intently to their leader. Awake now and shivering, POTUS was bewildered, but the Revolutionary War officers didn't seem to realize that he was there among them.

George noticed how pale his guest had become inside the sparsely equipped structure. POTUS had fallen asleep after dinner still dressed in his golf wear: an Ole Miss Rebels red and blue short-sleeve Polo shirt and lightweight khaki pants.

"Sir, I see I may be somewhat derelict in my duties as a Continental officer. When I accepted this chore, I promised to keep you alive—although now I wonder why! Let's thaw you out. We can edge closer to the large, crackling fireplace in the front of the room. I'm from the afterworld, so it won't make any difference to me, but it might help you better focus your feeble powers of concentration to grasp what's going on here. No one will notice because they can't see or hear us."

"I still don't understand why we are here in this smoke-infested log house lit only by candles, a fireplace, and moon beams shining through a few frosted windowpanes."

"Let's see if you can endeavor to figure it out. You are about to bear witness to one of the most important transitions in American history.

"See that man up front? He's General Horatio Gates. During the war, he reported to me. Before joining our cause, he served in the British army. He's imperialistic toward subordinates, scheming, and very ambitious. You two have much in common. Listen to what he has to say."

"Fellow patriots and officers, for purposes of this discussion I temporarily suspend my rank as second-in-command of the Continental Army. Why, you may ask? The answer is, I don't want you to feel obliged to undertake what I'm about to submit.

"Our military forces have been in stand-down for several months. Yet none of your charges have been released to go home to their families, farms, and businesses. It's not news to you that altercations have ground to a halt and that we may have prevailed in our revolution to end unjust dominion. I can report to you that the British are exhausted, and King George wants out. The peacemakers are in Paris, France. As I speak, they negotiate the terms of cessation. Until those terms are officially resolved, you and your men have been ordered to remain on alert in the event of renewed hostilities.

"Our Continental Army has been fighting for almost seven years without pay. As patriots committed to the cause, you have all run up debts. Your families are financially stressed and pained by your absence. I know how frustrated you are. I feel your misery.

"General Washington and I continue to petition the Continental Congress to fulfill its financial obligations to compensate the army with back pay and pensions. Our weak and fragile Congress has asked the thirteen colonies to help remunerate the army and its creditors. As some of you have already heard, the colonies voted on the matter. I am disappointed that they have rejected the referendum. They continue to resist the creation of a strong, centralized republic or agree to a system by which all federal debts can be honorably compensated.

"For those of us who have fought and witnessed the sacrifices, I know this news disturbs you. Frankly, under the Articles of Confederation that limit Congress, our central government is too weak to compel the colonies to assume their fair share of the cost of our revolution."

The officers began to swear about bureaucracy and the injustice of the situation.

"Gentlemen, I have a solution." They turn attentive. "I want you to know that I have not informed General Washington of this meeting. He fails to get the job done with the Continental Congress. I propose that we seize control of the legislature and use our military powers to force the colonies to give us justice and compensation. If you choose to follow me, I assure you that you will receive what is duly owed you."

Just then, all heads turned as General Washington walked to the front of the room. How did he know of this meeting? The officers glared at him. Washington asked permission to speak to the officers.

Reluctantly, Gates granted Washington's request. What were his options? He would dishonor himself if he refused to grant the Commander in Chief an opportunity to speak.

As Gates nervously stepped aside, Little Big Hands watched the events unfold as if it were a YouTube Video. He observed that the faces of the gathered officers showed surprise, resentment, and anger toward their Commander in Chief, and now confusion.

Washington said, "As both a citizen and a soldier, I too am conflicted about the present situation. I understand your anger and frustration and I share it. Despite what General Gates has just told you, I don't think he understands the lay of the land. I remain confident that our new government will, in the end, act responsibly toward us.

"Ask yourselves: if General Gates were successful in seizing control of the Continental Congress with your help, what happens afterwards? Too often in the course of history, military coups have evolved into dictatorships or monarchies. Most everyone the worse off. And who do you suppose would like to subvert the power of the people and usurp for themselves the reins of government?"

Washington paused to put on a pair of glasses and adjust them to his nose, then continued. "In the service of my country I have not only grown gray but almost blind. I want to share a recent letter from a powerful and persuasive congressman that I've known for years and trust with my life. He assures us that we will all get paid." Washington pulled the letter from his pocket and read it to the huddled warriors. Afterwards, he passed the letter around, removed his glasses and looked them straight in the eye as he spoke. "Fellow officers of the Continental Army, we have come too far to do what General Gates proposes. A military coup of our civilian government is not what we have fought and died for over the last seven years. We must not abandon what we have achieved, a free and just nation . . . unique in the history of mankind."

The hardened soldiers began to weep and applaud.

It slowly dawned on Little Big Hands that Washington had just prevented the United States from a sour turning point in history. A point where all that had been fought for might have ended in tyranny, civil eruption, and a home-ruled monarchy.

As the scene before him faded from view, Washington elbowed Little Big Hands to get his attention. "You know what my successor Thomas Jefferson said about this moment?"

"No," said POTUS. "You know I don't read history."

"Jefferson declared that the moderation and virtue of a single character prevented this revolution from failure, as most others have been around the world, by a subversion of the liberty it was intended to establish. After our victory, many wanted a monarchy. I refused their frequent invitations and appeals to wear a crown and govern like one."

"Hey," Little Big Hands asked, "After you settled things down at the Temple of Virtue, what did you do about General Gates? His conduct seems like insubordination to me. I fire people for a lot less than that."

"Well, if you really want to know, General Gates took—with some encouragement from me—what you might call early retirement from the Continental Army. Kind of you to ask, Little Big Hands. Now let's talk about the present. I'm haunted about the implications of your actions lately."

"What do you mean, my actions? If you ask me, they seem pretty consistent. Since your time government has gotten bloated and hard to control. Too many liberal bureaucrats that frustrate the will of the people. That makes it difficult for a president to exert his authority."

"Little Big Hands what you really desire is to become an autocrat. Admit it! After turning over four national security advisers, three chiefs of staff, three directors of Oval Office operations, five communications directors, and numerous cabinet members, the White House functions in a way that fits your personality and suits a monarchy! Your presidency looks like an executive office of one to me. No pun intended, you're a little short-handed for the task.

"Little Big Hands, had you studied some European history in college instead of theater and acting, you'd know that even kings, or at least the most revered ones, sought wise counsel. If you haven't already, you are soon going to find it very difficult to pass the blame for your errors in judgment. When I was a child, we concocted a game that fits your situation. Late in the nineteenth century, children called it pin-the-tail-on-the-donkey. If you don't rethink your presidency, the American public might like to pin one on you."

After a long silence, POTUS regained some of his composure and tried to change the subject. He became bolder and interrupted: "I know you are the founding father, but I refuse to believe you were without faults. No disrespect, Sir, I visited Mount Vernon on an obligatory school field trip and noticed those slave quarters . . ." Then he grew more contentious. "In case you haven't noticed, your image is a bit tarnished these days, even if you remain the honored Father of Our Nation. As it pertains to civil rights, you've slid down the pole a way. But don't worry George, I will defend you and all your monuments."

POTUS continued, "After all, don't you think what happened over 200 years ago should stay there? I mean those were your norms. We have different norms now. In the view of some of my most loyal constituents, they believe white people are now more discriminated against. They think their rights are under siege with all the rioting that's going on and the destruction of statues that earmarked our nation's development."

George briefly thought about Little Big Hands's question and then responded. "I must tell you that I regard Mount Vernon's dependency on slave labor as my misfortune. To this day, I remain haunted that in 1791 I expedited back to Mount Vernon a portion of my Black slaves who served me in the presidential mansion in Philadelphia.

"Pennsylvania had just passed a law that automatically freed slaves. To avoid it, I acted quickly, before it went into effect. I can never forget the disappointment in their faces when I returned those slaves to Virginia. However, I left some of my favorite house slaves behind, thus assuring their freedom.

"Of course, there were other regrets from my youth, when I unabashedly sought wealth. Just like you still do today. To that end, I even pursued a commission in the British army! Imagine the folly in that endeavor! Fortunately, the king's men arrogantly and rather quickly disposed of my application. They found my American birth unworthy, even though I had served them admirably during the French and Indian War. A commission would have given me access to a better military education. Perhaps they also sensed where my loyalties already lay, thinking that someday I just might use that education against them. As a former British Officer, General Gates certainly did.

"Little Big Hands, other past presidents are eager to confront you. I am not alone in this grand endeavor to save our beloved country. Be aware, be prepared, and be cautious when you hear in your head creatures approaching from the swamp. Your fate depends upon what you say and what you do. Expect more visitors. Some will not be as gentle or kind to you as I.

"When you get home, turn on that funny-looking box . . . that contraption that has all those talking pictures inside it. Perhaps you will get a glimpse of the future if you continue to pack the courts with judges who subscribe to your doctrines, gerrymander elections, and assume responsibilities belonging to Congress. Now I must return to the shadows of history."

***

Back at Belladonna, POTUS awoke frightened on the veranda. He was covered in perspiration. Hungover, he wondered, "Have I just had a bad dream?"

Then he noticed the soot from an ancient fireplace smeared on his hands and on the seat of his pants. The Ole Miss shirt had been singed by sparks from a roaring granite fireplace fueled by birch and oak to take the edge off a frigid late winter evening in the Hudson Highlands.

Little Big Hands remembered to switch on the television and stared in disbelief. At first, one part of him wanted to shout with joy and tweet about what he was hearing. He rationalized that for the good of all, sacrifices had to be made. Government wasn't working, and it was truly time for an autocrat.

"Hello again, ladies and gentlemen. This is Annie Oakely Remington for Channel 6666, an affiliate of Ferret and Opossum News. Daily we sharp-shoot the news to bring you bull's-eye reporting. Here's the latest on the riots occurring throughout the country since President Daniel Hands disbanded Congress and took military control of the government. He said today, and I quote, 'There has never been anyone in America's history better suited to make America great again.'

"Many Blue states are petitioning Canada to become provinces. The Canadian government has flung open its doors to immigrants from the United States. Over twenty-five thousand national and state congressmen have been jailed for insurrection. Their fate is unknown, and relatives have not heard from them.

"President Hands now refers to himself as His Majesty. At a rally in New Orleans yesterday, he explained why it is in the best interests of future generations that he serves in office for the rest of his life. He explains that if it is in Russia's best interests to let Vladimir Putin reign as president for life, then he advocates equal treatment to deal with him in the interests of world peace among nuclear giants.

"The president has mandated that American history, as we have known it since the Pilgrims came to this country, be eradicated from our educational system. That includes curriculum, books, and any other references to our last four centuries as a democracy. Beginning with his coronation and going forward, history will begin anew.

"It has been my privilege to report to you the evening news the last fifteen years. I am resigning. Tonight, I wish you farewell and God bless. By proclamation of His Majesty, all news stations have been nationalized and will be syndicated under the 'All Hands On For America' government broadcast network."

POTUS began to second-guess his initial self-congratulatory reaction to the news. He so often shot before aiming. He snapped off the television and thought, "Is this what I really want for my country?" Deep in his soul, another part of him silently wept for the impending loss of institutions that had once made America the greatest democracy on earth.

Had he imagined all this?

Ghost #3: Thomas Jefferson

THE NATIONAL ARCHIVES

Too exhausted to get up, Little Big Hands reached for a silver flask he kept under the couch pillow. The monogram on the flask read "The Boss Stops Here." He took a deep swig and swallowed the liquid courage in one gulp. The warmth trickled down his throat, stirred his gut, and staved off the terror from his sweaty nightmare. The alcohol momentarily dampened his senses. He quickly fell back into a welcome, deep slumber.

Time passed, but how much? POTUS's one exposed ear (the other burrowed deep in a pillow) detected the heavy purr of a cat, then a piercing growl, followed by a sharp hiss. The cacophony in the swamp got louder. His mind identified the creature as an eastern cougar, relatively rare in these parts, but not unheard of. Cougars, sometimes called ghost cats, creep up undetected if they are going for the kill.

Indeed, there was a ghost that hovered beside POTUS while he slumbered. Little Big Hands's sixth sense of survival prevailed as he pried open one puffy eyelid. Hungover, he became slowly aware of another ghastly, tall, and lanky nineteenth-century figure. His mind still fogged, Little Big Hands inquired, "Who, no, what are you?"

"Sir, I'm Thomas Jefferson. I see my catcalls to arouse you have succeeded. I lost a damn good hunting dog to one . . . ripped out his throat. I am not here to extend you any violence. I assure you that I have upright intentions. Believe me, I am no more thrilled to visit you than you are by my intrusion. In fact, I'm rather irritated. The delicacy of this arrangement must strike every portion of common sensibility. But duty calls."

It was by no coincidence from the heavens that the first two visitors were towering presidents who stood well over six feet two inches tall. The man beside Little Big Hands certainly didn't appear presidential. And like Washington, he spoke in a manner that Little Big Hands found hard to understand.

While in office, as often as he could, Jefferson had eschewed the pretentious ruffles, bows, scarves, and polished metal jacket buttons of his time. Although it was customary for formal occasions, neither he nor Washington liked wearing wigs. In the summer, they sweated and stank, and they collected fleas in the winter. For his journey to earth, Jefferson wore a simple muslin work shirt, a comfortable pair of relaxed-fit pants, and his long hair tied back at the nape of his neck.

"After my arduous service to the preservation of a young nation, I partook of a rather peaceful rest these last two centuries. But I owe it to my country to venture this journey through time as a vessel sent to help gauge your worthiness. Believe me, I would not recommend the mode of travel. Where you are headed, the route may prove more calamitous. I'm here to talk to you about that inevitable destination if you don't repent."

Impulsive and short-fused from lack of sleep, POTUS responded: "Repent from what? What the hell do you mean, worthy?" Referring to himself alternately in the third and first person, as he often did, he said, "Don't you know that President Hands holds the highest office in the land? I am the most powerful person on earth. I am the Chosen One." Trying to gather his fragmented recollection of history, he stammered, "As I vaguely recall, when you ruled this country it's population wasn't much bigger...than say...Louisiana is today."

Jefferson was indifferent to the reference to Louisiana, but he flinched at the word "ruled." Third person, like royalty. "Hmm," he mused to himself. "I thought George Washington set Little Big Hands straight on that one." Jefferson arched his ancient spine forward, and vented: "You fool, I have just begun to roast the likes of you. Wake up and pay attention, you presidential inchworm!"

Now he'd commanded POTUS's full and undivided attention.

Always a keen observer of his surroundings, Jefferson held a scroll in his left hand for inscribing impressions. Since his ink well had long gone dry, he borrowed a ballpoint pen and scribbled his initial assessment of POTUS's state of mind and pompous behavior. He rather liked that the ink didn't drizzle if he held it too long in place on the page; this was quite unlike a feather quill. "I desire to invite you on a journey of discovery."

Although Jefferson had politely extended the invitation, his tone of voice conveyed that it was not a choice.

Pushing back, POTUS exclaimed in a whiney voice, "Again? Where are we going? Wherever it is, I don't want to go."

"On an expedition to Des Moines, Iowa, to listen to a person whom you revere and adulate. Don't worry, I'll take care of transportation. The trip won't take long."

Whether the trip was inside his head or for real, POTUS never knew.

***

Suddenly, there he was with Jefferson on the fringes of a large crowd watching a political speech.

"Oh," POTUS realized admiringly as he pressed his handkerchief to the side of his mouth, "that's me talking before a sold-out stadium of partisans." A broad smile came to his face. "One of my best speeches . . . I sure told them what they wanted to hear. They loved my comments about filling the courts with like-minded people. A judiciary who will share the same fundamental values and conservative beliefs as their ancestors. One that's consistently tough on crime, rules in favor of less government, cuts back on wasteful social welfare, restores Christian values, bridles immigration, protects the rights of free enterprise and gun owners, and favors developing our God-given resources unencumbered by wishy-washy environmentalists."

POTUS silently congratulated himself that he had skillfully influenced the courts with appointments and Congress with political favors. Since he had always pushed the envelope between the edges of right and wrong to bend them to his will, he felt the effort was good insurance against scurrilous impeachment charges or, worse yet a trial for treason.

Glowing with pride, he asked Jefferson, "What did you think of my speech? I'm at my best when I'm freewheeling in front of a crowd . . . letting them know exactly what's on the top of my mind. And I love to get them chanting their support 'Lock her up' and 'Make American Great Again.' Then afterwards I tweet a few sentences to reinforce the message. Some of my best fans are from rural white areas and less educated, so they don't read much. Gotta keep thoughts short and sweet for them. They've felt disenfranchised for a long time. But, the Electoral College lets them punch above their weight."

"Sir, I must offer you credit. Few presidents have focused with such success on a narrative and then amplified and perpetuated it. Your uncanny and ruthless political instincts paint perception as more important than reality . . . especially for supporters who are tone-deaf to opposing ideas, facts, and politics. You then milk their blind loyalty dry . . . because they want so badly to believe in you. As much as it mortifies me, I confess you play certain segments of the public trust like a banjo.

"Just a moment, I want to make a few more notes . . . an old habit of mine, to write everything down so I don't contradict myself later. Might work for you, too.

"I know your disdain for history. If you cared for history, it might have dawned on you that I once shared your views about the judiciary branch. I felt certain it should be subject to the will of the people. Same for the justice department. And since it seemed to me that the president best represents the will of the people, I argued that the judiciary and all its branches should be subordinate to the executive branch.

"Our first two presidents, George Washington and John Adams, were members of the Federalist Party. They believed in more central control and regulation of the nation's business than I did. In that respect, you and I are also much akin. My election was the first time that running the country fell under the control of the Democratic-Republican Party. The whole transition became a delicate balance. Those dangerous times threatened our young and fragile democracy. The fear of change could have triggered another revolution. I observe with some irony that a similar fear of change among your fellow Neti Pot Wing members keeps you secure in office—at least for the time being.

"The Federalists harbored a lot of acrimony over losing the election and contested the outcome. Their vindictiveness and underhanded resistance almost led to a Constitutional crisis. All we fought for in the Revolutionary War could have been lost right there and then. Fortunately, the House of Representatives resolved the election in my favor.

"Do you think that if they were presented the opportunity today, the House would do the same for you?"

POTUS responded, "Certainly not, but I've got my puppets in the Senate. They pretty much hog-tie the House these days."

Jefferson pressed forward. "My most extreme political adversaries in the Federalist Party accused me of atheism or deism. To suppress my ideas, they tried to place restrictions on the press. I fought back. My enemies perverted every word that fell from my lips or flowed from my pen. They invented negative stories about me when facts failed them. Does this sound familiar?"

"Yes," POTUS said. "I tweet about it all the time. I fight back with my own fake news."

Jefferson said, "One clergyman believed that my election was going to destroy religion, introduce immorality, and loosen all the bonds of society. Believing what they wanted to believe, my adversaries completely ignored that I was an author and a signer of the Declaration of Independence! This explains why I adhered to the principle of separation of church and state. History proves churches are incapable of objectively governing nations.

"Little Big Hands, I've noticed that your opposition charges that you have exploited religion to fuel your popularity and manipulate perceptions of false virtue. As you might conclude, *my* foes never made that accusation." Jefferson couldn't help chuckle about his little attempt at a joke.

Feeling persecuted and unaccustomed to criticism from another dead man, Little Big Hands silently hoped Jefferson might have something better to do soon. He began to tune Jefferson out. No need to listen to him ramble on.

Jefferson sensed POTUS's thoughts and jerked him out of his mental retreat. "Come, you political weasel, say goodbye to Iowa. We are headed to the Capital, even if I have to drag your butt all the way there."

***

On Constitution Avenue, halfway between the White House and the Capitol, POTUS and Jefferson approached a white marble temple that gleamed with massive Doric columns on all four sides. As they entered, POTUS recognized the rotunda and interior of the National Archives. He had been there a couple of times but always found the place too stuffy. To him, it reeked of stale history...a waste of time. He was, after all, a businessman, more interested in making his next buck, cutting his next big deal for power and glory, and seeking bankruptcy protection from the courts.

As they walked past the Declaration of Independence, the Constitution, and the Bill of Rights, Jefferson steered and prodded Little Big Hands toward one particular document. Gruffly, Jefferson said, "Before you go back to Louisiana, you're about to get an education on why the 1803 Supreme Court decision *Marbury versus Madison* lies encased in this great hall of honor."

POTUS exclaimed, "I'm not familiar with this case."

"Of course you're not, you imbecile!" replied Jefferson. "What else can explain your despicable efforts to pressure and bend the courts to the will of the people . . . by that I mean the political beliefs of your partisan supporters.

"My colleagues harbor the impression that you desire to shape the courts in your political image. Now, that may not be unusual for many ruling parties. But it's the way you have tread on the matter that disturbs us.

"There are allegations that you may have corrupted the lower courts with bribes, favors, and political cronyism. And there are also accusations that you have placed many of your friends in the state and federal courts. Consequently, half the population views judicial rulings with cynicism. And to stir up controversary, with disdain you egregiously criticize the Supreme Court and call them ignorant when they rule against you. How can people respect the law when their president indulges in these kinds of shenanigans?

"The way you advanced your recent appointment of Supreme Court Justice Justin T. Daniels, your second cousin, was quite a coup! Facing allegations of sexual misconduct during his Senate confirmation hearing, your heavy hand squelched the FBI's investigation. They never followed up on all the allegations and your guy squeaked through. You displayed unusual sympathy for that man's plight. Then again, you dosey-do around similar charges yourself. Must be convenient to have a kindred soul sitting on the Supreme Court—just in case.

"What do you have to say about these charges? Anything to confess that might clear your conscience?"

Clearly irritated by this line of questions and ready to dodge the ramifications, Little Big Hands did what he does best: confront a personal attack with an even more aggressive counterattack, facts be damned. "Have you forgotten the Fifth Amendment?

After a couple of hundred years in the ground, senility might be a bit of a problem for you. So, I ask you the same question."

Jefferson responded, "I have made mistakes in office. What president hasn't? The best learn from them. I posed the question to give you an opportunity to clear the slate.

"As I look back on it, the Marbury and Madison case lingers as my biggest philosophical error. And that's quite a statement, since history remembers me as one of the greatest political thinkers of the eighteen and nineteenth centuries. To the end of my presidency, even after I accepted the verdict of *Marbury versus Madison*, I continued to argue—altruistically, I might add—that the courts should be subject to the political will of the people. History has proven me wrong. We stand before this document because you are making the same mistakes about separation of powers that I did when we were a young nation. The difference is that your efforts are for personal political gain.

"Our nation has survived, progressed, and become wiser because the judiciary is one of the three coequal branches of government. As an aside, we ghosts also hear rumblings from Congress that you have attempted to subordinate and undermine their relationship to the executive office.

"At the Constitutional Convention, our Founding Fathers established the Supreme Court as independent and equal to Congress and the president. However, neither Washington, Adams, nor I treated it that way until the case you are staring at was decided.

"Just like your sad presidency now, real enmity and acrimony split the Senate and the House of Representatives. *Marbury versus Madison* can be viewed as me versus Chief Justice John Marshall, the courts versus the executive, the Federalists versus the Republicans, and the advocates of a strong central government versus the proponents of states' rights. Now, two centuries later, you foment these conflicts over again . . . dividing Americans and polarizing any meaningful legislation from passing.

"On the eve of the Marbury case, I rose above myself and my personal beliefs, and became a bigger man for it. . . something I suggest you do. To quiet the nation, seek harmony, and unify Americans from all political persuasions, I declared that 'We are all Republicans, we are all Federalists.' Whatever the outcome of the case, I want to register that we are a people governed by the rule of law and a nation ennobled by an independent judiciary, even when we disagree.

"So, the decision in *Madison versus Marbury* went against me. It established that federal law was superior to state law and that the Supreme Court will be the final arbiter of the Constitution. As much as you would like it to have turned out otherwise, the trial also helped to establish the principle that judges cannot be impeached due to political disagreements or disagreements with particular rulings . . . another critical and enduring principle of judicial independence.

Rather than govern with anger and vindictiveness, I disciplined myself to exercise temperance, patience, and commitment to heal rifts between political parties and within them. Whenever I could, I sought common ground with my opponents.

"On the other hand, Little Big Hands, news reporters think you sow division and attempt to keep everybody off-balance. Are their allegations true or false?"

POTUS, less alert from his ordeal, missed the question. Instead, he blurted out, "Who says I can't impeach a judge who is worthless? I have a few liberals in mind who I intend to show the back door."

Glancing over at POTUS, Jefferson observed that he showed extreme signs of mental and physical fatigue. His eyes drooped and his jaw hung slack as he began to drool. POTUS's capacity to concentrate had always been short, and his recall of what he'd said, or what other people had told him, was notoriously limited.

Abandoning oratory, Jefferson stuck his finger in POTUS's ear to pipe one last message into his brain. "Little Big Hands, I want you to remember that the things you tamper with give strength to our national government and character. When you wake up, I want you to watch the morning news to see what lies ahead. If you keep befouling this great country, whose birthday I and President John Adams chose to honor the exact same day as our deaths, we will haunt you to infinity."

Jefferson inscribed a few more notes, then said, "I have no more remarks to make upon it and in this place." He left POTUS where he first found him.

***

When he awoke, POTUS dashed to the television set in the bathroom. Even though he desperately needed to relieve himself following his adventures with Jefferson, he had an inexplicable urge to flick on the news before he urinated. Out of habit, he began to scroll through a few stations to find Ferret News.

He misaimed, spraying the floor, when Miss Annie Oakely Remington began reporting the latest news for Channel 6666. "Thank God," he thought. "Hands On For America government broadcast network had simply been a figment of his imagination— he had not nationalized the news after all."

"Hello again, ladies and gentlemen. As you know, President Daniel Hands and Billy Brickell, the Republican Senate majority leader, recently delivered on another campaign promise to their loyal supporters. Just six months ago they filled the last vacancy on the Supreme Court. Rarely in our history have all judges on the court been of the same political persuasion. Like the cabinet members do now, they have announced that they will meet frequently with our president to assure that they are all on the same page when it comes to future rulings.

"This move gives these two leaders unprecedented power over our judicial system. In conjunction with the judges, the decisions President Hands and Senator Brickell from West Virginia make will affect the nation for several generations and reflect the will of the people who elected them. From their rulings, we may expect great changes to our medical care, social security, environmental protection, banking and business regulation, immigration, and civil rights.

"The opposition braces itself for the siege of PAC money to reshape the political landscape. As I speak, law schools, scholars, and political scientists already demonstrate in the streets. Students are violently registering their disapproval. As a result of this abuse of the public trust, the free press and most news broadcast networks have boldly vowed that they will no longer interview any Neti Pot candidate or give them political coverage in future elections. The stock market has tanked, and economists believe that we may be headed for a run on the banks.

"Until next time, this is Annie Oakely Remington, signing off for Bull's-Eye Headline News."

Upon hearing the broadcast, POTUS vacillated between euphoria and depression. Certainly, he thought, he was savvy enough to prevent the state of affairs from coming to this if he successfully reshaped the Supreme Court. Like so many other initiatives he tried to put in play, he had been stung by the law of unintended consequences. Or were they unseen? Either way, like Don Quixote, Little Big Hands convinced himself those consequences presented new opportunities to demonstrate his leadership.

He was physically and emotionally spent. Maybe this was just another dream? A nightmare?

Ghost #7: Andrew Jackson

THE BATTLE OF NEW ORLEANS

Little Big Hands once again stirred from his slumber on the couch. In a stupor, he remained hunkered down inside Belladonna's screened veranda, facing the swamp. With dull eyes, he viewed the wispy cypress wood trees along the bank of the swamp whose gnarly roots drank deep from the slow-moving currents.

The full moon penetrated the swamp and cast long beams of progressively dimmer light into the darkened interior. Here the creatures of the night fed and were fed upon in the battles of survival of the fittest. The laws of nature governed the quagmire that no man could long tame or drain.

POTUS had cottonmouth and was desperate for another shot of Jack Daniels Tennessee whiskey. While he stretched out to grab the bottle from the lamp table for another sip of fortitude, he heard in his head, for some incomprehensible reason, the lyrics from "The Battle of New Orleans" sung by Johnny Horton:

> *In 1814, we took a little trip with Colonel Jackson down the mighty Mississip'*
> *We took a little bacon and we took a little beans*
> *And we caught the bloody British in a town in New Orleans*
> *Ol' Hickory said we could take 'em by surprise*
> *If we didn't fire our muskets 'til we looked 'em in the eyes.*

The song was released in 1959 when the country was still very patriotic. As a statement of the country's mood then, "The Battle of New Orleans" won a Grammy for Song of the Year. A school principal in Arkansas had written the song in a creative attempt to get his students more interested in history. POTUS's grandfather on his mother's side, Jasper Johnson, loved the song. He played it often and thought the lyrics might instill a sense of heritage in his grandson, but the rebellious teenager grew bored. But repetition slowly made an impact on him, and he had come to idolize Jackson. Jasper was a descendant of President Andrew Johnson, who was the first president to face impeachment.

Lacking the two-thirds majority in the Senate, Johnson barely avoided impeachment for high crimes and misdemeanors.

So, POTUS wondered, after all these years since my grandfather passed away, why am I back hearing this song again? I never liked it. Just bits and fragmented pieces of it came into his head.

Then POTUS heard a figure approach humming the tune, along with what sounded like brittle tree branches snapping. But it wasn't the wind or the trees. It was a shriveled man in ancient military garb. With each aching step, the old soldier's bones groaned and crackled. He advanced with help from a cane symbolically hewed from—of course—a hickory tree.

The musty figure stiffly sidled up to POTUS. Cantankerous and pained by the years of his age, President Andrew Jackson spared few words: "Jackson here. Not by desire, damnit it to hell!"

Although Jackson spoke in a style as antiquated as previous ghosts, Little Big Hands related to his southern dialect and, in particular, his use of profanity. Ignoring the old man's grouchiness, POTUS blurted out, "Finally, a visitor who shares my sentiments and style, the seventh president of the United States! Welcome. Sir, it's nice to meet a no nonsense, outspoken American patriot. For inspiration, I've got your portrait in the Oval Office covering my back . . . if you know what I mean. And here you are! I promise that I won't let those lunatic liberals topple statues of you or deface them. I'll teach some respect...lock 'em all up. They see a former slave holder; I see a true American hero who sent the British packing.

"When I campaigned for office, I compared myself to the great man you were. And for good measure, I even passed out hickory toothpicks with a slogan on the boxes: 'Pick Your Troubles Away with Daniel Hands, the Second Coming of Ol' Hickory, and Just as Mean.' Can you believe I'm a politician? I can't either.

"Modestly, if I do say so myself, I ran a great campaign that now they say was better than yours, which was one of the best. We did a great job. The people loved it. I attributed my success to you. We have so much in common to discuss. Some bad things have been going on here lately, and I welcome your visit."

In an optimistic overture, POTUS said, "Perhaps we can get a few things worked out about these horrible apparitions. There's some misunderstanding going on. President Daniel Hands has been an extraordinary president. He's really a likable guy and a remarkable leader. Of all the ghosts, surely you know that!"

With a guffaw, Ol' Hickory burst into tears of laughter.

Not sure of what to make of Jackson's response, POTUS threw down two shots of Jack Daniels. Before he could get to a third, Jackson seized the bottle and guzzled the rest of it down. The long-forgotten taste lingered in his mouth. Jackson wiped his mouth with approval and cleared his throat and said, "I desire that fuel for where we are about to go."

Abruptly, a puzzled POTUS found himself beside Jackson on the ramparts of New Orleans, over 140 miles from Lafayette. While the old man chewed tobacco and spit it out the side of his mouth, a legion or more of invading British Redcoats approached, their brandished bayonets reflected the morning sun as they marched steadily forward. The beat of their drummers and the wail of bagpipes pierced the air and frightened POTUS. In the blink of an eye, the violent scene played out and Jackson was surrounded by admiring troops and bloody British troops dying in the mud.

Just as quickly, the battlefront dissipated and both men were back on the veranda.

"What just happened?" asked an astonished POTUS.

"Son, you've just borne witness to the conflict that essentially ended the War of 1812 in New Orleans. We rendered our justice to the British for torching our beloved White House. As you have just seen, when I withdraw my temper, my better side doesn't get mad—it settles the score. Took me a lot of duels and a trail of dead men to figure that out. We exacted our revenge on the British army, and their Indian and Spanish friends, for attempting to steal President Thomas Jefferson's Louisiana Purchase. They suffered upwards of two thousand casualties to our one hundred.

"Henceforth, I got the nickname Ol' Hickory for my stubbornness and unbending nature in times of crisis. That name, which I am so content to be considered, launched my popularity and cemented my bid for the presidency. The legend lived on after I survived the first attempted assassination of an American president. I confronted the dastardly villain with my cane and beat him senseless. I broke it over his head. I miss that gnarled piece of wood from the hills of Tennessee. We treaded a lot of ground together.

"When I led our troops to victory, my body had been compromised by dysentery, old dueling wounds, and an exhausting march through uninhabitable terrain. These inconveniences did not dissuade me from my duty. I remained a soldier for the good of my country. In regards to the matter of doing your duty, we have important matters to ascertain. Pardon my directness.

"You, sir, avoided the military by fabricating a disability. We both know that your broken tailbone was no excuse. Your family and privileged connections bought into the ploy. During your run for office, you claimed that you were a friend of the military and bragged about your desire to serve and respect them. And then, with no military service in your background, once you became Commander in Chief, you had the audacity to criticize the legacy of the McCain family. You are a cheap imitation, calling the US senator and son of Admiral McCain a coward for getting captured in Vietnam. Do you have any sense of decency?

At heart, are you a coward? There is a considerable majority who entertain the latter opinion.

Jackson thought to himself as he spat chewing tobacco. "If I could just raise my feeble foot waist-high, I'd give this weasel a military boot in the ass to remember to eternity!

Then he said "Little Big Hands, you remind me a bit of Aaron Burr, Jefferson's first vice president. Burr viewed politics as opportunity for fun, honor, and profit rather than an opportunity to serve a higher calling in the preservation of democracy and this great county. Like Jefferson, I found his attitude toward government disturbing.

"Many of your colleagues appear to have made a sport of politics, especially your hand-selected vice president, Poppy Morebucks. Burr killed Alexander Hamilton in a duel—one of the Founding Fathers of the United States, as well the founder of our country's financial system. Eventually, Jefferson rid himself of Burr. He came to the same conclusion as Hamilton: that Burr was untrustworthy, an opportunist like your Morebucks, and in government to serve himself. Sadly, those allegations cost Hamilton his life.

"After leaving government, Burr headed to the Louisiana Territory. He boldly invited Britain, who refused, and then Spain to finance him in raising an army to seize the territory from the United States. He even suggested that with their help he could march on Washington and unseat Jefferson. What do you suppose Jefferson did when he learned that his traitorous former vice president had engaged the British in a dialogue about taking over the Spanish territory—possibly including Texas—and carving out a separate country? If you had been Jefferson, what revenge would you have exacted on Burr?"

"I would have fired him. Oh, wait—he was already fired, right? Well, then, I would have used my powers to chase him down and crush him, like I do my political enemies and those who cross me or prove disloyal."

"Well, you're pretty close on that one," said Jackson. "For his alleged treachery, Jefferson made sure Burr was tried for treason. Remarkably, Burr was acquitted on some kind of technicality. That outcome didn't make Jefferson very happy with the justice system he'd once tried to control. His hatred toward Burr continued to fester. For some time, he persevered in efforts to retry him. The pressure Jefferson kept on Burr ran the scoundrel out of the country. To my satisfaction, he fled to Europe to live a life far from the president's grasp."

POTUS smiled. "I like revenge. Sure didn't know any of this about Jefferson. I got a different view of that note-taking bookworm. He never brought it up when he scared the hell out of me."

Jackson steered the conversation back to Burr and stopped pulling his punches. "Rumor has it that Burr had a lot of romantic affairs in New Orleans. Little Big Hands, you are so much akin to him that I wouldn't be surprised if DNA testing would reveal you as the bastard great-great-great-whatever-grandson. How you got away with blatantly inviting the Russians to interfere with our elections is beyond the comprehension of heaven and hell. I venture to say that in your own way, you are no better than Burr! Why you haven't you been tried for treason for inviting a foreign country to meddle in our elections defies my understanding."

"Ouch!" POTUS cast his eyes down, unable to look his longtime hero in the eye. Never a good listener, he managed to grasp the parallels.

"Let me share another story," Jackson said. "My hot temper and reputation for revenge often got the best of me. I inspired either love or hatred. But sometimes it kept me focused on what needed to be done. With no quarter given, I fought the British during the Revolutionary War and the War of 1812. They humiliated me when I was a young teenage prisoner of war for refusing to shine an officer's boots. He slashed me with his saber,

almost cut off two of my fingers and left a depression in the top
of my head that could cradle a cigar.

"Did I let my hate for the British fester forever, like you do for
those who oppose you? No! When I became president, I signed
new trade agreements with my former enemy. We stopped
restrictions on British ships sailing from the West Indies, and
they gave our ships access to the West Indies. Our new attitude
opened the door to trade with other European, Far East, and
South American countries. For the most part, our relationship
with Great Britain normalized. Consequently, our country's
exports grew seventy percent and the badly needed imports to
help fuel our growth rose over two hundred percent.

"I dwelled in a brutish time as America spread its frontiers.
Freedom and violence were flip sides of the coin. Social status
often offered very little protection. I prospered because I was
tough and ornery enough to strike before someone else could
land the first blow. However, I didn't see everyone who disagreed
with me as an enemy.

"Little Big Hands, there's a huge difference between restitution
and pure mean-spiritedness just for the sake of getting even. I've
heard rumors. If you are foolish enough to believe that you've
modeled your aggressive behavior after me, then I'd say that
you're mistaken. I was never a bully who threw my weight around
just because I could embarrass someone or feel good about myself.
Hear me well, and do not mistake my meaning. I am offended
and deeply resent your comparison to me! You make enemies or
invent them to rally and manipulate your partisans. Once you
make an enemy, you never find it in your heart to forgive. You
call them names, brand them losers, and belittle them."

POTUS slumped his shoulders and attempted to turn away,
deflated by this verbal lashing. But Jackson pointed his old
hickory cane at him, holding him in a metaphysical straitjacket.

"I confess that I did have a volatile personality, but not as extreme as yours. I was quick to personalize political disputes and see myself surrounded by dark conspiracies—the biggest one related to how I lost my first attempt at the presidency. A partisan House of Representatives decided the outcome, ignoring the Kentucky state legislature's recommendation to vote for me. Just the way you won the office, privileged political insiders voted for John Quincy Adams. They ignored the will of the people. But in honor of the office, I did attend Adams's inauguration.

"Your miserable, dark conspiracies about those who oppose you are simply concoctions to gain sympathy from a trusting, narrow-minded electorate. It baffles me how people can see and hear what you do and still jump to favorable conclusions about you.

" I too had my enemies, but I didn't hide behind walls, money, and words. By one account, I fought dozens of duels, partially due to my mercurial temper. I have the scars to bear witness. My dearest companions used to say: 'When he was on horseback, the lead in him rattled like a bag of marbles.' In 1806, I killed Mr. Charles Dickson over a debt he didn't pay and for insulting my wife. He fired first. As his pistol exhausted gun powder, his face framed a sinister smile while he watched a bullet burrow into my chest. I winced and calmly took aim and killed him on the spot. But as I grew older, I learned grace and forgiveness. Once I fought a duel with Thomas Hart Benton. Fortunately, we both missed and oddly enough, he became a political ally and a friend."

Little Big Hands, feeling braver once he realized how feeble the old warrior was, pushed back, saying, "Well, at least I never killed anyone."

Jackson roared back, "How do you know? Who knows what harm a lie, an insult, discrimination, and ignorance might do to another person? I believe you kill people's souls and break their hearts. If I were not a ghost, I'd slap you in the face and challenge you to a duel at twenty paces. Then we'd see how brave you really are."

POTUS's knees started to knock.

"You try what little remaining patience I possess. I feel the mercury rising in these brittle bones. When I accepted this odious errand, I made a promise not to harm you. So, to cut to the chase, your character lacks temperance and forbearance.

"All my life, I abhorred special interest groups. I appointed people who I knew and felt I could trust. Unlike you, I at least listened to their counsel. Even if I disagreed, they kept their jobs. Regrettably, I made some mistakes. I appointed an old friend, Samuel Swartwout, a New York City fixer, to the collectorship of the New York port. My vice president, Martin Van Buren, tried to warn me about Swartwout, but I didn't listen—a characteristic that you have perfected. Swartwout stole more than one million dollars on the job and fled to Europe before I could hang him.

"Nevertheless, I balanced the budget and paid off the national debt. You won't be able to do that coupling big tax cuts with huge expenditures for your pet projects. If I were you, I'd be cautious about comparing your presidency to mine. It might create the wrong expectations from your constituents.

"There were some other scandals, but I don't lose sleep over those affairs. But if I were you, I would discharge a lot of sleep over yours. Your scandals whittle away the trust and kind feelings that voters invested in you to serve them and to display to the world our precious democracy.

"You asked what haunts me from my eternal rest in the middle of the night on a half-moon? It's the beating of tom-tom drums in my ears. I ignored the Supreme Court's ruling in *Worcester versus Georgia* that decided that Native Americans could not be forced from their homeland. I approved US troops leading over fifteen thousand Cherokees from Georgia to reservations in Oklahoma, now remembered in history as the Trail of Tears. Thousands of Cherokees died on that march. Many wanted to become US citizens and live a humble life while they farmed the land they were born on.

"Although I detest your comparisons to me, perhaps in some ways we are alike. The people who voted for me in the South wanted these Native Americans assembled and evicted so they could expand their plantations. I wanted to clear the way for an American empire. They called them savages and deemed the red man, by birth, incapable of amalgamating into our society or becoming Christians. If I am honest about it, what I did to appease my constituents is not unlike your promises to build a wall, evict immigrants, and open up national parks for exploitation.

"Little Big Hands, I cannot refrain from suggesting to you that you will have no eternal rest unless you reform your ways. I beg of you, go to the American people and your imagined enemies, and plead for their forgiveness as you deem proper. Tell them you've had an epiphany. Ask for a do-over. Maybe resign. If you pay heed to my warnings, perhaps you can salvage your soul. I discharge you now and take my leave."

***

Back at Belladonna, as POTUS slumbered, his restless mind glimpsed the future. Or was it yet another nightmare? He dreamed that all his former cabinet members and senior staff had conspired against him. They had gone to Congress to share instances that supported grounds for impeachment or worse yet, treason. Even his shapely, trusted twenty-eight-year-old personal assistant shared a video captured on her cell phone of him encouraging the Russians to dig up dirt on his political opponents and to use social media to sully his opposition. Hadn't he hugged her like a daughter?

Why the betrayal? He'd promised them all executive immunity!

Ghost #16: Abraham Lincoln

THE PEORIA COURTHOUSE

Jackson's chewing-tobacco spittle clung to the toes of Little Big Hands shoes. In disarray, he wobbled to the bathroom to wash the memory off his shoes. Secure in this sanctuary, he positioned himself on the throne, the only seat of power he could find at the moment, to contemplate recent events. What could he do to shake these nightmares?

After an indeterminable period of time, POTUS heard the distinct sound of wood being chopped. Then somewhere on the property he thought a tree crashed to the ground. The sharp snap of brittle timber pierced the air.

Frightened and curious, POTUS left the bathroom and grabbed a pistol to join his security forces on the lawn. None of his protectors were there, and no tree lay on the ground. A tall, gaunt, bearded figure stood in the distance with a black stovepipe hat on his head. The handle of an ax rested on his shoulder. As the man approached, POTUS recognized the famous black jacket with tails that fell below the knee.

Astonished, POTUS thought to himself, "This has to be Abraham Lincoln, back from the tomb."

Lincoln's complexion appeared ashen. He had a bullet hole in his hat. Towering at six feet four inches, plus the hat, Lincoln dwarfed POTUS.

Lincoln noticed that POTUS was fixated on his hat. His wide mouth grinned as he said, "Oh, the bullet hole. It's from a previous endeavor to assassinate me. I didn't wear this one at the Ford Theatre. I had multiple enemies. No doubt you do too. You better pocket that gun. It won't protect you here. Oh, and put it on safety or you might shoot off the crown jewels."

Then his tone abruptly changed. "My dear sir, I have an ax to grind with you regarding one of your speeches." Lincoln's lanky arms suddenly pounded the rusty ax-head between POTUS's shoes. The ground erupted before his eyes. "No need to fret," exclaimed Lincoln. "In Kentucky and Illinois, I became the object of attention as an expert log splitter—and not a bad wrestler."

Once again POTUS's ear struggled to understand 19th century dialect. But he knew a clear and present danger when he saw it. He turned pale and started to bolt for the back door of the veranda.

In a recent speech in Georgia, he had compared himself to Lincoln and boasted that his poll numbers were better than Sixteen's. Then he belittled Lincoln because the union almost lost the war to General Robert E. Lee. To add insult to intended injury, POTUS bragged that he could be more presidential than any president in history, maybe except for Lincoln. He'd added, "All you have to do is act like a stiff." Then he mocked Lincoln by moving robotically around the stage with an imaginary stovepipe hat on his head. Afterwards, the speaker of the House reprimanded President Hands. He said that POTUS was no Lincoln and scolded him for maligning Lincoln's reputation as well as the dignity of the Oval Office.

In an authoritative voice, Lincoln commanded, "Do not entertain escape. I wish for you to climb into my carriage immediately. I have plans for you and wish to waste no further words."

Paralyzed with fear, Little Big Hands complied. He hoped they weren't headed to the bloody battlefields of Gettysburg or to witness another assassination at Ford Theatre.

Suddenly, they stood behind a crowd of mostly men from all walks of life, some who wore their Sunday best and others in overalls. They had gathered in front of the courthouse in Peoria, Illinois. POTUS remembered the old expression, "If it plays in Peoria, it will play anywhere."

What played out in front of them was Lincoln making his case against the Kansas-Nebraska Act in direct response to Stephen A. Douglas. It was Monday, October 16, 1854. Normally on that day, most of the merchants and farmers would work their trades, but this event had been well publicized. The anxious crowd sensed an epic battle of words. It didn't hurt that the corn whiskey poured freely, the custom of the day when politicians wanted to draw a crowd.

With some gratification, Lincoln whispered in POTUS's ear, "That's me up there. My speech lasted three hours, and history records it exceeded seventeen thousand words. I know from your previous visitors that you can't concentrate that long, so I'll just give you the highlights.

"US Senator Douglas, a Democrat from Illinois and the chairman of the Committee on Territories, shepherded the bill that let settlers decide among themselves when they entered the Union whether to become free or slave states. Congress approved the act in May of 1854. Many people thought that slavery had waned in popularity."

Lincoln explained, "Douglas championed the bill in hopes it would quell further friction between the North and South over the extension of slavery. Just the opposite happened. It reignited the issue, and the tensions that resulted eventually led to the Civil War."

Lincoln said, "I had always opposed slavery. I avow that I was practically an indentured servant myself when my father sold my services to help feed the family. When I learned of the passage of this act, it infuriated me. It roused me as never before. My vigorous opposition relaunched a dormant political career and led to the Oval Office six years later.

"Douglas and I debated one another seven times in Illinois to rounds of cheers, laughter, boos, and applause. On the issues, we were bitter political enemies. As we championed our different political beliefs, we hit each other with all we had.

"Later I opposed him for the Senate in 1858 and lost because of what you now call gerrymandering. I had won the popular vote. Isn't that how you won the White House . . . by gerrymandering to get the electoral votes even though you lost the popular vote by almost three million? Sadly, another 100 million eligible voters never bothered to go to the polls.

"So, you might say I had every right to carry a grudge and demonstrate animosity toward Douglas over losing my run at the Senate. But after I won the presidency, did I make cries of 'Lock them all up,' like you? Or invite a foreign government to dig up dirt on my political foes?

"In fact, Douglas and I respected each other. When we weren't debating each other—I might add, in a civil and respectful manner—we had great fun. I once told an audience that he and I are about the best of friends when we get together and that he would no more think of fighting me than his wife!

"After I lost the run at the Senate seat to Douglas, I even wrote a personal letter of recommendation encouraging the president of Harvard to admit his son. Whether we win or lose an election, the honorable thing is to pull together to calm and unify the electorate.

"So, may I ask why you persist to shadowbox with defeated opponents? What satisfaction do you find in reopening old wounds? It is my observation that autocrats, dictators, and monarchs peer over their shoulders. Insecure, they visualize the next revolution that could unseat them."

Little Big Hands swallowed hard and then stuck his chin out and said, "I learned from my pa to never let an enemy get the upper hand. Or when you have him down, get off the ground. Just keep sticking it to him. The man who makes the most noise wins.

"I thought you said you were a skilled wrestler. I bet you didn't let 'em up. I learned there's always someone who wants to take your place. Don't turn your back, and don't trust anyone. It's a dog-eat-dog world. And honestly, I thrive on the verbal combat. A little guy like me has to do what he has to do to get ahead. There may be smarter people than I am out there, but they don't have the moxie and street sense to prevail. Voters don't like a lot of words or big ideas. They like sideshows."

"Little Big Hands, I implore you to rethink your philosophy of life. I wish you to do nothing in life merely for revenge, but that what you do shall be solely done with reference to the security of the future. Otherwise, generations to follow may only remember you as a malicious, combative, and shallow man who let opportunities to reconcile pass him by.

"I never manifested bitter hatred toward my enemies. Nor did I punish the friends of my opponents. I reinstated Army Captain Edward Andrews, who was a political supporter of George B. McClellan. McClellan and I disagreed on many key issues when he opposed me in my run for reelection in 1864. I said supporting General McClellan is no violation of army regulations, and as a question of taste of choosing between him and me, well, I'm the tallest and he's better looking. I learned that humor and wit serve better than acrimony.

"What did you do when that young Lt. Colonel working in the White House reported a potential security breach as a result of one of your whacky phone conversations? His superior agreed that the officer was clearly duty bound to report the potential violation. Out of spite you fired the officer and his brother, an uninvolved civil servant. But being a vengeful man, when the officer subsequently became eligible for promotion you tried to dissuade the Pentagon. They stood firm. You're a mean-spirited man."

Unable to constrain himself, Little Big Hands snapped back: "You don't expect me to believe that you didn't strike back at those who were disloyal to you or didn't support the cause of making America great again. Politics is a game of hard ball. I'm loyal to those who pledge allegiance to me. That's why I commuted Paul McCavity's sentence. My friend and former campaign manager was convicted on eight felony counts. Falsely, I might add! He refused to testify against me. Craig Millert, the special counsel who investigated whether the Russians meddled in the last election, can say whatever he wants to about my friend having committed a federal crime. I have no reservations about bending the legal system for a good cause, nor does Tony Bark, my attorney general. Different treatment for Roger Yikes, my personal attorney who blabbered about me. He's languishing in prison. Deserves him right for crossing me. I also delivered justice to Dominic York, the United States Attorney for Southern District of New York. He wasted government time and money investigating me on trumped up charges. So, I had my attorney general use his means to remove him from office."

Lincoln cast a cynical eye on POTUS and responded, "Believe me, Little Big Hands, we know from the heavens what's true and not. Your ledger sheet on the matter is pretty one sided. Along the way, you've made enemies of a lot of former friends and allies. And, it doesn't help that you play at politics like it's a game, winner take all. In getting your friend out of jail, 'you crossed a line that even President Richard Nixon dared not in the depths of the Watergate scandal.' You are a rogue president.

"I saw victory as an opportunity to restore old friendships. Immediately after Richmond fell to Union soldiers in April 1865, I visited Confederate general George Pickett's wife in her home. And if you remember any of your history, after the war we sent our defeated enemy home to their families and let General Robert E. Lee retire in peace and mercy.

"I had no appetite and derived no pleasure from revenge. I've come to warn you that people who feed on revenge get consumed by it. Leaders who resort to dirty politics and call someone stupid or un-American, or label the press the enemy of the people, or accuse the networks of being liars, will get someone killed. One of your deranged followers may take matters into their own hands. I should know—I bear witness as a victim.

"Surely if you want to get something done in a government that endures, you must learn there's no time for childish name-calling. It depreciates the US in the eyes of the world and denigrates the office.

"Your tit for tat in the media has to stop. Only a thin-skinned, shallow fellow behaves that way toward criticism. A confident man, sure in his direction, won't waste his time with trivial tweets and tricks. In the final year of the Civil War, Republicans and Democrats alike hated me and, of course the South. Did I let that bother me? Did I react like you? No.

"Before I drop you off at Belladonna, I have one more bone to pick with you. You do know that my nickname is Honest Abe. We couldn't be further adrift in character or reputation. Fabrications, alternative facts, and outright lies won't continue to blind the American people forever. Although you have some competition, do you want to go down in history as the nation's most dishonest man ever to serve as president?

"I have regrets, but nothing like you may have in the afterlife. I wish I hadn't gone to that theatre. I was in a celebratory mood and felt that I owed Mrs. Lincoln more of my time. The South festered from the humiliation of defeat. With death threats I received from disgruntled victors and vanquished, perhaps I should have exercised more caution.

"Then there was my vice president, Andrew Johnson. For eternity, come every future presidential election, I'm compelled as my penance to relive his appointment. I should never have chosen that hard-drinking, impulsive, and ill-tempered Johnson, drunk at his own inauguration, to be next in line to succeed me. He was a small-minded man who lacked vision, and he fell under the influence of Southern politicians. On the heels of my assassination, he had the audacity to declare that 'the US is a country for white men, and by God, as long as I am president, it shall be a government for white men!'

"The radical Republicans, who favored more punitive Reconstruction than I, tried to impeach Johnson. They missed by one vote. Rather than alternately employing a carrot and a stick, that milquetoast Johnson ruined any opportunity for a balanced reconstruction. Under Grant it had to be more stick because of Johnson's temerity. It was my dream to heal the nation's wounds after the Civil War. I think I could have gotten that job done. I had formulated a vision for peace in anticipation of victory.

"I foresee that your political career may soon grind to an end. If so, it will come from the powerful and steadily aimed words of a free press, both from the left and the right. Facts, by nature, are nonpartisan. Unless you change course, those facts will catch up and overwhelm you. I have stated my piece to you, Little Big Hands, and grant you a respite and safe passage home."

***

On the ride back to Belladonna, the steady cadence from the horses' hooves and the sway of the carriage lulled POTUS into a fitful nap. He dreamed that all the enemies he'd accumulated over his career in business and his short time in politics had collaborated with the hated press to dig up dirt on him. In the dream, he was wearing nothing but a G-string, fully exposed to the world, with only a pole to cling to.

Ghost #18: Ulysses Grant

FORT WAGNER

As Lincoln's carriage faded from sight, POTUS stood disheveled, haggard, and confused on the lawn. When he recovered his bearing, he hustled to the security of the veranda. The moonlight revealed that the sole on the inside edge of his right shoe had been split open, as if cleaved by an ax. The shoe flopped with each rapid step. The log splitter had left a permanent reminder of his ghostly visit.

Just as he reached the decorative paved stones and landscaped gardens that lead up to the veranda, a man galloped up on the largest high-spirited thoroughbred POTUS had ever seen. The rider, firmly in control of his mount, wore a dark blue Yankee uniform with gold stars embroidered on each shoulder. A cloud of cigar smoke hovered over the scene. The red glow on the tip of the cigar spit ashes onto POTUS's brow and singed his rumpled hair.

Overwhelmed by the situation he just left and the dangerous one before him, Little Big Hands oddly expressed compassion for the trampled camellias, cyclamen, and roses. Disgusted, General Grant spun his steed around several more times in the garden, stomping everything green underfoot. Then he reared his mount, whose front hooves pawed high above POTUS's head. Little Big Hands cowered. His mind flashed, "My life ends here, with a cleaved skull."

Instead, the general swooped POTUS off his diminutive feet and threw him on the back of Cincinnati, his great war horse. The animal was a gift from a wealthy businessman and admirer from St. Louis. Grant announced that they were going for a ride.

POTUS had a fear of horses and avoided them whenever he could. As a child, the first time he rode a pony it bucked him out of the saddle. He landed hard on his rump and it ached for days.

Grant was a superb horseman, one of the best at West Point, and Cincinnati had little difficulty galloping at a full pace with two riders on his back. POTUS gripped the saddle blanket so hard that his knuckles turned white as his hind end grew sore from the pounding. The riders disappeared into a cloud, ghost riders in the sky, as Little Big Hands screamed, "Where are my security guards? I'll fire you bastards for this!"

Grant shouted out over the howling wind, "Don't look down and don't fall off. Below you lies eternal damnation."

POTUS closed his eyes, but he soon detected the roar of cannons and smelled acrid gunpowder smoke that choked the life out of the air. When he forced his eyes open, they watered in the dense sulfur that blanketed the ground. Cincinnati pranced nervously on a narrow strip of sandy beach between the Atlantic Ocean and an impassable swamp. Before them, the Union army executed a full-frontal attack on Fort Wagner, whose Confederate defenses were legendary.

Fourteen cannons bellowed at the approaching soldiers. The sand before them had been mined and spiked. The earthen fort rose thirty feet above the sand dunes and was essentially bomb-proof, with ten feet of sand above the fort's ceiling.

The only way for the Union to gain control of the entrance to Charleston Bay, South Carolina, and continue their march south was to seize control of this fort.

POTUS wondered why they were here. What could be the point of bearing witness to these strange events?

General Grant could read POTUS's thoughts. "I always wanted to see this battle but was elsewhere. I felt these soldiers would fight harder than anyone on earth to earn freedom for their people. I helped recruit some of the poor devils who bravely go forward. That's the Fifty-fourth Massachusetts regiment whose blood stains the sand red. In reflection, I am responsible for their sacrifices.

"Can you see that all but one of these men are black soldiers?"

The men of the 54th had their bayonets pointed forward in a charge as the sand exploded around them and cannon balls and bullets from the fort crumbled their targets. Before POTUS's eyes, the 54th managed to breech the first wall of defense and engaged in brutal hand-to-hand combat with the Confederates before being slaughtered to a man.

Grant said, "These freed men, formerly slaves, volunteered to serve their country as proudly as any other. They weakened the fort's manpower and set the stage for subsequent assaults. Eventually the Confederates had no recourse other than to abandon the fort.

"The Union owes a debt of gratitude to these fearless black soldiers who laid down their lives in this war, and to every other minority and immigrant who sacrificed themselves in every war after this one. By the conclusion of our great domestic struggle, one hundred and eighty thousand Blacks served. They transformed the war and provided a clear path to their emancipation and established new identities as American citizens. Those who died did so, however unwittingly, to give their descendants the opportunity to vote the likes of people like you out of office someday!"

Of course, POTUS knew very little about these details of American history, particularly this engagement.

Grant turned to POTUS and said, "I wanted you to see this battle. The next time you get set to disparage minorities, think again about how these soldiers died to give you the freedom of speech to infer from the sins of the few that they are all rapists, murderers, and criminals.

"I command you to give serious thought to your speech, behavior, policies, and hiring practices toward minorities and immigrants. You tell voters that you are not bigoted. But we know your daddy and granddaddy were, and they shaped you into the man you are today.

"The soldiers before you are both minorities and immigrants, however originally unwilling to first come here. Their ancestors deserve better from you. The Fifty-fourth were some of the bravest men in our army. They fought to preserve the Union that you poorly govern now.

"And I want you to know whilst they were dying for their country, draft dodgers in New York rioted and lynched several black people, including the nephew of a sergeant in the Fifty-fourth who was just killed in this attack. Many of my Republican colleagues in New York contrasted the heroes of the Fifty-fourth with the cowardly murderers. They shouted out that the soldiers of the Fifty-fourth who fought for the Union earned more respect than the white men who rioted against it.

"So, when people behave in a hostile manner toward minorities, the blacks sure seemed willing to fight for them. I gave my wholehearted support to arm the Blacks. President Lincoln and I remain forever grateful for their service."

No longer able to keep his mouth shut, POTUS asked, "Why did they riot? Perhaps they had justifiable reasons."

"Ahh, now that's a good question. It goes to the root of the matter. In your eyes, and those who think like you, they might have had good cause to riot. You have made speeches around the country that insinuate immigrants have flooded the country, committed crimes, and taken away jobs.

"Here's the real reasons for those riots. New York City was and remains the business capital of the nation. In the early stages of the Civil War, New Yorkers resented losing the South as one of its main trading partners. Before the war, cotton constituted forty percent of all goods shipped out of the city's port. When the war started in 1861, businessmen with selfish interests advocated seceding from the Union. They put the almighty dollar in their pocket ahead of the nation's best interests. Then antiwar merchants, manufacturers, traders, and newspapers kept warning working-class white citizens that emancipation would result in their replacement in the labor force by thousands of freed black slaves from the South. They stressed that these same workers would be drafted into the army to help make this happen.

"So, what was the result? The New York draft riots remain the deadliest riots in US history, even worse than the 1992 Los

Angeles riots and the 1967 Detroit riots. I want you to know that if you continue to manipulate your base of supporters with lies and half-truths about losing jobs to immigrants and minorities, your fearmongering could precipitate riots greater than all those past ones put together.

"There's one more thing I want to show you. Put this sheet over your head. We're headed incognito to a Ku Klux Klan meeting. You see that group of people who all look just the same? They are cowards. They're about to hang a young boy, perhaps thirteen years old, who accidently strayed into the wrong neighborhood. He's soaked in his own sweat, blood and urine. Neither you nor I can intervene since we're in a time warp."

Grant said, "I don't want to watch any more of this. I will tell you what I did about it when I became president.

"Immediately after the Civil War, the Klan flourished in the southern United States. Their conduct appalled me, particularly because so many freed slaves fought and died so valiantly and honorably to preserve the Union. I used every resource available to me to right the wrongs. I put my foot down on the Klan's neck. I signed legislation aimed at shutting down the activities of these white terrorists. And I stationed federal troops throughout the eleven southern states that had seceded from the Union. As a result, by the early 1870s, the Klan died out.

"But we must remain diligent. The Klan reemerged in the first half of the twentieth century—with the help of your grandfather and father, I might add—and then became visible again in the early twenty-first century. In the latter instance, it was because you failed to denounce the white supremacists ralliers in Charlottesville, Virginia. No quarter should ever have been given to the Klan's existence. Now you give new life to this group by fomenting bigotry and hatred of minority groups. Your thoughtless comments fuel animosities among mostly poor, less-educated workers in industries that have passed their prime and that cannot survive without huge subsidies. If you don't stop this now, you will go down in infamy as a deconstructionist and a violator of the Constitution.

"Another thing I want you to know. I worked hard to foster a peaceful reconciliation between the good people of the North and South. I pardoned Confederate leaders. I wanted them to understand their pardon included protecting the civil rights of freed slaves. I'm as proud of the Fifteenth Amendment, which gave black men the right to vote, as I am of serving as a general that ended the Civil War. A great debt has been contracted to secure to us and our posterity our united nation.

"So, tell me. Why are you not doing something about the gerrymandering that continues even today, in the modern age of the twenty-first century? Some of the worst still exists in these states: North Carolina, Texas, Michigan, California, Pennsylvania, Ohio, New York, Florida, and Virginia. But I am sure you know that. You can see both parties have blame. Who knows how many good people's talents are lost to the service of our country due to gerrymandering?"

POTUS responded, "Don't tell me you didn't try every trick in the book to get elected. Let's get real. Jefferson told me that gerrymandering has been around since his time, and so did Lincoln. I welcome the help of my good friends to serve this great country. If we didn't do this to the Democrats and Free Ticket Wing, they'd do it to the Republicans and Neti Pot Wing."

Grant coughed, then replied with a measure of disgust, "My time with you is almost up. Thank God! I want to show you one more thing. Let's go to Wilton, New York.

"Do you see that old man propped up in a bed trying to finish his memoirs before he dies of esophageal cancer as a result of a lifelong enjoyment of smoking cigars and chewing tobacco?

That's me. In one of my last pages, dated July 19, 1883, I register comments on the use of cocaine to relieve my pain as I race to round out my memoirs.

"I noticed your drool. Former cancer patient, right? Perhaps it's time for you to start work on your memoirs. Only the Lord knows what their redeeming value may be.

"So, I ask you, POTUS, How do you want to be remembered? How will the lens of history record your time in and out of office? From what I've seen from afar, it may not be kindly unless you mend your ways."

POTUS cavalierly said, "Thanks for the advice. I hope that's not an omen. Surely you must have your own share of regrets."

"You want to know what regrets I have? Although nothing quite like the scale of yours, my administration, particularly my cabinet, suffered too many scandals. I constantly shuffled my officials for one reason or another. When I look back at it, my standards were too low. In a spirit of participation, I allowed my trusted associates to have too much influence on my personnel appointments. I admit I failed to recognize that some of my trusted associates could be so dishonest or self-serving. Does that sound familiar? I was also too autocratic. Does that strike a note?

"In an unprecedented way, I ran the presidency in a military fashion. I didn't know how to stop being a general, just as you may not know how to stop being a business tyrant. However, I earnestly endeavored to respect the powers of the coordinate branches of government, neither encroaching upon them nor allowing encroachment upon the proper powers of the office which the citizens of the United States conferred on me.

"I rarely consulted with my cabinet or other experts when I made decisions. Some of those decisions proved disastrous. I am sad to say that corruption was discovered in seven federal departments, including the navy, justice, war, treasury, interior, state, and the post office.

"And I also regret nepotism. Over forty of my family members got government appointments. To my everlasting regret, the press and my enemies labeled the corruption 'Grantism,' and it ate away at my legacy. Although I corrected as many of these travesties as I could during my second term, I am eternally forced to defend my record in office. How about you, POTUS?"

Little Big Hands replied: "I'm more interested in loyalty and meeting the needs of my political stalwarts than a little profiteering. I've been around the latter most of my adult life. Know how to deal with it. When necessary...get even from those who steal from me. I trust my colleagues and their family employed here. It doesn't bother me one bit that Vice President Morebucks's daughter has a job in the State department or that the Chinese granted her licenses to market a new line of cosmetics there. The attorney general has his son-in-law working in my White House and a daughter at the Treasury. As long as we're are all pulling on the same rope, supporting my agenda, I'm happy. Aren't we all opportunists in one form or another? Government jobs have to have some benefits to draw those who are accustomed to big salaries and bonuses in the private sector. How else can you attract them? It's the big picture that counts."

Astonished at Little Big Hands's shameful diatribe and defense of nepotism, Grant decided any more time with him was wasted. He delivered POTUS back to Belladonna. As they rode up the lane to the estate, Little Big Hand's chin bobbed on his chest. He suffered from exhaustion and overstimulation—like a child who had eaten too much sugar and stayed up way past his bedtime. POTUS awkwardly slid off Cincinnati's hindquarters. General Grant's great war horse made a quick attempt to kick him where the sun doesn't shine. Fortunately, Cincinnati missed.

Grant chuckled while he watched poor POTUS stagger toward the house. Perched high on the saddle, Grant shouted: "Want you to know that Cincinnati is a great judge of character.

He is the son of Lexington, the fastest four-mile thoroughbred in the country. He recognizes bad breeding when he sees it."

***

The front of the home was ostentatious, even for a Southern mansion. Over the top, like a mafia wedding cake. As Little Big Hands approached the entranceway a little after two AM, he greeted his security guards in a sullen and accusatory voice.

"Where in the hell have you lard heads been when I called for you? Dozing again on the job? Look down that driveway . . . do something—catch that guy on the big horse."

The guards looked blank as they stared ahead. There was nothing there. The compound had been put on lockdown and tightly guarded due to the increased threats and insults from American citizens. Somehow, some way, all security protocol had been violated by the president.

"Look, boss, we patrolled the premises all evening. We have no record of you leaving the mansion, and the alarms were set to alert us if any of the doors were opened. We're as dumbfounded as you seem baffled. Where have you been?"

POTUS didn't answer. He knew they would never believe him, and he didn't know how to explain it without them thinking he had gone insane.

Overwhelmed, he collapsed into bed. Little Big Hands switched on the news, hoping that he might be treated kindlier there than he had been by Grant. Miss Annie Oakely Remington began a flash news announcement for Channel 6666. Normally she would have been off the air at this hour, so Little Big Hands discerned that some sort of crisis must have occurred. What he heard next sent a chill down his spine.

"Annie Oakely here. We bring you ground-breaking reporting anywhere, any time. This just in. Unprecedented rioting continues to occur in a dozen major cities . . . New York City, Atlanta, New Orleans, Chicago, Dallas, Denver, Houston, Seattle, Portland, San Francisco, Los Angeles, and of all places, Palm Beach, Florida. A coordinated uprising among minorities and their sympathetic supporters has reached epic proportions. They scream for social justice and blame President Daniel Hands for driving them to such drastic actions. Thus far there has been little looting, but millions have taken to the streets to demand that the president, his vice president, and the Senate majority leader resign."

POTUS's multiple phones began to ring. Caller ID showed calls from his vice president in D.C., the head of the Neti Pot Wing in South Carolina, and the Senate majority leader in West Virginia. He answered none and wondered if this is just another hallucination.

Ghost #20: James Abram Garfield

A VISIT TO A DEATHBED

Just as he almost drifted off to sleep, Little Big Hands detected the eerie call of a whippoorwill…a bird which makes the same sound as its name. From his southern lore, he knew the legend that this bird senses a soul about to depart and captures it. Superstitious Native Americans believed the Whippoorwill's serenade to be a death omen. POTUS stirred and then awoke to the tall presence of a forlorn bearded figure before him. He wore a white cotton hospital gown smeared in blood.

Little Big Hands thought "My time is up. So many rounds of golf not played. Buildings unfinished and restaurants unopened. Women unloved. Before me stands the grim reaper." The ghost acknowledged POTUS's fears and forced a smile in spite of his own agony. He introduced himself as James Garfield. "Never heard of you," POTUS responded.

"Your previous visitors predicted as much. Not many remember me since I only served in office a few months. I was the second president to die from an assassin's bullet. The perpetrator, like many assassins, was delusional. He failed as a lawyer and an evangelist. Sadly, just like in your times, he found it easy to find a cheap gun."

"Wait a minute!" Little Big Hands interrupted. "It's not the gun's fault. Garfield, you know as well as I the second amendment grants the right for citizens to own guns."

"We don't have time to debate the point, and you wouldn't listen anyway. Some truths are not self-evident. Come with me and I will show you the room in the White House where they attempted to save my life."

They entered a darkened space that had been curtained off. The air smelled stale and rotten. Gruesome nineteen century medical devices sat on tables next to a man lying in agony on a bed. Garfield spoke up. "See that hysterical woman who weeps and holds my hand? That's Lucretia, my wife. For almost 90 days I have endured every torture that medical care and knowledge of the time could inflict on a gun-shot victim.

"My doctor, Willard Bliss, can't find the bullet. He thinks it's on the left side of my abdomen. But there is nothing blissful about his treatment. He and his assistants continue to stick their ungloved fingers inside me to probe where the bullet has lodged.

The instruments they used are not sterilized. In frustration they slit me open almost 20 inches from my stomach to my groin to make the search easier. Septic shock invades my core. Much of my body is infected and swollen. A weaker man would have succumbed long ago. The doctors and nurses force me to eat. Yet, I can no longer control my bowels."

Nausea and panic overcame POTUS. Sweat trickled down his brow. Air conditioning did not exist. Except Garfield's sick room, the midsummer heat and humidity toasted the vermin infested residence. An enterprising engineer had invented a method of blowing air over ice to comfort the president. But the cold air could not curb the stench that permeated the room from Garfield's open wound nor the stink from broken sewage pipes beneath the building.

"I am pleading with Lucretia to transport my bed to our seaside cottage in New Jersey. I want no more effort to save my life. One last time I want to inhale the salty ocean air, see the water's blue hue stretch out into infinity and witness the majesty of one more sunrise. She consents, provided I will allow the doctor to try a new imaging device that Alexander Graham Bell has just created to locate metal embedded in my flesh. Bell has worked around the clock to complete his invention in hopes of saving my life. Convinced that the bullet is burrowed in my left side, the doctor deploys the device. He finds nothing. He doubts its effectiveness. Later an autopsy will reveal that the bullet lay hidden deep in my right side. Likely, Bell's invention would have found it had my physician not been so skeptical of the science and so sure of himself. It will eventually save many lives."

POTUS interrupted, "What's the point of telling me all this? I feel sorry for you and your family, but I don't understand why we are here."

Garfield sighed. "I'll be brief since my presidency was too. The physician who treats me ignores what modern medicine of the time offers. He refuses to embrace the latest in science and technology. Dr. Joseph Lister, a British surgeon and a pioneer of antiseptic surgery, had already proven that washing hands and instruments could prevent infection and save lives. American doctors largely paid no attention to his findings and seminars."

"I still don't get your point and I would rather prefer to leave this room. It disgusts me."

"You Sir are no different than Dr. Bliss and his colleagues."

"What do you mean by that?"

"Let me be specific. When Covid-19 erupted in China, you largely ignored what scientists said about the potential spread of a virus for which mankind had no immunity. You paid little attention to your daily presidential briefings about the implications for America. Didn't read most of them. Then, you initially said the virus would have little effect on our citizens. Making light of the matter and angering the Chinese, you named Covid-19 the Kung Flu. If the Chinese wanted to help America benefit from what they've learned about treatments, your lack of diplomacy certainly removed any incentive.

"Once it's recognized that Covid-19 invaded our country, you appoint yourself an authority. Like the doctor who ignored scientific evidence when he treated me, you suggest people should use hydroxychloroquine to prevent Covid-19 on the basis of antidotal claims. You call it a game changer.

"Because of your public profile, scientists working for the government feel compelled to try to prove your recommendation. They sacrifice valuable time that could be better used to find a real cure. Their studies show that the drug is ineffective against the virus. But you didn't stop practicing medicine without a license. You horrify doctors when you also speculate that a disinfectant injected into the veins might prevent or cure the virus. After he heard you, one of your fanatical followers actually does that and dies. A few months later you falsely claim that 99% of Covid-

19 cases are totally harmless, even though the World Health Organization provides evidence that 20% of all cases are severe enough to require oxygen or hospital care.

"Then to insulate the country from bad news, you attempt to muffle Dr. Stanley Steward, the director of the National Institute of Allergy and Infectious Diseases, who has advised six presidents on HIV/AIDS and other infectious diseases. And, one of your dear supporters, Jerome Buster the Lt. Governor of Texas says there is something more important than living. Hmmm, did you hear him or any party stalwarts volunteer for the alternative?

"Echoing your rhetoric, the back-up governor declares that he's sick and tired of listening to Dr. Steward, even though the Coronavirus leads cause of death in the U.S. You and he put dollars ahead of life. Did either you or Buster ever stop to think that about 80% of Covid-19 related deaths in the U.S. are people over 65 years old? These citizens make up a large part of your campaign base and financial support. Have you given any thought to how they may respond at the polls when you make them your sacrificial lambs?

"To further deny the impact, you claim that this will all be over soon and refuse to wear a mask. Rather than lead by example, you choose to politicize the matter. You stick out your chest and crow that the Constitution protects freedom of choice not to wear a mask even though scientists tell you that to wear one protects others, not just yourself from Covid-19. Little Big Hands, I wonder how many more people will die because of your ignorance?"

Red in the face, he could barely conceal his anger. Little Big Hands shouts "The virus is all the fault of those Chinese weasels. They should have done more to contain it. They should have told us about its spread sooner. And the World Health Organization napped while the virus creeped up on them too. Or, perhaps they are in bed with the Chinese? They won't get any more funding from the U.S. while I am president."

"Little Big Hands, you never accept that you're culpable. Prior to the eruption of Covid-19, didn't you give a financial haircut to our Center for Disease Control and Prevention? By arbitrarily slashing their budget, as you've done to many other government entities that your party wants to shrink, you gutted the Center's ability to respond to the crisis on a timely basis."

POTUS pushed back: "All the Center does is scare people. It's a money pit. They fly off to this country or that to treat some third world disease we've never heard of. Private enterprise could just as well be doing their jobs."

"Little Big Hands, I find you tiresome. I need to return to the Cosmos to give an updated report on your frame of mind. I implore you to consider what I said. American lives depend on what you do.

"Before I go, I'll share a couple of regrets. First, I wish I could have completed my first term in office. In my inaugural address, I meant what I said about my intent to restore dignity to African Americans brought to this country in bondage and grant them full citizenship. Had I been able to fulfill that promise, perhaps Jim Crow laws that propagated racial segregation in the south never would have found fertile soil. I might have starved the racial attitudes that eventually shaped your presidency, Woodrow Wilson's, and Richard Nixon's."

"Last, I regret my brief infidelity. It was a troubled and stressful time in our marriage. I acted irresponsibly. We lost our first child and I sought solace from a female reporter for the New York Times. I later accepted the blame and pledged eternal loyalty to my wife. Stood by it. In return, she found it in her heart to go forward. On conclusion of my time in office, we dreamed of returning to the splendid shores of Lake Erie and our peaceful and abundant farm in rural Mentor, Ohio where we raised our five children. Instead, I went back in a coffin.

"So, POTUS does the press treat you with the same grace they did me? Do all your wives forgive you? I don't know about the women in your life, but if you focused on a constructive and believable solution for the Covid-19 problem and stopped making it a political issue, the press might give you more room to breathe.

"On a totally different subject, if you make the display of the Confederate flag a key campaign issue, it will leave a bitter taste in a lot of mouths. Even NASCAR, a bunch of good old boys who play hard and run fast, supports the ban. I was a General in the Union Army. Saw a lot of people die to save the Union. The people who carried that flag did not want to make America great. Do you know how many people died because of that flag? On both sides, 618,000. If you don't give better leadership to combat the Covid-19 war, the number of fatalities here could conceivably swell to half that level. Is that how you want to be remembered?

Our nation needs a bold leader with command of the resources to heal the wounds you have inflicted upon it the last four years.

Ghost #26: Teddy Roosevelt

A TRIP ON THE ELYSIAN

The back to back experiences with Grant and Garfield left POTUS depleted. He smelled horsey after the hard ride on Cincinnati's rump and he ached from head to toe from the experience with Grant. After the previous ordeal with Garfield, he looked at the sheets to see if they were coated in blood. Unable to sleep, he decided a blissful soak in a full tub of therapeutic warm water might cure him. If nothing else, it might cleanse him of bad memories.

He thought, "In the morning I'll deal harshly with those pesky rioters, when I'm more presidential. Give them something to remember me by. I'll send in the National Guard and make those mealy-mouthed bastard socialists pay for crossing me. Or maybe I won't, if all this is just another nightmare."

Frustrated that everyone looked at him like he was nuts, POTUS washed away his cares with a bottle of Scotch and a bar of soap. In a deep slumber and pickled in the tub from the booze, he distanced himself from time, space, and reality.

As he soaked in the tepid water, POTUS sank deep into his subconscious. He fantasized about an early twentieth-century train headed to Belladonna. He visualized an ancient steam engine as it huffed and puffed and belched a trail of steam high into the sky. The rails shuddered and a shrill whistle erupted in the quite presence of the estate like a fire alarm.

In a trance, Little Big Hands bolted out of the tub. Naked and hung over, he started to slip on the wet tile floor just as a firm hand saved him from a fall. Then he was startled by a bold, authoritative shout: "Bull Moose here. For God's sake, man, get dressed. We're about to miss the train. Cover that dinky thing up. It's time to go!"

***

For the adventure, Roosevelt wore his cavalry tan jacket, belt pack, leggings, and famous rough rider campaign hat. The war uniform had been made for him by Brooks Brothers with their best wishes for success in the Spanish American War of 1898. He had wedged on his nose a pair of armless Pince-Nez wire-framed glasses. With a wince or a wrinkle of his brow, he could pop them right off his nose. Only a neck chain prevented the lenses from tumbling to the ground.

Teddy Roosevelt herded POTUS into his Private Pullman Palace car, the Elysian.

"We are going to take a little trip back up north. I want you to ride in comfort. May take a while, since about a hundred eighty privately owned railroads existed in my time—each its own little monopoly. We'll need to make some transfers, but don't worry about tickets."

With a tip of his campaign hat toward POTUS, Roosevelt said, "All aboard, the tab's on me. In my world, time's irrelevant, so we'll get there when we get there."

In the presence of Bull Moose, Little Big Hands sobered up. He recalled the riots reported in the news before he fell asleep. He said, "Before we go, I've got an important conference call to make to Vice President Poppy Warbucks and Senate Majority Leader Billy Brickell. It pertains to a national emergency that I've methodically deliberated over. Time to take some action. Certainly, when you were in office, you must have had a few of those yourself, old-timer."

Roosevelt scrunched up his cheeks, which prompted his spectacles to spring off his nose. He snorted. "Bully for you. Go ahead. But lest you forget, in my eyes and your last six visitors', you are the subject of a national emergency. I want it distinctly understood that you don't have much time."

When POTUS ordered Vice President Warbucks and Senate Majority Leader Brickell to send in the National Guard to crush the riots, both acted perplexed. Brickell replied, "Sir, this the fifth time you've called us in the last couple of days about an emergency and demanded intervention. If I may be blunt with you, there are no riots going on now, unless they're in your head. Nor were there the last time you called. And none of your cabinet members conspire to bring your presidency to an end. We've still got in our pockets the people who count.

"Warbucks and I think you need to come back to Washington. We'll arrange for a thorough medical exam at Walter Reed. Keep the whole thing quiet. Send you over on a Saturday night when the press sleeps. The docs may prescribe a few more pills. Until they get you right-sided, we'll happily take care of your executive duties."

Brickell thought to herself, "We've already handled your crap for most of your administration anyway. Maybe those good doctors can just keep you sedated through the rest of your presidency. A clandestine military coup."

Out loud, Billy said, "Nobody will ever know you've experienced these illusions. May I set up a confidential appointment for you?"

POTUS threw down the phone. The hotline went dead.

While he admired the luxury of the Pullman car, a number of disturbing storm clouds crept into his head. "Why back north? Is this trip a precursor to an impeachment? Am I being escorted back to Washington in the company of the Rough Rider to testify before Congress?"

Roosevelt, always up for an adventure, and also a gracious host, put his traveling companion at ease. "I've always enjoyed this coach and know how you appreciate luxury. Come, take a stroll with me."

As they walked down the aisle, Roosevelt said, "I had this car built for me when I set out on the longest train ride ever taken by a US president. For nine weeks, I bivouacked in these seventy paneled feet of virgin-forested mahogany, equipped with the finest leather and velvet chairs, two sleeping chambers, two bathrooms, a private kitchen with my own five-star chef, a dining room, a stateroom with picture windows, and a rear platform to deliver whistle-stop speeches. He laughed. If you're going to rough it on the trail, this is how to travel!

Without provocation, Roosevelt's bull terrier, Pete who often rode the rails with his owner, tore at Little Big Hands's pants cuffs. "Damn it Pete, stop that! I'm sorry. Pete doesn't trust foreigners. Just a few weeks ago he almost ripped the pants off the French ambassador.

"I don't want you to misunderstand me, or Pete. These plush arrangements might fool a person like you. Although I savored the finest life had to offer, I campaigned to protect, preserve, and replenish Mother Earth. I set out on a mission to see the American people from coast to coast. Along the way, I wanted to tour and personally inspect this great country's vast natural beauty and the depth of its unlimited resources. I also conceived of this trip as a marketing campaign to test my concept of a square deal; a way to express and test my vision for a domestic policy that would benefit the purity of our blessed land and its people.

"Little Big Hands, you know about marketing campaigns, don't you? If you had to make a wager, did you seriously ever think you'd win the primaries and then the Oval Office? From the get-go, your campaign was more about the glorification of the Belladonna brands of meats, restaurants, hotels and real estate. If you accidentally won the presidency, all the better for your brand. But whatever the outcome, how could you resist all those campaign donors who generously paid for your free advertising?

"I am here to confirm whether what others say about you is true. Some say that you never had much appetite for running the country, or even a deep-rooted vision for the nation. They claim that your campaign to denigrate your opponents was a front to promote and feed your carnivorous hunger for power, wealth, and fame. They say you fooled the people who were ready to be fooled, talking in great generalities about what you would do for them."

Hearing this, POTUS sniffled, "Aren't we all about marketing campaigns? Look at that silly hat that you wear, curled up on one side, and those shiny boots. Don't lecture me about brand image. If we don't look after ourselves, who will? If I hadn't done what I did, someone else would have. This isn't the first time I've been called the Elmer Gantry of politics.

"Those claims you mention lack substance. I have big plans for a wall, extracting energy from the earth, creating vast pipelines across the country to transport oil and gas, uprooting the deep state, protecting the right to bear arms, and exporting the human rubbish causing all the crimes across America. And that's just the beginning.

"In my second and third terms, I'll run the country like a laundromat. The people will thank me. I'll cleanse the country of what ails it and wash the refuse down the drain. When I'm done, I'll be eulogized on Mount Rushmore. One of you has-beens may have to move over."

Roosevelt ignored this nonsense and calmly repositioned the Pince-Nez glasses on the bridge of his nose. He continued in a soft but firm voice. "I want to tell you more about my historic train expedition across America. You'll soon see the significance, even if I have to sport a big stick to enlighten you.

"During the trip, I took along the famous naturalist John Burroughs and camped with John Muir, founder of the Sierra Club. We progressed westward through the most scenic landscapes and small towns whenever possible, stopping to explore the East Coast, Midwest, Northwest, far West, and Southwest.

"In Indiana, they loved it when I said, 'Speak softly and carry a big stick.' You, Sir, speak loudly and swing a small stick.

"When I spoke in South Dakota, I talked about the qualities they should look for in a public figure: a man who keeps his word and never promises what he can't deliver. The crowd whistled their approval.

"Little Big Hands, can you understand this? Didn't you promise that the trucking industry would pay to repair our nation's highways, knowing full well that would never happen? Or if it did, that the American people would ultimately pay through chargebacks from the industry?

"In Oregon, they cheered when I said, 'Do not like hardness of heart, nor softness of head.' In Arizona, I spoke of the Indians in my Rough Riders regiment from Texas. I stated since they were good enough to fight and die by my side during the Spanish American War, I owe them the exact same deal as any white man. I felt obligated to integrate them into our society, with all the rights and privileges of any other citizen even though I once said fourteen years earlier in a speech in New York that 'I don't go as far as to think that the only good Indians are dead Indians, but I believe nine out of ten are.' I had to eat those words and I'm glad I did.

"When I reached Yellowstone and Yosemite, I stepped up my campaign to preserve America from exploitation. When I arrived at the Grand Canyon, special interest groups, powerful lobbyists, and congressmen pushed to make the land available for mining precious metals. I disagreed. I urged with the sturdiest of rigor that our countrymen leave it as it is for children and generations to come as one of the greatest sights everyone should see. I resolved that this natural beauty must become forever a national park."

For emphasis, Roosevelt swung his big stick in the air and bellowed. "It infuriates me with the keenest indignation, Little Big Hands, that you now sully the national parks with talk of granting oil, gas, and mineral rights. Have you no sense of guilt for what you will rob from future generations? Think of your own grandchildren and those who come after."

Lamely, POTUS mumbled a preposterous fundamentalist belief. God had made the earth for the dominion of man and people mattered more than the planet.

Bull Moose refused to even acknowledge such ignorance and continued. "Upon entering the San Lorenzo Valley, I admired the majestic beauty of giant sequoias, some dated back to the time when the first Egyptians penetrated the valley of the Euphrates. I began to see that unregulated lumber practices threatened these timbers and exhausted our forests elsewhere. And I made the connection between forests and water conservation. Forests absorb water and help control floods. During my trip, I concluded that we must prevent speculators from ruining this beautiful land. I pushed policies to avert America's forests and waters from destruction by the hands of a few men of great wealth."

Unable to focus or synthesize information except in small bites, when he heard the word 'water,' POTUS blurted out, "I'm going to deregulate energy-efficient dishwashers, showers, toilets and sinks. I'm rolling back Obama Department of Energy efficiency standards so that you can actually wash and rinse your dishes without having to do it ten times. I took a dump the other day and it took four flushes to say 'goodbye.' We've got plenty of water. Look at that California Governor. He sends all that water out to the Pacific and then he limits people to 50 gallons of water. Before you know it goes to 47, 46, 45."

In reaction, Roosevelt again wrinkled his nose and popped off his Pince-Nez glasses. After a deep breath, he responded, "That's absurd! 'Our forefathers faced certain perils that we have outgrown. We now face other perils, the very existence of which it was impossible for them to foresee. Modern life is complex and intense. Our success at this grand experiment called democracy depends not only on our personal welfare, but on the welfare of mankind. That includes the environment.'

"So, having told you all this, am I angry? Damn right! Yes— with you, especially. To win votes, Little Big Hands, you cater to special interest groups, like coal. You know coal's useful life cycle will come to an end. To promise those miners you'll restore their jobs is pure poppycock. You could have offered them education for jobs in viable and sustainable forms of energy.

"Under your direction, the Environmental Protection Agency has once again relaxed its enforcement. Your appointment of Jamie Leaks to head the EPA mocks all the work that I and many of my successors have done to preserve our natural and rapidly diminishing resources. Little Big Hands, why did you appoint such a scoundrel to head the EPA? He has publicly denied the findings of the world's top scientists on climate change, opposed environmental regulations, and lobbied on behalf of industries that pollute our lands. Never have the air and the nation's drinking water been so violated. Lung cancer, other environmental cancers, and related illnesses are multiplying. Killing people. Have you no shame or sense of responsibility? These deceased souls will surely seek you out and haunt you.

"Look at the evidence! In Russia, we have increased instances of black rain and snow colored by pollution from industrial, petroleum, and mining sectors. Children suffer hideous skin rashes and other ailments. And, more and more mothers give birth to deformed children. The glaciers continue to melt, and cities like New York, Houston, New Orleans, and Miami suffer catastrophic floods. All this rests on you and your predecessors' heads, all of you who ignored Mother Nature's pleas for help.

"There are over twenty-six thousand indicators of global warming on this planet and many go back well over a hundred years. Scientists haven't just lectured conservatives. They warned President Johnson of impending disaster, and every president since him. How can you possibly hide the evidence for political gain? What could possibly justify it? No bribe is big enough for such a travesty. Are you under the influence of those who have paid scientists to deny climate change and claim it's a liberal concoction? If so, I want you to know that thirty-eight conservative studies that repudiated climate change were analyzed from scratch. It was found that each one contained one or more errors in calculation. When these errors were acknowledged and corrected, these amended studies agreed with thousands of other studies: dramatic climate change is underway. For what it's worth to you, we ghosts can see it from the heavens."

POTUS pushed back. "I must admit, I was unaware that our fabulous Neti Pot scientists might have made some errors in their calculations. Are you sure the data hasn't been manipulated? People do that to support what they want to believe. Our scientists came up with some compelling reasons why much of climate change is just a big liberal hoax that scares people about fracking and investment in fossil fuels.

"Their findings made sense to me and discounted the impact of carbon dioxide emissions. I'll give the matter more thought, but my energy plan will make American great again, and independent of all that Middle East oil and their hostage-takers. That's a good thing."

Persisting in what he had chosen to believe, POTUS continued. "I still believe that the earth is just going through weather cycles that have repeated themselves over time. We've been here before. You know, one year hot in one part of the globe and another cold. One year dry another wet."

Bull Moose shook his head. "I don't know if you really believe the garbage that comes out of your mouth or if it's just convenient for you to help your friends get rich or elected. A thermometer doesn't know the difference between a liberal or a conservative. Look at the evidence in your own home state of Louisiana, with hurricanes and repeated five-hundred-year floods just a few years apart. Hurricane precipitation rates are increasing. Storms are intensifying faster. They're stronger and move more slowly as they drown everything in their path. And they are bigger.

"Let's take your flawed, dastardly logic about natural cycles. All evidence shows that the sun is getting cooler, so global warming can't be caused by that. And global warming can't be attributed to the earth's orbit, because the current path should be gradually taking us into an ice age. The only explanation is that man has placed a blanket of carbon dioxide around the planet. How can your administration hide behind lies about climate change? We are more backward than China and India. They are shutting down coal plants as quickly as they can and investing billions of dollars to replace them with clean energy.

"Little Big Hands, find your soul. Exercise some leadership. Remove the blindfolds and earplugs you share with your voters. Enlighten them about the true causes of climate change and the consequences. They want so badly to believe everything you say. Such a campaign might help you gain some independent voters and win reelection.

"Furthermore, stop targeting and insulting Breta Youngburg, that sixteen-year-old climate activist from Sweden who *Time Magazine* put on its annual cover for her stellar work on behalf of slowing global climate change. Instead of wishful thinking that you'd grace the cover, she won *Time's* 2019 person of the year. Even Ferret News had the common sense to apologize for calling Breta a mentally ill Swedish child on one of its programs.

"I implore you to do something right and of real service to humanity with the awesome power invested in your office. Although some may question it, you too are a creature of God. Caring about God's creation—the earth and people and other living things—is a genuine expression of faith and gratitude, an acceptance of responsibility to the nation and world."

Under the full weight of Roosevelt's bully pulpit, POTUS became speechless. Momentarily, he lost ability to utter a sound. He just stood there and drooled, with his handkerchief pressed to the corner of his mouth. With some relief he felt the train begin to grind to a halt. Then the lights went out. The next thing he heard was Roosevelt's voice announce, "Bully, we've arrived."

They stood by the American Museum of Natural History's entrance on Central Park, Upper Manhattan. Beside the steps, Roosevelt pointed to a dominant sculpture of himself on horseback gazing across the park and into the future of America. The size, scale, and significance of the mounted rider dwarfed POTUS.

With great pride, Bull Moose said, "This museum remains one of my proudest achievements. It upholds everything I stood for in life and memorializes the work I did on behalf of conservation. My father, Theodore Roosevelt, Senior, was one of the founders."

POTUS was relieved to find that he wasn't in Washington, D.C., about to face a congressional hearing or an impeachment trial.

"Come on in, it's just going to be us—a night at the museum, just like the movie Ben Stiller and Robin Williams star in. I must say, Robin did a good imitation of me. We can't possibly visit all the exhibits here in the time we have left together. So, you and I will concentrate on just a few of my personal favorites: the Theodore Roosevelt Memorial Hall and the Biodiversity and Environments Halls."

With renewed vigor, and unshackled by ghostly confines, Roosevelt dragged POTUS through the four stages of his life. First, they stopped by to view insects, small creatures, and rocks he collected as a young naturalist. Bull Moose suggested that POTUS reminded him a bit of a bloodsucker he found in a stream.

Then they advanced to the Badlands of North Dakota, where Roosevelt first became alarmed about the extinction of the American bison and other wildlife. Bull Moose took this opportunity to grimly point out to POTUS that he was endorsing policies that would eventually extinguish man from the planet.

Roosevelt became even more animated when they stopped by the conservation exhibit on his unprecedented action to place some 230 million acres of public lands under federal protection.

Then he provided a glimpse of the future. Bull Moose showed POTUS much of that same land stripped, ripped, gouged and laid barren as the projected result of his reckless policies to exploit timber, minerals, and fossil fuels.

Gathered round the sordid scene, children wept over the spoiled lands. Even in their innocence, they sensed what they had lost to POTUS and the Republican Party and Neti Pot Wing's policies that ruined the earth for future generations. In the background, their parents shed tears over POTUS's recent decision to roll back clean water rules. Favoring private enterprise over the protests from the EPA Science Advisory Board, Little Big Hands had repealed or weakened nearly one hundred environmental regulations.

As moisture gathered in his eyes, an agitated Roosevelt popped the glasses off his nose again, and cried, "Little Big Hands, you've even screwed Mother Nature. You violate the objective to restore and maintain the chemical, physical, and biological integrity of the nation's watershed and wetlands."

His mission almost over, Bull Moose began to atrophy in the presence of the fourth exhibit that honored him as a lifelong explorer. It portrayed his last great expedition on the River of Doubt in Brazil, a journey that had almost cost him his life. He'd returned home permanently weakened.

Roosevelt turned to POTUS and said, "Like the River of Doubt, I cannot see where your course as a president will take the nation. If I had had better guides on my last journey, so many bad things might not have happened on that river. It is my fervent wish that you find better political appointees to help you and your administration navigate—even avoid—the savage and swollen political streams that lie ahead of you."

A notoriously poor student, with grades to prove it, Little Big Hands was forced by the gravity of Roosevelt's presence to discover things about the environment he'd never cared about.

Along the way, he learned about Roosevelt's passion for trust-busting to protect the American people and the land.

Roosevelt made frequent references to POTUS being in bed with big business, then added, "It is well to keep in mind that exactly as the anarchist is the worst enemy of liberty and the reactionary the worst enemy of order, so the men who defend property rights have the most to fear from wealthy wrongdoers—and those who champion popular rights have the most to fear from demagogues who would oppress honest businessmen, honest men of wealth in the name of those popular rights; for the success of either type of wrongdoer invites a violent reaction."

POTUS wasn't sure he fully understood what Roosevelt was saying. He ventured, "Are you saying that the political party in power should be cautious about imposing too much of their will on the loser?"

Bull Moose grinned.

Roosevelt finished the tour well before daybreak on the east side of the museum. He said to POTUS, "It may not be too late. When you get back to the present, I want you to think hard about changing your course on the environment. I don't like it that you have broken environmental agreements with other nations. You still have time to make a big difference in the world. Use your bully pulpit to save the environment before you have to face our Creator.

"More than my presidential library and national parks, this museum is my greatest legacy. What will be your legacy, Little Big Hands? Perhaps you still have time to make it something significant and honorable. Time's a-wasting. Perhaps your legacy will just be the Belladonna burger—an overhyped marketing campaign for a cheap piece of branded meat.

"I have regrets. To show you that I was once human, I'll share one that still haunts me. I encouraged the Japanese to embrace a Monroe Doctrine for Asia like ours for the Americas. That may have precipitated Japan's Greater East Asia Co-Prosperity Sphere. They began to dominate their Asian neighbors, and it led to Pearl Harbor and World War Two. That's my recurring nightmare in the afterlife."

***

As promised, POTUS's round-trip train ticket got him back to Belladonna. He stood before the mirror in his hallway. He hardly recognized himself. His reflection looked a lot like a 1930s mug shot of Al Capone, only shorter and pudgier. POTUS vaguely recalled eating constantly, mostly out of anxiety, while he shared the train with Roosevelt. He remembered Roosevelt feasted at the dining table with as much gusto as everything else in life.

Ghost #28: Woodrow Wilson

THE NATIONAL CATHEDRAL

The security guards, alarmed by POTUS's erratic and flummoxed behavior, alerted the White House's personal physician, Dr. Wots Themater. Themater always traveled with the president to keep him properly medicated for a personality disorder that he concealed from the public.

Around 3:30 AM, Dr. Themater found Little Big Hands curled up in a ball with a throw pillow over his head in the lounge on the veranda. POTUS's legs twitched as he whimpered and babbled about something that sounded like confrontations with ghosts. The doctor woke him up enough to administer a sleeping pill that had proved effective in the past.

Dr. Themater noticed on a side table a series of tweets on POTUS's iPad that rambled on about apparitions. The garbled sentences and broken phrases littered with dot-dot-dots made no sense. Themater turned off the table lamps and draped a blanket over Little Big Hands, hoping that he would sleep soundly in the three hours that remained before dawn.

***

In his sedated state, POTUS dreamed that he stood by a gray-haired, long-faced man in an unobtrusive dark corner of a nave inside a cavernous church. Outside, the winter day chilled the bones. People could see their breath escape as their shoes and boots crunched on fresh snow. Wind quickly filled in any evidence of footprints in the white powder. The gaunt, pale man gripped a cane as he observed a funeral through his gold-wire-framed glasses. The man whispered in POTUS's ear, "Talk quietly. I have things of importance to say to you, but I don't want nonbelievers to realize there's an afterlife. We are here to talk about yours."

Immediately, Little Big Hands thought he was about to witness his own funeral. Then he came to his senses when it dawned on him that nowhere near this number of solemn people would come to say farewell to him. Maybe to celebrate his death, but not to mourn.

The vaulted ceilings overhead stretched into the heavens. The cathedral was wrapped in 360 degrees of stained glass with a magnificent rose window as the focal point. Grievers packed the church to honor the loss of a prominent person. The minister delivered the eulogy as he stood by a closed casket blanketed in an array of deep red, yellow, and pink roses laid over evergreen boughs. On the floor, peace lilies ringed the casket.

"Where are we," POTUS inquired, "and whose funeral is this?"

The ashen man curtly replied, "You don't recognize this place? Rumors must be true! All these years in office and you have never attended a service or a memorial at the Washington National Cathedral. George Washington first conceived of a national cathedral as a place of worship for people of all faiths. This is my funeral."

In wonderment, POTUS asked, "What's your name?"

"I'm Woodrow Wilson. History shows that I'm the only president ever entombed here. It's kind of lonely. When I died, the bishop of the National Cathedral approached my wife and asked her to bury me here. He hoped the cathedral would become the American version of Westminster Abbey, where monarchs were laid to rest. No other presidents followed me, but don't get any ideas. Better no company than the wrong company.

"I want to share some concerns I have about you and your presidency. I know you've heard this line before from others.

"Academically, you squeaked into college on probation. Your dad purchased your degree by funding a chair for the department of animal husbandry. And you've kept your grades and SAT scores under wraps ever since. I graduated from Princeton, earned a doctorate in political science from Johns Hopkins, and once served as president of Princeton. I don't mean to brag. I just want to convey that I pursued my education by listening to others and absorbing their knowledge to better the human condition.

POTUS could no longer restrain himself. "Look Wilson, my education doesn't matter. I'm proof that in becoming the president of the United States, it doesn't seem to matter what I did or didn't do in college. Street sense matters. The ability to read people and get inside their ear. No, I don't read history books, seldom read any books. I'm just not a book worm. I leave that to old people…those who are retired and have nothing better to do. If people can't tell me or show me their point quickly, then they don't deserve my attention.

"I'm a visual person. And, most ladies know that. Television is my medium. That's how I learn what's going on and I used it damned effectively to win the Republican nomination and then the White House. Got lots of free airtime from the networks for my showmanship. Even those who didn't adore me quickly came to realize that if they didn't cover my campaign, they'd tumble in the network ratings.

Ignoring the man's self-infatuation and ignorance, Wilson continued: "As the nation's president, I owed much of my success to the study of politics. In particular, how does power really work? And how, in a democracy, can power be made to work more efficiently, with more accountability to the people?

"Some leaders infatuated with power become bullies. Power corrupts them. They don't feel the need to listen to or take advice from anyone. They don't know what they don't know, and that makes them dangerous leaders. They become narrow-minded, self-righteous dictators. Do you know anybody like that?

In one of my speeches I said: "With great government went many deep secrets that we too long delayed to scrutinize with candid, fearless eyes. The great government we loved has too often been abused for private and selfish purposes, and those who used it had forgotten the people. The rule of law should protect the weakest in our society.

"There has been something crude and heartless and unfeeling in our haste to succeed and be great. Our thought has been to let every man look out for himself. Let every generation look out for itself. We reared giant machinery that made it impossible for any but those who stood at the levers to have a chance to look out for themselves.

"I'm here to determine what kind of leader you are and what levers you push."

This news made POTUS very uncomfortable. He responded, "I'm the kind of president who listens to the will of the people."

Wilson said, "I served as the governor New Jersey before I sought the presidency. Did you ever serve in any public capacity to truly understand the innards of government? When I stepped into the highest office in the land, I had identified and established a portfolio of human talent to fill critical cabinet positions. People who understood how to make government work for the people. While it's easy to criticize government, it's a lot more difficult to run a government.

"A president is only as good as the people he appoints to serve in office and how effectively he retains them. By that count, history will judge some of us harshly. I must express my concern that you, Sir, have had the highest turnover of cabinet positions and department heads in our country's history. Many have proven to be crooks and others are under indictment.

"I'm buried in this cathedral because I was a very religious man. But I strongly believe that anybody who presumes to know God's will commits blasphemy. So, I governed in a manner that separated church and state and religion and society. Thomas Jefferson did likewise. I do not feel that the religious views of religious tribes should be forced upon others, especially by government. Yet from what I can see, you seem comfortable using that strategy to win votes.

"To make my point, you recently used the military to clear the streets and sidewalks of peaceful demonstrators so that you could hold up a Bible in front of St. John's Church for a photo op. What do you think the evangelists will think of you if they learn you don't read books, particularly that Bible? They are enamored with you, intoxicated by your spell over them. I dare say that it never occurred to them that you used the military to violate the Constitutional rights of their fellow citizens. With sweet talk, you Juicy Fruit your partisan fans and, for their entertainment gumshoe others of different religious persuasions.

POTUS responded: "A lot of presidents have used that church for photo ops to convey their belief in Christianity and their commitment to the Ten Commandments."

Wilson couldn't help laughing: "We are not present here now to determine how closely you've followed any of those commandments nor count the violations. That's between you and your Maker who must have some regrets by now.

"When leaders blur the lines between church and state, they jeopardize objectivity and polarize the nation. Great nations don't stoop to narrow issues. They are dynamic and adjust to the times. Some of the most atrocious deeds have been—and are yet today being—performed on others in the name of religion… whether they be Christians, Jews, Muslims, or Hindus. It has been my experience that some of the most self-righteous people stumble the most. You only have to go as far as your news to see a vast number of hypocritical religious, business, and government leaders going to jail for abusing women and children.

"Unlike your ugly statement about Muslims and Hindus in this country, I tolerated both religious liberals and fundamentalists. I respected their rights as long as they didn't inflict their beliefs upon others. Although I was a Presbyterian and my wife an Episcopalian, I counted Jews and Catholics among my closest political associates. I'm proud that I became the first president to visit the Vatican and the first to appoint a Jew to the Supreme Court, Louis D. Brandeis.

"I abhor people who say they do certain things because God told them to. In the spirit of America First, I kept the US out of World War One for three years. Some people would implore me in the name of God and humanity to declare war on Germany. I rebuffed their requests. War isn't declared in the name of God; it is a human affair entirely. And that's exactly what was happening—a war of national interests, ancient grudges, rivalries, religious and cultural clashes.

"When I took the nation into World War One, it wasn't because our homeland had been attacked. I did it to restore governments by choice, to protect democracies where they already existed, and to stop endless bloodshed. Of course, I also had some other goals: restore international waters and freedoms on the high seas. Promote free trade, not protective borders and tariffs. I called my vision for the world Peace Without Victory. It meant equality of rights among nations and freely chosen governments. The vehicle to do all this I called League of Nations. It would have included former enemies. I championed it with all my heart and soul.

"I believe the League could have prevented World War Two. It would have established a new world order. But afterwards, the victors and my political opponents decided to impose punitive sanctions on the Central Powers. Those measures choked the life out of Germany, Austria-Hungary, Bulgaria, and the Ottoman Empire's recovery. Rather than build a bridge to lasting peace, they left sore winners and unrepentant losers.

"Instead of a League of Nations in which the US would have participated, our country walked away from the mess in Europe. The League of Nations, ahead of its time, died on the vine. Once again, we isolated ourselves from our world neighbors. And here's the irony: isolationist-minded conservatives in Congress believed that the league would limit America's autonomy and draw the country into another war. Now we know that a second world war happened anyway.

"The biggest decision I made during my second term in office was to take America into World War One. That decision shortened the war and saved millions of lives. Unfortunately, it came at a high price.

"In my single-minded pursuit of victory, the most consequential mistake I made was to ignore the Spanish Flu epidemic. The first recorded case in the world broke out in Kansas in 1918, where we were training 56,000 American troops to go abroad. When they departed Kansas, the exposed troops spread the disease across the country and then to Europe. There it mutated and became even more deadly. It didn't choose sides, and eventually also killed French and German troops. I regret that I never uttered a public statement about the Spanish Flu. Both Allied and Central power nations censored reports of it to avoid affecting morale. Since Spain was a neutral country, they weren't restricted and alerted the world to the pandemic. That's how the flu got its name. So, don't point your finger at Spain for a calamity that possibly began in the U.S.

"More of our troops died of the flu than the war. Before it was over, 675,000 American and maybe 50 million people worldwide perished in an invasion by the Spanish Flu that came in three waves. And, here's the clincher. While in Paris April 1919 to negotiate the Treaty of Versailles, I suffered a debilitating case of the Spanish Flu. And, it's too coincidental that six months later I suffered a massive stroke. As I lay bedridden and unable to rally support for my treasured League of Nations, Congress decided not to approve its formation.

"Little Big Hands I implore you to re-consider how you handle the outbreak of Covid-19. My administration's failure offers you lessons. Please don't let this nasty segment of our history repeat itself.

"I didn't provide leadership to the states nor act on medical advice. You now repeat my errors in judgment. You've de-centralized the primary responsibility to the fifty states to combat the virus. They lack the collective ability to predict and plan medical supplies, let alone the means to efficiently distribute them. Consequently, each state blindly goes its separate way without the benefit of the others' insights. The results of your administration's dereliction to duty magnify loss of life. Your failure to squelch the virus explains why the U.S., with only four to five percent of the world's population, has twenty-five percent of its cases. As a side note, be careful you don't catch the latest virus circling the globe. Like the Spanish Flu it can disable administrations and cripple governments. It did mine. If I were you, I would wear a mask.

The message barely registered with Little Big Hands. He always received criticism as a personal affront and rarely admitted he was wrong about anything. POTUS shot back, "I believe the less government involved in public medical care and insurance, the better. These things need to be delegated to private industry who know how to satisfy markets when they see them. The only exception is the high cost of prescription drugs. That's the real problem in this country. I did promise my loyal base to find a solution. Any day now the Coronavirus will be gone, but not those high prices for drugs."

Wilson realized his allotted time with POTUS was about to run out. He made one last effort to redeem him, or at least score a point or two with Little Big Hands. "The most long-lasting decision I think I made was to reverse my position and stand behind women's suffrage. I pushed Congress to pass the Nineteenth Amendment, and they did, in my last year as president.

"And here's another irony. In their first time at the national polls, women rejected my party. Women were very instrumental in helping Republican Warren Harding win the next election. He ran on a campaign that opposed the League of Nations and favored a return to a more insular society separated from the catastrophe in Europe. Can I fault them for that? Philosophically, no! Those women lost many of their fathers, sons, and husbands in a war not of their making."

POTUS responded, "Well, I like and respect women, too. Many voted for me, attended my rallies, serve in my administration, and say nice things about me on Ferret News."

Wilson hesitated to find the right words, and then, ignoring decorum, quipped, "You also famously grabbed them by the pussy! And I don't think you have been very sympathetic to those coming across the border . . . especially those with children whose fathers were murdered.

"You and I are about as fundamentally opposed as two people can get. You have strayed far from the role I felt a president should play regarding the duty laid upon him by the Constitution. It was my belief that the president should be the representative of no constituency, but of the whole people. In contrast, you speak for special interests and wrongly interpret national thought. In hindsight, my party lost to the Republicans because we failed to make a strong case for a vision of the future. And if your vision is likewise flawed and out of sync with the times, you cannot secure it by voter suppression. Inevitably, the tide turns against you.

POTUS laughed at Wilson. "I can't take you seriously! If I tried to represent the whole people and act on their collective behalf, my feverish, loyal voters would abandon me. My ass would be out on the street. I won the election by catering to less than fifty percent of those who voted. The ones who mattered. I fed them what they wanted to hear. And I'm not going to cross them now."

Wilson plowed ahead. He noticed that POTUS's capacity to assimilate information, never a strength, had rapidly dissipated. He had to cut to the chase. "Don't count on all those voters again. Once they discovered the real you, many have become discontented. Look at the Lincoln Project. All long time Republicans, their members threaten your administration. The

Project actively campaigns against you. They make a lot of noise and have raised a lot of money to get the job done.

"Listen up Little Big Hands. I have one other major regret which, in the light of history, I cannot atone for and need to share. I did very little to improve racial relations. While on the campaign trail to get elected for a second term, I assured African Americans of my wish to see justice done for them. I told them that should I remain president, I would advance the interests of their race. Most of my cabinet members, like me, were born in the South, along with nearly all the congressional leadership. Some tried to segregate governmental workers, which I put on hold. However, I did little to intervene in the race riots around the country in 1919 other to state my shame that they had happened under my watch.

Here's one more warning to you POTUS. You have one hundred years of racial history and progress available to learn from the mistakes of your predecessors. Don't blow it for the sake of those not ready to embrace the 21st century.

President Johnson, born and raised in the deep South, took a bold step to end discrimination. But now I fear you ignite old prejudices and cultural divides that he tried to tame. Your most recent examples are speeches at Mt. Rushmore and then on the Washington Mall, July 4th. If Princeton University has to remove my name from the Woodrow School of Public and International Affairs to make the point that injustices have been done, so be it!

"So, POTUS, my time with you is spent. What will your funeral look like? There are many things you've done to splinter the country. I can't predict whether enough time remains on the clock for you to undo the harm you've caused. I hope so, for the good of the nation and your presidency.

"On its anniversary, I attend this funeral. And it's almost always on a cold, bitter day in February. I sit in the pews and contemplate what more I could have done to create the League of Nations, secure world peace, and end racial injustices. Had I been successful, perhaps I could have turned aside the march to World War Two.

***

"Before we part ways, let's take a look at what your funeral may look like." As they glimpsed the future, before them stood thousands of cheering grandmothers, mothers, and daughters at the foot of the crumbling wall that POTUS had tried to construct. The avowed purposed was to protect the capital from those he deemed left wing protestors, vagrants, rabble-rousers, and criminal minorities. The woman minister, overseeing the shortest presidential funeral in history, helped the national park rangers install a huge bronze plaque in the distant shadows of the Lincoln Memorial. It said, "Here for eternity lie the ashes of Daniel Hands, President of the United States. May this remnant serve as a permanent reminder of the perils of political greed, ego, folly, duplicity, racial discrimination, debauchery, and the travesties of unbridled partisanship. This is the second of two walls he attempted to build during his time in office. May he be known in history as the Walled-In President."

POTUS overheard a young daughter asking her mom how the president had died. The mom replied, "Well, Sweetie, he died on what they call the nineteenth hole in golf, eating a Belladonna burger. Ate too fast, swallowed the wrong way, and then choked to death." Then the mom warned her daughter, "Honey, never bite off more than you can chew."

Ghost #30: Calvin Coolidge

STANDING ROCK

While asleep, POTUS's arms and legs thrashed like a palmetto bug flipped over on its back. He dreamed that he was clutching President Woodrow Wilson's funeral service program in his hands. Then he felt a sharp peck on his cheek. He opened one eye and came face-to-beak with a large, charcoal-colored bird. Was he about to lose an eye?

The raven meant him no further harm. As his sight came into focus, Little Big Hands looked down at a pair of leather moccasins that had tiptoed up to him without a sound. Propping himself up on one elbow, he observed a mysterious man dressed conservatively in a dark double-breasted suit. His dark tie and white shirt made him look like a life-size silhouette lifted from an aged black-and-white 1920s photo.

What distinguished the figure before him, other than the brightly beaded moccasins, was an elaborate eagle-feathered headdress that trailed down the back of his suit to his knees. The black, white, red, yellow, and blue feathers stood out against the dark suit. As a breeze cut through the screened porch, the headdress fluttered and came to life.

Calvin Coolidge introduced himself. "Of course, this wasn't my normal dress in the White House." Accustomed to his role as the big chief, Coolidge bellowed with a tribal authority that pierced Little Big Hands's ears and woke him from his stupor. "Rise and shine from your teepee. Hurry, we're headed to the sacred headquarters of the Standing Rock Sioux Tribe. I want you to see my formal adoption into the Lakota Nation. The ceremonies are about to start in Deadwood, South Dakota. This event will be quite different from your inauguration day on the Washington Mall, where you famously claimed hundreds of thousands of people exalted in your election, setting a new record."

Was Coolidge paying him a compliment? Hearing what he wanted to hear, POTUS perceived it as favorable. A warm glow of self-satisfaction came over his face and he relaxed. Perhaps Coolidge was here to praise him.

***

Coolidge and POTUS soon stood to the side of a ring of tribal leaders who were involved in an elaborate ancient Lakota ceremony. As the drums beat a sacred rhythm, Chauncey Yellow Robe, a prominent Lakota activist and teacher, conducted the ritual in Sioux, his native tongue. His beautiful daughter's lustrous long black hair glowed in the moon light as she positioned an eagle-feather headdress on President Coolidge's head. The headdress was a potent symbol of Lakota culture and, with it, the Lakotas gave Coolidge the name Wanbi Tokahe, which meant Leading Eagle.

Clearly pleased, the apparition nudged POTUS with his elbow when Yellow Robe translated the name into English. He said, "When my staff arranged for me to visit the Black Hills of North Dakota, Chief Yellow Robe, a descendant of Sitting Bull, wanted to give me a warm welcome. POTUS, I know history doesn't move you much. Surely you must have some recall that Sitting Bull crushed General Custer at the Battle of Little Bighorn. It was certainly reenacted enough on TV when you were a kid. Times have changed. Now China, Iran, Pakistan, Russia, North Korea Venezuela and a few other countries would like to scalp you.

"I became the first president to visit an Indian reservation. Keep in mind that the tribe adopted me a mere forty years after US troops massacred a hundred and fifty-three Lakota on the banks of Wounded Knee Creek—mostly women and children. There were still hard feelings about that among tribal elders, but no hostility was shown toward me. Only graciousness. The aftermath of that slaughter triggered public outrage. Most Americans felt the Indians had already been successfully pacified, so why kick a man when he is down?

"While president, I helped usher in the Indian Citizenship Act of 1924, which automatically gave full US citizenship to American Indians. Whenever I could, I acted as a strong proponent of tribal rights. For obvious reasons, I could not let the Sioux Nation stand equal to the US government as many Indians wanted. Where would that ever end?

"I expressed regret at their poverty. I leave it to the historians to ask whether I could have done more to address the travesty of the US government's forced assimilation of Native American children. They were systematically being placed in federally funded boarding schools that stripped them of their language and culture. As ill-conceived as those boarding schools were, at least we tried to give the children a better education. We just didn't understand the significance of separating children from their land, families, and culture, or its enduring effects.

"The nation should have learned its lesson from my era. Then you came along and ripped immigrant children from their parents. Imagine the indelible trauma that created in the minds of those children. Imagine how it distressed the parents who traveled with their children at great risk through so many countries only to have their children torn away from them. And then the travesty of the US government not being able to reconcile hundreds, if not thousands, of children with their parents. At least we knew who and where the parents were when we forcefully integrated those children into our society.

"To make matters worse, Little Big Hands, you started to send immigrants who had already secured responsible jobs and contributed to our economy, back to their broken countries. Your perverted policy also punished children, the DREAMERs, who grew up and were educated here.

The times are different than my era. Over ninety years later yours should be more enlightened. But it isn't! You've repeated a sordid history, separated immigrant children from families and then confined the little ones in cages like animals."

POTUS stammered and then found his voice. "Who in their right mind would drag their children on foot and expose them to the perils of crossing central American and Mexico to come to the U.S.? We don't need crazy people like that here. What kind of parents are they? Illegal immigrants take jobs away from our citizens because they work for lower wages. Many find jobs just long enough to go on welfare and then turn to crime. They milk Medicaid and hospital emergency rooms. Those whose children get a college education in the U.S. should go back to their own country and contribute to their own society."

As he waived a ceremonial tomahawk in the air, Coolidge shouted, "Your niece who wrote that book about you is right. You have no sense of humanity or empathy. And you lack the vision and wherewithal to solve the immigration issue in a constructive and compassionate way. Life has been handed to you on a silver spoon. And now it is tarnished and useless.

"Pay attention, Little Big Hands. For the first time in our history, you have U.S. citizens trying to leave our country for a better life. They want to flee the chaos and uncertainty your administration has created. No thanks to you, they get discriminated against on the other side of the border. Give some thought to apologizing for your miserable conduct and demand better treatment for your own citizens. Some may want to return if you can come up with a real vision to renew America and make it happen."

In a rare but delusionary moment of introspection, POTUS said, "I fear no man or god. I am sure I can turn around the country if the damn liberals and the press would get off my ass. I'm a bit shorthanded right now. Can't get good help to follow my orders. All those indictments either put all my good people in jail or prompted them to resign from my administration. Others fail to understand the vision I have to make America truly great again.

"To compound the problem, the Federal Reserve won't lower the interest rates any further because they say I caused the problem. My people know that's not true. If we can get those coal and steel workers back to work, nuclear plants fired up again, silly regulations lowered, and shut up all those tree huggers while we exploit our natural resources, we can compete and grow."

Skeptical, Coolidge considered POTUS's reply for a brief moment, then said, "How can you do that with your popularity at an all-time low? Unlike you, I remained popular throughout my presidency. The people appreciated that I had a dry sense of humor and said little that I couldn't back up. They laughed with me when Teddy Roosevelt's daughter described me as a man who appeared to have been weaned on a pickle. Pardon my brevity, but voters crave something you lack: authenticity.

"The Roaring Twenties was a fast-paced time of social, cultural, and technological changes. An emerging airline industry accelerated those changes. Many Americans spent money as if it were a renewable resource before the crash of the stock market and the American economy. Are you too self-centered and myopic to recognize the parallels between then and now? As best I could, I tried to stabilize the economy through rapid change. What is your road map?"

Pissed off, POTUS answered in a shrill voice and waived his huge hands in threatening manner toward Coolidge, "My constituents are confident in me. They will follow me anywhere."

Coolidge ignored him. POTUS failed to process the question. Coolidge dug the needle deeper in hopes of finding a nerve...a live person. "One of the things I'm most proud of is that I appointed a special counsel to investigate the Teapot Dome oil-lease scandal. That scandal was one of the sins of an unchecked economy. Power corrupts. I sent my Secretary of State to jail for accepting bribes to lease federal oil reserves without competitive bidding. That is where he belonged. I also cleaned up a lot of sleaze that occurred under the Republican Harding administration before me. Let me tell you, corruption is not exclusive to either Republicans or Democrats.

"I was an honest guy, lived frugally, and did my best to restore public trust in government. Under your administration, corruption and collusion seemed to have reached a historic high. Everybody knows why you commuted the sentence of your buddy who lied to Congress. Not even Nixon stooped to that. Also, why you fired the head of the FBI. dismissed your Attorney General, and belittled the Special Counsel investigating obstruction of justice. You relieved the Ambassador to the Ukraine and her boss. Should I go on?

"Here's your problem—and it has to do with all those shallow campaign promises you made about draining the swamp. Along the way you morphed into the beast who dwelled in the swamp. You built your campaign around shallow slogans and phrases that have been turned against you. You never learned that it is not the adjective, but the substantive, which is of real importance. It is not the name of the action, but the result of the action, that is the chief concern.

"Let me end with a little story before we part. In 1749 there was an ad in a London newspaper inviting the public to come see the most amazing magician ever at the Theatre Royal Haymarket. That theater stands yet today. The advertisement promised that ticketholders would witness magic never before seen anywhere else. The magician would take a walking stick from any member of the audience and play it like any musical instrument. He would take a common wine bottle and in full sight of the audience insert himself into it. For an encore, he would turn himself into any person, dead or alive. On the evening of January sixteenth, the theatre was sold out, with a large crowd waiting outside. When the great illusionist failed to show up, people realized they had been duped. One man looked on in amusement. He was John, the second duke of Montague, who had just won a bet with his friend Lord Chesterfield that he could fill a theater by promising the public the impossible. That, sir, is how I feel about your presidency.

"Unless you act promptly and wisely, your regrets in the afterlife will haunt you forever. My only regret is that a year after the next president came into office, the Great Depression arrived. Looking back on it, there were signs late in my administration that unparalleled economic growth, high living, high debt, excessive spending on luxuries, and high-risk business ventures could not go on forever. Born and bred as a conservative, I was loath to intervene. I had cut taxes four times, slashed government spending, and balanced the budget like a good Republican. But there were no surpluses. In 1928, under my direction, departments began saving all they could out of present appropriations, which further reduced government services. Business cycles come and go. I started to raise interest rates in hopes of calming inflation.

"As politicians, we like to take credit when things go well and blame others when they don't. You grew up in Louisiana. You do speak some French, right? As they say in New Orleans, laissez les bon temps rouler. Now every night I have the same nightmares of people queued up for blocks waiting to withdraw hard-earned deposits before their banks default, lock their doors, and destroy their lives. The tranquility and harmonious relationship between business and government rapidly dissipated, along with the goodwill extended me while in office. Afterwards, many blamed my tax cuts and minimal regulation of industry as factors that triggered the Great Depression."

When he levitated to a parallel universe of ghosts, Coolidge did not bother to offer POTUS a puff on his ceremonial peace pipe.

***

Back from the reservation, POTUS dreamed that he was sleeping on a bed of feathers until a dark thought blossomed into another nightmare. In the recesses of his mind, he pictured his grandchildren caged like monkeys across the Mexican border. Without a word to him, his own son and daughter had made the decision to flee the country. The President of Mexico refused to release them unless POTUS would reveal dirt on his political opponent in Mexico's upcoming election.

Ghost #31: Herbert Hoover

THE MANURE PILE

L ittle Big Hands had just reached REM sleep when the clock-radio started to jabber about some economic calamity. With one eye open, he caught the motion of a hand dialing up the volume. When he realized it wasn't his own, he shot out of bed, turned down the annoying volume, and came face to face with the hologram of a man in a dark-gray three-piece suit. Briefly, everything went out of focus, then the hologram took a step back and introduced himself as President Herbert Hoover.

"I couldn't resist the temptation to fiddle with your radio. I'm very fond of radios, and it's been a long time since I've touched one. As secretary of commerce during the 1920s, my radio conferences played a key role in organizing, developing, and regulating broadcast networks. We went from three hundred thousand people owning radios to over ten million."

POTUS, fully awake now, said, "I don't listen to radio much anymore. National Public Radio makes me feel uncomfortable. Besides, I need visual stimulation. You've probably never seen a television or ever tweeted over the internet . . . that's how we communicate now. Hey, you really need to get that suit dry-cleaned . . . it's pretty wrinkled and reeks of stale cigarette smoke, mold, rotten wood, and, maybe garlic."

"Well then, I suggest that we go out and get some fresh air. If you have a pair of boots, you'd better put them on."

POTUS thought, "What a strange comment," until he glanced down at the hologram's feet. Hoover wore a pair of buckled-on, ankle-high, black rubber boots. His pants were tucked tightly inside. POTUS laughed out loud, and commented, "Did your mommy make you wear those?"

***

In the flash of a time warp, Hoover and Little Big Hands were ankle-deep in manure in a cattle yard in West Branch, Iowa, not far from Hoover's birthplace. POTUS, as was his habit when distressed, pressed his handkerchief to the corner of his mouth as he started to drool.

"Careful where you step," said Hoover. "Manure, like politicians, can either stink things up or make things grow.

Let's watch this conversation with the farmers talking to their president."

Spud Oehler, a prominent grain farmer, spoke first for the group. "Mr. President, we are in crisis. You reassured us over the radio last year that the 1930 Smoot-Hawley Act you signed into law might not be perfect, but that you were confident that it would help. That gave us all hope. And now, here we are. None of us has reaped the benefit of all those tariffs you placed on agricultural products from other countries. In fact, we are pretty much starving.

"As far as we can see, the counter tariffs Canada and Europe imposed on our products has made our circumstances worse, and also for those folks in town. Damn Senators Smoot and Hawley for their industrial tariffs they added on top of the ones for agriculture."

Martin Swisher, a dairy farmer, snarled, "Mr. President, we trusted what you said about these tariffs. You're from Iowa. We thought you were one of us. Now we have a trade war. Yes, a goddam war.

"Look what happened to the British when they levied taxes on the colonies' goods and services. Beginning with the Boston Tea Party, those tariffs led to armed conflict. We aren't ready to shoot our guns yet, but sure enough, people have lost their jobs and fallen into disease, poverty, and despair. Mr. President, people are dying."

President Hoover hung his head in shame. Hoover said to POTUS, "Then and there I realized I stood over my boot tops in shit. I couldn't look those Iowa farmers in the eye. When other countries retaliated with their own tariffs on the United States, our exports fell by sixty-one percent in 1933. The impact of the Smoot-Hawley Act stalled economic recovery from the worst recession in our history. To be honest with you, and I hope you listen to me, I ignored a petition signed by over a thousand US economists who all begged me to veto the act. Guess what? Come next election I was out of a job. And many of those farmers lost the land their forefathers had homesteaded. Many committed suicides rather than face their loved ones with the consequences.

"When I ran for a second term, I felt certain that the expressions of the so-called New Deal that my opponent Franklin Roosevelt espoused would destroy the very foundations of our American system. I believed we must go deeper than platitudes and emotional appeals in the campaign. If the Democrats' frivolous promises were implemented, America would no longer be the America we knew. Even with ten million people unemployed, the New Deal would make the government the master of people's souls and thoughts. Reluctantly, I had to admit that history proved me wrong. Monumental measures were needed to turn the nation around."

Little Big Hands responded, "Well, I can see why. You guys were already spiraling into a recession when you passed those tariffs. Kind of stupid, don't you think, looking back on it? I won't make those kinds of mistakes. After I win my trade wars, the United States will never have been economically stronger. Everybody will want to do business with us. And the dollar will remain the standard for global trade. I still have that on my side. Probably, my face will end up on the front side of a buck when all is said and done."

"Little Big Hands, you've already repeated those mistakes. I fear that your America First movement will excite old animosities and promote new trade wars that do great harm to the American people. With what happened in my administration, we have plenty of evidence to show that trade wars and tariffs raise prices to consumers, create shortages, and stifle innovation. More often than not, they protect businesses who choose to profit rather than invest in innovation and growth. But you ignore history. Take steel, for example. Your tariffs on steel cost US consumers and businesses more than nine hundred thousand dollars each year for every job created. The cost was more than thirteen times the typical salary of a steelworker. Jobs in steel-using industries outnumbered those in steel production by about eighty to one. Hit hard by your tariffs, steel users were forced to absorb costs or pass them onto consumers. Many lost market shares to overseas competitors who replaced US exports. And very few steel-producing jobs were added because modern mills don't require more manpower.

"You fancy yourself an economist, but you don't do your homework or listen to the experts. The Federal Reserve studies showed that tariffs led to reductions in manufacturing and increases in producer prices. Both do harm to employees and consumers. And they found your tit-for-tat retaliation against other countries is an idea best relegated to the past, given interlocking global supply chains. You've created a trade war that you neither comprehend nor will win. But to distract your critics, you wanted a war, and you got it. The cost to the nation is disastrous.

"My predecessor, President Calvin Coolidge, once famously said that the chief business of the American people is business. He and I set high tariffs on imported goods to protect American industry, not unlike your America First policies.

"I was the third Republican president in a row. With years of prosperity under Republican leadership, we thought we knew what we were doing. Unfortunately, we hardly saw the Great Depression of 1929 coming until it was up close and hit us on the nose. As I look back on it, our protective tariffs on imports concealed structural problems—inflation, low savings, and high debt. Those tariffs fed inflation and made imports more expensive for consumers. They artificially raised prices on domestic goods that benefited from lack of competition. I'd advise you not to continue to make those mistakes. Nobody wins."

Shaking the manure off his boots, Hoover pointed to hogs in an adjacent pasture. "Little Big Hands, do you see those pigs in the mud squabbling around the trough for their next meal? Take a good look. There may be a message there for you. I see you just fired your campaign manager because your brand's reputation in the political polls appears mired in the mud. How original of you to announce that move over Facebook. I don't expect his replacement will have much success either, because as the old expression goes, 'you can't make a silk purse from a sow's ear.'

"Let's get you back to Belladonna. It disheartens me to think or talk much about the Depression of the 1930s, and even more to talk to you. I volunteered to share my misery in the afterlife with you, and I have done my duty."

As his hologram began to fade from view, Hoover couldn't resist touching the radio one last time. He turned it on and boosted the volume. On the way out, he said to POTUS, "I think you should listen to this broadcast right now. You might get a glimpse of the future."

***

Even though discombobulated, Little Big Hands's ears perked up when he realized that a macroeconomist and a Harvard Business professor were about to talk about him on the radio. Surely it must be something flattering.

The host of the early morning PBS news began: "We bring you an update on the current state of President Daniel Hands's trade wars with Asia, Europe, Africa, the Middle East, Canada, Mexico, and Latin America. Yesterday the United Nations imposed sanctions on the US for starting this war. Effective immediately, no goods or services will be exchanged with America. The United States has been excluded from current trade pacts. Our country will be treated as a least-favored nation."

The economist said, "Bear with us while we put President Hands's trade war into perspective and give you our view of what to expect. Our country has been involved in seven contentious trade wars. How should you plan to weather the current war? Most of our past wars, with the exception of the first, produced more losers than winners.

"Here are our most significant trade wars to date. Number one, the Boston Tea Party of 1773. Two, the Smoot-Hawley Tariff Act of 1930. Three, the chicken tariff war of the 1960s. Four, the 1987 trade war with Japan. Five, the Canada-US lumber wars of the 1980s. Six, the 1993 banana wars. And, Seven, the 2002 steel tariff war. Now we have Eight, the Daniel Hands tariff war with China, Canada, Mexico, and Europe.

"Our current war takes the world to the edge of a global recession. Unemployment has skyrocketed, prices have soared, goods and services suffer short supply, and stock prices have plummeted. The result is the biggest de facto income reduction to the middle class in the history of the United States. The resultant riots are unprecedented. Many politicians may go to jail for conspiring with lobbyists to gain special treatment and protection for products and services."

The professor added, "The future of the dollar is highly uncertain. It is rapidly losing its value in relation to other currencies. If our predictions are correct, we recommend that you do whatever you can to protect yourself from the inevitable free fall, including buying scarce minerals, and yes, planting your own gardens and raising chickens.

"And now a word from our sponsor, the US Government Bond Fund."

POTUS immediately started to tweet bullets over his dissatisfaction with the sloppy coverage from the liberal news station. How dare they broadcast that his trade war looked increasingly like a suicide vest about to detonate the global economy and that all the Federal Reserve's horses and all the president's men may not be able to put the economy together again?

He found it particularly insulting that the economist described him as a self-proclaimed tariff man using eighteenth-century coercion in the globalized twenty-first century. POTUS shut his eyes after the talk show host summarized, "President Hands plays with a small yellow rubber ducky in a large pond full of big green menacing alligators." He turned the radio off to the sound of laughter.

Ghost #32: Franklin Roosevelt

THE OVAL OFFICE

"**M**r. President, how can you sleep on the veranda with the midmorning sun in your eyes? You could go blind. May I bring you something to eat?"

Charles Pastor, POTUS's personal assistant, had searched for him for the last hour, ever since the kitchen staff reported Little Big Hands had failed to show up for breakfast. Weaned on grits, country ham, fried eggs smothered in Tabasco sauce, and biscuits topped with cream gravy, Little Big Hands hadn't missed his daily ritual of a big breakfast since he occupied the White House. He usually chased it all down with a shot of bourbon, which he called his inspiration to begin a new day. He got the idea when someone told him that Winston Churchill usually got things rolling with a brandy.

Haggard and the scent of manure still in his nostrils, POTUS replied, "God awful of you to wake me up, Charles. I feel like I've just gone to bed. Since I'm awake now, could you please have the kitchen staff just leave a cup of coffee, some toast, and three aspirins in the lounge? No eggs today. I need to take a shower and go watch the rest of the morning news. Oh, don't forget the bourbon. I need fortification.

"Charles, before you leave, what's the latest on the international boycott of American goods I heard earlier this morning?"

"Sir, I don't know where you heard that. It's not true. We couldn't figure out what you were tweeting about. Your angry reference to a small rubber ducky made no sense. Have you forgotten, Mr. President, that you have a tee time scheduled with party loyalists from South Carolina, Florida, and Texas at eleven AM?"

When he was at Belladonna, POTUS played a round of golf every day, and he expected his guests to stay at his lodge. None of this struck him as a conflict of interest. In his first term in office, POTUS eclipsed all records of time spent by a president at golf resorts. No accounting was available on how much of this was on the taxpayer's dime. But as a yardstick, a *Forbes* reporter estimated that at the rate Little Big Hands was going, his dalliances on the golf course would cost taxpayers over $340 million. Few CEOs ever spared this much time away from their jobs without losing touch with their businesses or getting sacked.

"Charles, I don't think I will putt for the American people today. Please tell our visitors to enjoy the course, and don't forget to tell them about our fabulous nineteenth hole, where they can make a campaign contribution."

Charles shrugged. To stroke the president's ego, he had already negotiated a huge handicap with the boys from South Carolina, plus the promise of several mulligans. In return for guaranteeing Little Big Hands another reelection victory, Charles had already given them free golf balls with provocative images of the beauty queens POTUS had sponsored in the annual Belladonna Miss Garter pageant. Talent was not a requirement.

Charles wondered whether the boss suffered a nervous breakdown. He looked terrible; puffy face, skin the color of gray putty, and shaky hands. Not even the thought of a post-golf victory parade to the bar, to suck up celebratory drinks at his guests' expense, aroused his appetite for the game.

***

POTUS spent the rest of the day by himself in the lounge. As he watched the various network news reporters cover his presidency, he'd shout back at the screen, "Fake news! A president who is doing a great job cannot be impeached! If they don't like it here, they can go back to where they came from! My polls show my ratings are up, not down! We are winning the trade war! That guy who just resigned from my cabinet was a dummy. He wore glasses to make himself look smart! What a bunch of socialists!"

As he ranted and raved about being underappreciated, a fountain of drool frothed from the corner of POTUS's mouth. Oddly, he felt relieved, as if he was purging himself of enemies.

He carried on a conversation with Alexa and his multiple television sets until dinnertime. He complained how unfairly he was being treated for his significant accomplishment. When Alexa said, "I didn't get that. Would you repeat it, please?" he shouted, "Shut up, bitch. I'm not talking to you."

That evening, POTUS sat at the dinner table alone. He said, "Hello, friends," to two Big Macs with extra pickles and a double serving of French fries. Then "Welcome to my house" to a large milkshake size container of red wine that McDonald's now served on tap. His tolerance for alcohol had been heavily compromised by events that had unfolded over the last several nights. Although he drank himself into a stupor, POTUS had sufficient command of his faculties to avoid a second evening on the veranda. With mustard stains all over his white linen guayabera shirt, POTUS thought, "I've been betrayed and smeared by a hamburger." He retreated to the master bathroom. There, he deposited his clothing in a pile that no one was allowed to touch. The staff speculated that POTUS didn't want anyone going through his pockets to see what mysteries they might contain, like the telephone number of a Russian contact or a local massage lady.

After a long steamy shower, the day's tensions eased. POTUS crawled into bed to begin a nonsensical barrage of tweets about fake news, denials of affairs, and whose head might be next on the chopping block in his administration. His twisted sentences were incomplete, words misspelled, and thoughts scrambled.

Exhausted and fully vented from tweeting, POTUS slumbered in the upstairs master bedroom surrounded on both sides by the columned wraparound porch facing the wetlands in the distance. He had left the windows and French doors open to the porch to allow the evening breeze to flow through the screens.

He awoke to what sounded like an alligator hissing in the room as its jaws crunched open and shut. The thought terrified him. A moment later, he perceived the silhouette of a man standing by his side, whispering, "Little Big Hands, wake up!"

For a few seconds, POTUS thought the figure was a security guard in pursuit of the gator. He clutched an assault rifle. It seemed pointed at him. The rifle appeared to be the kind that the press, left-wing liberals and now even a few conservatives wanted to make illegal. Just last week, twenty-four children were slain by such a weapon at a primary school in Jacksonville, Mississippi. As usual, the NRA offered their prayers and sympathies. Not much ever happened after that because politicians, like junkies, had come to depend on the NRA to shore up their campaign coffers.

Pale as cream, Little Big Hands bolted upright and hollered, "Don't shoot! We can make a deal!" Frightened that this might be his final moment on earth, his own liquidation in process—just like some of his bankrupt real-estate properties—he fell out of bed and promptly threw up all over his bedroom slippers.

As he raised his head in agony, POTUS mumbled, "You look familiar. I've seen you before." The unearthly presence gripped a wooden cane in his left hand and resembled a portrait of President Franklin Roosevelt that hung in the White House.

All the outdoor creatures were eerily silent except for the owls who hooted for their mates in the shadows and decay of the desolate swamp.

Out of the darkness, Roosevelt asked, "Why do you persist in calling the press enemies of the people?"

POTUS sputtered, "Because they are! They disparage the people's elected leader—me. They distort, ridicule, and subvert my leadership. They won't listen to or believe hardly a thing I say. And they disrespectfully dig up all this dirt about my past. Why can't they let bygones be bygones? Fortunately, my constituents have turned a deaf ear to them. Thank God for them, for the sake of my administration. If I can deliver the promises I made to my loyal voters, they'll accept that the means justify the end."

Roosevelt playfully said, "Hop into my presidential carriage, the Queen Elizabeth. It's one of two Cadillacs designated for my use. The other I named the Queen Mary. I thought it be more appropriate if I picked you up in Al Capone's armored 1928

Caddy Town Sedan, but the IRS sold it off before I could object. It was the Depression, and not even the government could afford three cars for presidential use. I did love that car. It's been quite a while since the Queen and I took a ride together, if you know what I mean. Lately, I'm a little unaccustomed to driving, but shall we go?"

Little Big Hands, like a lamb, climbed into the car with no idea where they were headed. He cringed as Roosevelt floored the old and rusted Caddy. On earth Roosevelt had been a two-pack-a-day smoker; now, he clutched an ivory cigarette at a jaunty forty-five-degree angle between his teeth and blew smoke inside the car. As they rode along, bits and pieces of trim peeled off the old girl from the vibration, abrupt turns, and frequent braking. Roosevelt drove like he was immortal!

Once in front of the White House, Roosevelt plopped himself into a wheelchair and beckoned POTUS to follow as he wheeled himself into the Oval Office. A pungent odor of Camel unfiltered smoke lingered in the hallway. He whispered, "It's December seventh, 1941. Shall we watch some history here? You'll get the drift soon enough. I think you will profit from it.

"Look over there. In my earthly life, I sit at my desk, surrounded by my collections of rare stamps and whimsical trinkets. . . tense, shocked, and forlorn. Why? Japan has just staged a surprise attack on Pearl Harbor. Thousands of military personnel and civilians have been slaughtered on a Sunday morning, a day consecrated to God. And I stew over how our generals and admirals could allow this to happen. My first instincts are to give in to anger. And, like you have so impulsively done in your administration, fire the lot of them.

"My only companion in this hour of extreme loneliness is Fala, a Scottish Terrier who receives more fan mail than I do. POTUS, I understand you've never had a dog. I find it hard to trust a man who has never had one for a friend.

"As I gaze into Fala's eyes, I realize my own culpability. It does no good to lie to a dog. At Winston Churchill's request, I had imposed trade sanctions and embargos on Japan. I did it to give Great Britain some relief from Japan's aggressive military expansion in the Pacific that encroached on British protectorates. I may have accelerated an inevitable war. Before the sanctions, we provided over seventy percent of Japan's scrap, eighty percent of their oil, and over ninety percent of their copper. When we cut them off, we placed a stranglehold on their ambitions. And now that we had just been attacked, I would further demoralize the country if I fired our key commanders in the Pacific. As you can see, there was plenty of fault to go around. I'd advise you to be careful with your trade wars. Never can tell where they might lead.

"Now watch this. See that gentleman coming into my office around midnight? I've summoned him to the White House even though I'm distraught and exhausted from the longest and saddest day in my life. I pour Edward R. Murrow, the top reporter for CBS and an old friend, a stiff shot of Jack Daniels to help disconnect from the horrible reality of the day. I know we are going to need the press on our side to help win the war. I've invited him to support me in my darkest hour. We light up cigarettes, exhale the demons of the day, and briefly let the smoke permeate the silence of a world gone mad and cold. Compulsively and with little self-awareness, I tap my cane on the floor in a steady cadence to let the stress of the day dissipate.

"I need to know how Murrow thinks the American people will react when I announce to them the next day that the nation must go to war. For another unspoken reason, at this moment in time I also crave a close companion to share the overpowering loneliness I feel in this job, and to protect my sanity.

"Little Big Hands, do you ever have such moments?"

POTUS replied, "I never give the consequences of my decisions much deep thought. No sense to agonize over a decision once it's made. Besides, to do otherwise would convey a sense of personal weakness. Can't have that with all my enemies milling around. Got to keep up the right image with the boys . . . my conservative fundamentalists who aren't deep thinkers either. They are very intuitive."

"I pretty much expected that answer. I'll continue my story. Murrow understands my need for a friend in the uneasy calm before the storm. He senses my guilt and sense of shame. He says, 'We may make mistakes . . . but they must never be mistakes that result from faintness of heart or abandonment of moral principle.'

"Then he assures me that the American people, including most of those who didn't vote for me, will back me one hundred percent. He says that their latent fortitude, strength, and resourcefulness will mushroom. He swears their resolve and desire for revenge will make Emperor Hirohito, Prime Minister Hideki Tojo, and Admiral Isoroku Yamamoto deeply regret their despicable actions.

"To serve the nation in every way possible, Murrow pledges his full support to use his powerful voice and sharp pen to help focus the American people on the tasks ahead. For this I am most grateful and thank him for his visit at such a late hour. He strengthens my resolve to make our enemies pay dearly.

"Little Big Hands, I want you to keep that picture of me and Murrow in your head. When we declare war on Japan, an ally of Germany, Hitler immediately declares war on us. We step into the fight...a global conflict of unheralded proportions.

"Now we will advance the date to December twenty-third, 1941. At great peril, Winston Churchill has just sailed the high seas in the midst of German submarines hunting for prey. They would have considered it a windfall to send him to the bottom of the Atlantic Ocean. He's come to see me so that we may begin planning with our joint chief of staff the destruction of our shared enemies. On his first full day in Washington, I arrange for a press conference to demonstrate to the world that we, the British Empire, the Chinese, and the Russians are united in a common cause."

Roosevelt pointed to Churchill. "There he stands on a chair in the White House press room surrounded by admiring newspaper, magazine, and radio reporters. They cheer him on and furiously take notes for the evening and morning news. The press room reeks of stale cigarette smoke, garlic breath, whiskey, dust, and sweat. England's fourth estate has been a tremendous ally and boon to Churchill while Britain was the sole resistance to the Axis forces in western Europe. Now he's cultivating and courting the American press, as am I. Like the press, I cheer him on as he helps me rally our courageous nation to persevere, sacrifice, and march onward to victory. Unlike yours, Little Big Hands, his words are meaningful. The nation solemnly knows it's not bluster. They are primed . . . ready to follow Churchill and myself to hell and back, wherever and however we may lead them. And the press played an honorable and instrumental role in getting the job done.

"Let's flash forward to the present. There you are, Little Big Hands, tweeting in the middle of the night about the press being the enemy of the people. And there you are again on national television and then at a rally, poisoning the minds of your partisans, exhorting them to take their anger out on the press, when it should be at you. You cry out and whine that the press should be gagged or worse. What's the result? Your spiteful conduct sends a message to dictators, despots, and corrupt leaders around the world that it is okay to suppress the free press. Courageous reporters, men and women who dare to tell the truth are being assassinated around the world . . . in places like Venezuela, Saudi Arabia, Honduras, Guatemala, Mexico, China, Iran, Egypt, Russia, and Turkey.

"Take for example that American journalist who was murdered at the Saudi consulate in Istanbul. The CIA concluded that the Saudi Prince was personally involved. But you questioned the findings. Then to defuse the outrage, you say something to the effect that no one can know the truth . . . and even if we did know the truth, it wouldn't be worth risking our financial relationship with Saudi Arabia. What a gutless response. It sent chills down the backs of the fourth estate.

"In my day, we united in a common cause to rebuild the economy, reduce human suffering, and fight global tyranny irrespective of our liberal or conservative leanings. In January 1941, eleven months before we entered the war, I delivered my Four Freedoms Speech to Congress: . . . freedom from want, hunger, and fear, and freedom of worship. Congress mostly yawned—until Norman Rockwell visualized those freedoms in a way that connected emotionally with the public and Congress. His Four Freedoms oil paintings became bond posters and raised a hundred and thirty-four million dollars to help underwrite war expenses. In your dollars, that's over two billion, two hundred sixty-four million generated from four paintings.

As I see it, Little Big Hands your administration threatens these Four Freedoms that I held so dear.

"One of my administration's everlasting accomplishments was to give the American people a sense of financial security and dignity if they would but invest in themselves. We invented Social Security so the elderly could retire without wolves lurking at the door. Now you desire to undermine that safety net.

"Do you have any sense of the chaos and hardship you will impose on the American people if you end this program? The only ones who will benefit are the wealthy, employers who will no longer have to pay into the program, and shyster financial schemers. Social Security worked just fine until the government started borrowing from it and never repaying. That fund should have been untouchable!

"Excluding what Eleanor might say about our private life, I made other mistakes. Russia was one of my biggest. I see that you also kowtow to the Russians. They will take advantage of you. I know! Despite Winston Churchill's warnings, I trusted Uncle Joseph Stalin. I conceded too much. The consequence of my poor health, favorable impressions of Stalin, and overconfidence led to the Iron Curtain. Then what followed was a long, protracted Cold War my successors had to deal with. The world now knows the human suffering from those episodes.

"Little Big Hands, I fear for our nation's children under your presidency. As for me, I now return to an afterlife of infinite annual meetings in Yalta with Joseph Stalin. I'm weary and sick of him!"

***

Half-awake, POTUS trembled uncontrollably. He wondered if his most recent experience was just a bad nightmare triggered by gluttony at the dinner table. It must have been that last helping of chocolate cake, he thought.

In a stupor, he restlessly dozed off again. He dwelled in a twilight zone half-asleep, half-awake while listening to the late-night news. Although he hated the press, he was addicted to Ferret News. He thought it was better that they say something bad about him than nothing at all. "Gotta keep my name in front of the American people and counterpunch the bad stuff." He felt supremely confident that he could convince his constituency that there was always another side to the story to retain their support and blind loyalty. Blame all the bad press as something concocted by the deep state in government and the media.

Then he heard, "Hello again, ladies and gentlemen. This is Annie Oakely Remington for Channel 6666. Daily we bring you sharpshooting news. This just in. By consensus of the American Press Association, the executives of all the major networks have just decided an hour ago that they will no longer report on anything President Daniel Hands has to say. They are cutting off his access to radio, television, and newspapers. He will no longer exist in their vocabulary. This decision was difficult, even unprecedented, but so is the man who denigrates the highest office in the land. They concluded that the President's litany of half-truths, distortions, outright lies, and inflammatory comments were too toxic to publish or repeat, therefore, we will ignore all the presidential remarks. Twitter and Facebook's executives are also coming under pressure to pull the plug on President Daniel Hands."

Ghost #33: Harry Truman

THE GYMNASIUM

As the gray fog softly enveloped the swamp and clouded the windows of his Belladonna bedroom, POTUS's inner ear detected in the distance the harsh yip and sharp howl of coyotes that hung around the fringes of the swamp in pursuit of a meal. Then another noise stirred him. A melodious one. He awoke to a piano played somewhere in the house. Curious, he cautiously went barefoot down the stairway that wound to the first floor. Was he the only one in the house who heard the sweet sounds of a piano? In the Belladonna's grand ballroom sat a ghostly figure enraptured with Chopin's A-flat waltz, which he skillfully coaxed from the ivory keys. POTUS was startled to see that this apparition, whose elbows were flung out as he leaned into the keyboard, looked a lot like a portrait of President Harry Truman he'd seen in the National Gallery.

Truman, the finest piano player among all the presidents, said, "Glad you finally woke up, you sleepyhead! My bony fingers have practically etched the ivory off these piano keys." With a wide grin, he said, "When I played this piece for Stalin, he signed the Potsdam Agreement. Oh, I forgot, you don't know much about history and how it continues to affect our lives.

"Quick lesson. At the end of World War Two, an agreement was made between the United Kingdom, the United States, and the Soviet Union that addressed the military occupation and reconstruction of Germany, its borders, and the entire European theater of war. I have some important things to tell you! Come sit on the bench next to me."

***

Lulled by this gifted musician, the next thing POTUS knew, he had been transported to the gymnasium at Westminster College in Fulton, Missouri. As they entered, through a side door, Truman playfully pinched Little Big Hands's love handles, commenting, "These are getting flabby. Perhaps you need to work out more."

POTUS jerked with surprise. He knew that in the stress of recent events he'd over indulged, particularly with McDonald's burgers and fries. He still prided himself on being able to close his zipper, although his belt was now set on the last notch and his belly sagged over the top of his pants the way yeast dough rises from a bowl.

Inside the gym, Winston Churchill stood at an elaborate podium draped with American and British flags. He began his famous Iron Curtain speech. The date was March 5, 1946.

Truman whispered in POTUS's ear, "I know you've never heard this speech or read it, but he's talking about the Soviet Union figuratively and literally building an impenetrable iron curtain to separate eastern Europe from western. To staunch the flow of humanity, Stalin has begun to install a concrete wall that divides East Germany from West and separates friends and family. Churchill tells us the implications of this descending curtain and what it means to the future of the world. Now I want you to think about another absurd wall that you have begun building around Washington, D.C., to keep protestors out and to protect your unpopular government. Wasn't the one on the Mexican border controversial enough? This second wall will only further divide Americans and lead to harsh political consequences. You did this over the advice of both the Senate and the House."

Little Big Hands lied, "Not a nickel comes from the US budget. The government isn't paying for this wall. All my cronies and true patriots from the NRA, the American Lobby Association, the John Birch Society, Citizens United, Eagle Forum, and the Neti Pot Wing fund it. This wall, poured in red, white, and blue concrete, will be a beautiful thing—the legacy of a free and unencumbered government. If the Vatican can have a wall to protect the pope, we certainly should have one to protect the president of the United States, his administration, and Congress."

With the bluntness for which he was famous, Truman replied, "Little Big Hands, leave the Vatican out of this. You are so ignorant of history that you misapply what little you do know. Their wall was designed to welcome and to draw people in, like two open arms. Pope Leo IV built some portions of the original in the ninth century to protect the church from pirates and other marauders. The only thing your wall will do is protect pirates and marauders like yourself. Mark my words, both of your walls will crumble and become a monument to your follies. By the way, that Berlin Wall eventually came tumbling down, and so did the Iron Curtain that tried to prevent the advancement of civilization.

"Another matter, if you please. On second thought, I don't care if it pleases you. I want to know what is this nonsense is about you, under the antiquated, imperialistic Monroe Doctrine, threatening to nuke Venezuela and turn Guatemala, El Salvador, and Honduras into protectorates to rid them of dictatorships and criminal activity? Like a bully at school who brags what's in his pants is bigger than all his buddies', you bluster that your nuclear arsenal is more lethal than that of their Russian ally. Don't you realize lethal is an absolute term? Dead is dead."

POTUS replied, "Something has to be done about all these immigrants who flood the country and feed our high unemployment rate. And Venezuela has a sick, sick leader who is nothing but a Commie dictator like that former Chinese leader. Ol' what's-his-name. Uh, Chairman Mays . . . Mao . . Mayonnaise?"

Ignoring POTUS, Truman continued. "There are real and human consequences to such banter. I know! I used a nuclear bomb once and hope to never see another one detonated. But I never second-guessed that decision to drop the atom bomb on Japan, nor any of my decisions, because I truly understood my alternatives and the sum of their costs on human life, however they might pain me. Let me show you the human suffering. Look at this film clip showing a sinister and rapidly swelling cloud sucking into its dark soul the breath of life from all who dwell there."

POTUS stared blankly at the image Truman showed him of humanity swept away in the glow of a humongous red and gray cloud that rose to infinity. He jerked his head away. He didn't want to see or hear about it, nor did he register any emotional reaction.

"Some people learn from history, but you don't. Is it true you never read books? Your regime continues to play badminton with the North Koreans over serving up a nuclear strike. That's scary. You and their leader alternate between threats and mutual admiration. Right now, we have two bullies calling each other's bluffs.

"I'd be very careful if I were you about North Korea's back door neighbors, the Chinese. They came to the rescue of the North Koreans during the Korean War. Douglas MacArthur exercised some brilliant maneuvers to stave off the invasion initiated by the North Koreans. He drove them back across the border and then lobbied me publicly to bomb the Chinese and completely defeat communist forces. I disagreed with him. The result was the most famous confrontation ever between civilians and the military. I fired MacArthur before another nuclear war happened. The conflict in Korea remained a limited war and, eventually, a quasi-truce emerged with the help of the Chinese.

POTUS interrupted, missed the point and responded, "Aha! We do have some things in common. I have pressured a lot of generals and admirals to leave my administration who didn't toe the line with my vision for America. They had to learn the hard way, that is my way or the highway."

Truman ignored the comment and continued, "But rather than lead in a constructive way, you would rather swing a club than exert any effort at bipartisanship and diplomacy to find creative solutions. In your infinite wisdom, you have decided to pull the U.S. out of the UN Human Rights Council and from the World Health Organization. And to further downplay the importance of the UN, you have removed our Ambassador from serving on your cabinet.

"Fortunately, the United Nations, that you mock will continue without you. They pledge to effect positive, innovative change in regions of the world that suffer from poverty, moral and political decay, disease, drug trafficking, and climate change. The U.S. could benefit from this body of diplomats who could perhaps even help in North Korea. Instead, you make noises about pulling out of the United Nations all together if you don't get your way. If you would throw your weight behind the United Nations that Franklin Roosevelt and Winston Churchill conceived during World War II and that I helped implement after FDR's death, humanity could take a significant turn for the better.

"In Churchill's words about the adolescent organization while speaking here in Fulton, 'We must make sure that the United Nations' work is fruitful, that it is a reality and not a sham, that it is a force for action, and not merely a frothing of words, that it is a true temple of peace in which the shields of many nations can someday be hung up, and not merely a cockpit in a Tower of Babel.' If you were more a visionary, you might reach out to the UN to help you solve the problems in Central and South America as well as North Korea.

"I promise you that before the night is over, you will hear only the sounds of bats as they flutter around this room and dart about your head. Then expect company. As for me, I return to an afterlife every sixth of August watching films of a mushroom cloud over Japan. The images torture, torment, and never leave me. But the buck stops here with me. I fully accept my responsibility and this dark night of the soul because, in the end, I knew that it would shorten the war and save more lives, including those of the Japanese.

"I ask you, when your presidency ends, where do you think you are going? Do you want to be haunted into eternity by the image of another mushroom cloud that you set off? I implore you to check your knee-jerk responses to global crises.

"President Hands, I fear for the children of the world. That is why in my final days in office, I worked closely with my successor, General Eisenhower, to demonstrate how simply and peacefully our American system could transfer the presidency from my hands to his. Even though we were from different political parties, I met with Ike to brief him on current foreign and domestic affairs. I instructed my cabinet to do the same with their successors. He and his associates participated enthusiastically in these discussions to effect an orderly transfer of leadership. Our cooperation calmed the nation and helped heal division.

"In contrast, you shunned your predecessor and ignored any constructive input he could give you to assure a smooth transition of power, with the least disruption in the everyday affairs of the American people. The fact that you appointed only a very few cabinet members immediately when you assumed power made the transition even bumpier. For too many months, you shot from the seat of your pants, and your lack of expertise in domestic and foreign affairs paralyzed the nation."

***

Asleep on the piano bench in Belladonna's grand ballroom with his head resting on E-flat, Little Big Hands dreamed that he had triggered World War III. Try as he might, he could find no one to pin the blame on. When the war ended, he saw a future in which he was draped in chains and about to be tried for war crimes. In the dream, he berated himself. Why hadn't he listened to Truman's ghost? Little Big Hands's niece, Charla Hands, was correct. Until this brief dreamy moment of regret, POTUS never expressed remorse, acknowledged errors, or empathized with the plight of others unless it was to his advantage. He also greatly resented that his legal team failed to stop his niece from publishing her book that told all the dirt about the Hands' family history.

Ghost #34: Dwight Eisenhower

THE CONGRESSIONAL COUNTRY CLUB

An hour later, Little Big Hands awoke in a sweat, his Polo shirt soaked in perspiration. He thought he saw dark objects soaring around the room and vaguely recalled a warning about bats. Or was he just going batty? The details were sketchy in his mind and his skull ached. He turned around to find a ghostly figure that looked a lot like President Dwight D. Eisenhower with a bat on his shoulder. The ghost was lightly tapping him on the head with a putter.

"President Hands, your head is denser than I thought. Come, let's play a round of golf."

***

The next moment, POTUS found himself bouncing around like a bowl full of jelly with Ike behind the wheel of a golf cart at the Congressional Country Club in Bethesda, Maryland. Ike was quite impressed with the modern carts that told him the distance to the greens. He played with a set of 1960 Spalding Bobby Jones clubs. He patiently waited for POTUS to dig himself out of one sand trap after another. Clearly, POTUS had understated his handicap to look like a big shot, playing thirteen strokes worse a round. Ike refused to concede the ten-foot putts POTUS had been getting from those who sucked up to him.

Ike was also quick to get to the greenside first. He knew POTUS had a reputation for kicking his opponents' golf balls into sand traps if they hadn't seen where their balls landed.

Afterwards, Ike magnanimously suggested they go to the nineteenth hole and take a corner table. Ike, a chain-smoker who had suffered multiple heart attacks during his life, loved Scotch. He had become an aficionado while in Europe during World War II. After the heart attacks, his doc had limited his consumption. But when you're dead, does it matter?

After savoring the trademark bite of a Glenlivet, the taste of which he had not experienced in over fifty years, Ike got down to business. He questioned POTUS about his leadership style. He asked why the administration had such a high turnover of cabinet and top administration personnel and why so many people had been indicted for criminal activity.

As POTUS slumped forward in his chair like he was about to take a crap, Ike sat ramrod straight. He continued the conversation with "You do know that I was a five-star general?"

POTUS responded with sarcasm. "Of course, I do, but what's the relevance? Being president is more notable. I'm the president now, and you are the has-been. I fire generals all the time."

Ike, who could swear with the best of them when the occasion called for it, responded, "Goddamn, you're an infamous ignoramus! You are the Commander in Chief and don't have a speck of common sense on how to manage your role. You claim to be successful. A commander and master of the business world. The only thing I see that you have accomplished are five bankruptcies and hidden behind tax scandals to line your pockets.

"Six months into your administration, your military chiefs of staff offered to discuss with you strategy and alternatives in South and Central America and elsewhere around the world. They were alarmed by your take on history, particularly our key alliances that had been carefully forged over two decades. Instead of listening, you discounted those important alliances by labeling them worthless. You had no idea what you were talking about. Impulsively and ignorantly, you called the chiefs of staff a bunch of dopes and babies. Losers, to be exact. You told them you would never want to go to war with such losers.

Here's an even bigger fallout from that travesty...perhaps a first in our nation's history. Your Pentagon advisers now hesitate to give you military options because you might select the most extreme response. When events heated up with North Korea, China and Iran, they didn't trust your judgment and feared that you might accidentally take the U.S. to war. To contain some of your worst impulses when confronted with military actions abroad, they resorted to a new tactic. They by-pass you and directly contact their counterparts in adversarial countries. Your advisors warn them to exercise more caution because President Hands is too unpredictable and capricious. He might impetuously make a decision that would escalate conflict beyond either side's intentions. That's pretty sad Little Big Hands.

"Good God, Man, get control of yourself! In a fit of rage, you've offended these brave, talented, and dedicated men in the worst possible way because they don't agree with your stupid thoughts. You cut them off and don't even give them the courtesy of listening to the reasons for their recommendations.

POTUS blurted out, "Don't call me stupid! I'm the smartest man I know. In fact, I'd say I am a genius. A very stable genius. Look at my lifetime success in building the Belladonna chain of restaurants, hotels, and resorts. Those accomplishments required a very high IQ. And what other president do you know who graduated from the Wharton School of Finance?"

"Little Big Hands, stop the bull shit! Your brother Bubba had to help you with your homework. Because your grades were poor, you needed a high SAT score. So, you paid a friend to take the test for you. I'll give you credit for picking a prestigious school and not flunking out. But, the hardest part is getting accepted at a school like Wharton. After that, they rarely admit they made an admissions error. Instead they push you through the system and hope you don't embarrass them later. What was your grade point there? I understand you've sworn them to secrecy.

"In truth, you are the enemy within. I fear that you lack the capability to continue to grow, learn, or evolve in your job as Commander in Chief. Like just now, you can't control your emotions, moderate your responses, or absorb and synthesize the information given to you.

"Let me steer this conversation back to the military before we move on. To make matters worse, POTUS, you badgered them to charge the countries where we have troops to pay our government for their services. How could you prostitute our military like that? You risk their lives to turn them into paid mercenaries as a revenue source to supplement your beleaguered budget? The idea disgusts me. To think like that, one must be morally bankrupt!

"One measure of a leader is the quality and character of those he chooses to serve under him and his ability to keep them on his team. It seems to me that you don't really care about the personnel turnover in your government because you prefer to make the decisions yourself. Don't be surprised if the generals you try to browbeat quit. Also, your Secretary of State and Secretary of Defense. My God, man, when you mishandle personnel the way you do it puts the nation in harm's way and tempts our enemies to test our defenses around the world. You will regret every impulsive word you have uttered.

It's no small coincidence that China has chosen 2020 as a perfect year to suppress Hong Kong's democratic tendencies. Or that the Belarus dictator in Eastern Europe has just tightened his grip having mysteriously won over 80% of the popular vote. His opposition leader just fled for the sake of her children.

"Without the benefit of expertise, many of your decisions prove ill-founded. Nonetheless, through your own special magic, you flimflam your faithful followers to believe otherwise. You convince them that they can expect nothing less than the greatest outcome from your unparalleled decision-making ability. But your decisions often prove catastrophic. Take that incident when you shut down the government for almost three months over construction of a wall around Washington, D.C. because you could not get funding for your pet project. When things went from bad to even worse, you shifted the dialogue and blamed people who protested in nearby poor neighborhoods for holding up progress. You directed your attorney general to take them to court. We ghosts understand your formula, and it disgusts us.

"Let me tell you about a real leader in my life who forever shaped my military career and presidency. In December 1941, Army Chief of Staff General George C. Marshall called me to the Pentagon. Although he might have chosen many of my superiors, he asked me to plan the war in the Pacific. He knew that I had demonstrated a talent for leadership. When he laid this daunting task on my shoulders, Marshall, with cold, penetrating blue eyes, looked squarely at me and said the army has many capable men who analyze problems well but who bring them to him for final resolution. I must have assistants who solve their own problems and tell me the outcome later.

"Unhappily for this great country, Little Big Hands, you have failed to lead. You make poor personnel selections, lack a plan for the country's future, and foolishly make most of the decisions yourself. When you constantly override your staff's suggestions, you stifle their willingness to give you professional input. Worse yet, if something goes wrong as a consequence of your decisions, you pass the blame and throw your own people under the bus to disguise the truth.

"I hear you bluster about making war on Venezuela, Guatemala, El Salvador, and Honduras because they collaborate on the drug trade, mock you, and through their corrupt governments, force civilians to flee. What do you know about war? You never served in the military or studied strategy or tactics. Perhaps you played with toy soldiers as a child. I can tell you about war. And I assure you that it's a miserable course of last resort only to be used when all other alternatives fail.

"Why don't you listen to congressional leaders on both sides of the aisle, and to the Pentagon personnel who could suggest a banquet of more constructive ideas than war? In my time, Congress and my administration took a joint approach to the most vital issues so the business of the nation could go forward for the greater good.

"General MacArthur, who Truman relieved of command in the Pacific, and my own secretary of state, John Foster Dulles, tried to persuade me to push our military forces through North Korea and China to stop the spread of communism. They even advocated the option of nuclear weapons. Both were confident of victory since we were the world's premiere nuclear power. But I listened to alternatives from congress on both sides of the aisle. Consequently, I flew to South Korea to assess the situation. Yes, the Chinese and Russians both enabled North Korea's invasion. Although we might have won, it became apparent to me that we would be engaged in a war with all of them . . . a war for which the American people would have little appetite.

"I instructed our diplomats to negotiate an armistice to end the conflict. While they pressed hard for a truce and a reasonable approach to a neutral dividing line between north and south, I passed the word through India to convey to Mao Zedong that if China didn't back off in Korea, I may have to drop another nuclear bomb. I certainly didn't want to take such action, but it did get his attention. Although China had the advantage of manpower, we possessed unmatched technology. That threat accelerated the armistice.

"Why you cozy up to the Russians perplexes me. Although I don't believe they want to rule the world, they always meddle in others' affairs to protect their own paranoid interests. They provided North Korea and China weapons to fight us in Korea. Stalin told Mao to drag out the Korean War to damage the reputations of Great Britain and the United States. Thousands more lives were lost because of this gamesmanship. Because you have no grasp of cause and effect, you have enabled them to fiddle in Venezuela's affairs. With or without Russian aid, Venezuela will collapse under its corruption and mismanagement. Similar regimes have caved in over the years . . . without detonating a bomb.

"I am here to warn you about the far-right-wing zealots who would bend church and state to their narrow and self-righteous views of a complex world. Let me tell you about few of them.

"Out of fear of the spread of Communism, our country believed in the domino theory. That is one country after another would fall prey to this form of government. Senator Joseph McCarthy, my political enemy, crusaded against perceived enemies from within. He falsely accused people wrongly of being Communists. His accusations and lies—not unlike yours, POTUS—ruined a lot of innocent lives, particularly in the State Department and the CIA.

"Unrestrained, McCarthy grilled, harassed, and defamed Americans guilty of no offense. Truman denounced him for besmirching the loyalty of General Marshall and trying to destroy Dean Acheson, one of the greatest secretaries of state in the history of this country. Since I was initially aligned with some of McCarthy's conservative supporters, it took me a while to fully recognize his evil.

"Finally, out of disgust, I worked behind the scenes to isolate McCarthy from his colleagues, the media, and the mainstream Republican Party. Then I exposed him to the American people as the fraud and the coward he was.

"You remind me of McCarthy. In your own way, you are just as mean, heartless and petty. To deflect criticism and sow confusion, you disparage past presidents and first ladies, senators, past candidates, and people who work throughout the government. I think you may deservedly meet the same fate as McCarthy if you continue this familiar pattern of behavior.

"I listened for too long to the ultra-religious hawks in my government, in particular the brothers John Foster Dulles, Secretary of State, and Allen Dulles, Director of the CIA. Their persuasive influence launched violent campaigns against foreign leaders they perceived to be threats to democracy, Christianity, and the right of large American corporations to operate freely worldwide. General Motor's CEO, "Engine Charley" Wilson, epitomized the Dulles brothers' position when he famously uttered in 1953, 'I think what is good for the country is good for General Motors, and vice versa.'

"Allen Dulles put in play the Bay of Pigs invasion of Cuba and provided financial aid to help the French fight off Vietnamese Communists. When the imperialistic French left with their tails between their legs, we financially supported the corrupt South Vietnam regime. At the time, no one foresaw the consequences or the thousands of American lives that would be lost there. I did refuse direct military involvement, despite pleas from our military and the Dulles brothers to engage directly.

"History shows the Dulles brothers as bad boys who only saw the world in black and white, good and evil. They did more than anyone to manufacture the Cold War and lead us into Vietnam. The brothers ignored Winston Churchill's advice in the mid-1950s that Ho Chi Minh was unbeatable and that we should accept his victory and try to make the best of it. When Stalin died, they ignored his successor's periodic overtures for peaceful coexistence, believing it to be a ruse.

"When they could, the Dulles boys attempted to install dictators friendly to America. And by God, man, you are playing with the same kind of devils in the Middle East, Eastern Europe, Africa, and Central and South America!

"You have your own equivalent of the Dulles brothers operating in the Ukraine and elsewhere. Your special emissaries tried to cut deals in return for favors regarding your political opponents. Paul McCavity and Marcus Valentini learned some people can go to the slammer for that. I think that sordid affair may still catch up with you. There are other ways to deal with maverick third world countries, but I am not sure you are smart enough. I caution you about intervention in their affairs.

I am forever doomed to read once a month the book *The Ugly American* by William Lederer and Eugene Burdick."

POTUS finally screwed up the courage to ask, "Who was the ugly American? I don't think I ever heard of him. Tell me who he is, and I'll lock him up."

Ike laughed. "I think you are well acquainted with him. Speaking of that, there's one other matter involving an ugly American that recently came to my attention. It involves military self-governance. I am uniquely qualified as a general and a president to speak to you about the disrespect and lack of trust you show the armed forces when you intervene and override their disciplinary actions. Other than your egotistical compulsion to flaunt your power and satisfy your outsized ego, you had no business telling the secretary of the army to free that Green Beret who stabbed to death a captured wounded enemy soldier.

"You lack military experience and are out of your element. As a result, you fail to comprehend the necessity of military law to maintain discipline and moral integrity within the ranks. I salute the secretary of the army for telling you where to shove it and then resigning. You know what I think? You have an inferiority complex about dodging military service and respond with a perverse need to make generals and admirals fear you. You can't force respect; you have to earn it. Pulling rank will not get that job done for you.

"Throughout history our military officers have primarily led by example. You probably never even thought about what kind of example you sent to our enemies when you freed a maverick soldier. They'll point to you for lowering the standards for rules of engagement and violating the Geneva Convention. You dishonor those who took a sacred oath to protect the Constitution with dignity. If you were in charge of high-profile court martials, we would have fired you for calling into question the chain of command's commitment to the rule of law. You should consider a career change, Little Big Hands. You have the wrong temperament for this job.

"When you suddenly hear a bullfrog croak, I promise you that another visitor will appear. Be fearful! Meanwhile, keep your head down when you swing a club out of those sand traps, and stop throwing others' golf balls into the traps when they aren't looking. As I leave you, I pray that you will come to your senses. Peace and prosperity for our nation depend on a president who uses his enormous power and America's great resources in the best interests of human betterment."

***

For the rest of the night, Little Big Hands hallucinated that all his senior administrators and White House staff had abandoned him. Without warning, they had just vacated their offices and workspaces and left their keys on his desk in the Oval Office. Suddenly, he was a commander of a bunch of empty chairs, a chief without anyone to direct, abuse, or fire. And all the phones began to ring at once.

POTUS woke up lethargic, disoriented, and hungover. He was surprised he'd finished the night on the veranda once again when he had gone to bed upstairs. He wondered why he had on golf shoes. Perhaps he'd mistaken them for slippers. He could not explain the gritty sand that clung uncomfortably to his sweaty body. And why did he wear a golf glove? He remembered only brief sketches of the long night behind, and he felt like a black veil hung over him.

POTUS graved sympathetic company. To the surprise of his cook, he staggered into the kitchen. Although Angelica Hernandez had worked for Belladonna for over ten years, he'd never inquired about her personal life, and he didn't know where she was from. He had never had any interest in social discourse with his servants. Angelica wondered if she was about to be fired for some offense which she could hardly imagine—except for one dark secret. She desperately needed this job to support her family in Guatemala, to whom she sent more than half of her earnings.

Seeing her startled look and desperate for companionship after his string of unearthly visitors, Little Big Hands said, "Do you mind if I sit for a moment at the kitchen table? Come join me for a cup of coffee. Please remind me where you are from. And oh, whatever became of your beautiful daughter who used to help you in the kitchen? I can find a job for her at the club."

As her hands shook, Angelica brought two cups of coffee and sat down. She broke into tears, afraid that POTUS knew she had come into the country illegally and was about to send her back to Guatemala.

With a scowl, Little Big Hands instinctively said, "You are here illegally, aren't you? I never knew."

"Sir, I beg of you, for the sake of my daughter Sarah, please let me work. You can cut my pay. If you send me back, my daughter, who is in her first year of medical school at LSU, will have to leave the country, too. And I won't be able to support my elderly widowed mother in Guatemala. I've given my whole life to help Sarah get an education and, God willing, to someday become a productive U.S. citizen. She's so smart and wants to be a pediatrician to help poor children in this country get medical care."

To demonstrate to his voters that he would honor his pledge to be tough on illegal immigration, POTUS had just ruthlessly fired and deported a dozen employees —some who had worked for him for more than twenty year. Finished with his cup of coffee, Little Big Hands rose to leave the table, saying, "Angelica, you present a dilemma for me . . . a conflict of interest. For now, let's just keep this conversation between us."

As he left the kitchen, POTUS asked himself, "Why didn't I just fire her?" He wondered if his fond memory of watching Sarah from afar working in the kitchen alongside her mother had softened him. Or was he hooked on Angelica's skills cooking? Or was it because she was the first illegal immigrant he had gotten to know as a human being?

In hopes of cleansing himself of the memories of last night's events, POTUS went upstairs to shower and shave. Then he retreated to his office to prepare his State of the Union Address. Because he had alienated the press, he doubted that any of the big news networks would broadcast his message to Congress. They hadn't last year. He had butchered the historical job description of the presidency and discarded many of its duties, but he had been unable yet to shed this one.

Later that day, his first draft of his speech half-finished, Little Big Hands escaped to the golf course to play a round. He had called the mayor and several local members of the Neti Pot reelection campaign to join him. All had declined with excuses They knew his handicap was bogus and they didn't enjoy his braying over every shot. The last thing they wanted to do was get roped into buying POTUS drinks again in his own club.

"Well," POTUS thought, "I might as well have a little fun with Miss Josephine Greensmith." An athletic, hourglass-figured brunette with emerald eyes, she had been runner-up in the Miss World contest before she went on to college.

"Hello, Josephine. Working as a press secretary intern for me can be rather stressful. Let's play some golf. Why don't you drop what you're doing, change into your cute little pink caddy skirt and halter, and get some exercise on the course with me? The sunshine will do you good. Vitamin D, you know."

As they went from green to green, Little Big Hands bounced his eyes and his random thoughts off Josephine about his pending State of the Union Address. She inspired his putting; he loved to sink putts and then stare at her shapely backside as she squeezed her knees together and leaned forward to pull the ball out of the cup. Hoping she would get his meaning, he asked, "Do you think it's too long? I don't want to be too stiff in my delivery."

Josephine found it a chore to lug POTUS's bag around the course. It exceeded the USGA's limit of fourteen clubs and was as big around as his girth. As they left each greenside, Little Big Hands offered, "May I help you put the bag over your shoulder?"

Josephine declined. "No, thank you, Sir. Just part of the job to spend this special time with you." She knew he was looking for an excuse to get more intimate.

Just in case she might need it someday, Josephine kept a daily log of all Little Big Hands's remarks and innuendos on the back of his scorecard, which he never asked to look at. Silently, she thought to herself, "He's never going to score with me."

Thus far, POTUS had been unsuccessful in groping her. Many other women were not as fortunate or as clever. Some were just opportunists, like the president. Josephine instinctively knew to keep her distance. She deeply resented Little Big Hands for telling her what to wear on the golf course, or anywhere else. She thought to herself, "What's a girl to do? I need this job to service the debt from the student loans I accumulated to get degrees in political science and save for law school. Who would have thought it would come to this? Soon I will tell this monster I plan to resign like most of his other staff."

Many mulligans later and exhausted from digging out of almost every sand trap on the course, POTUS returned to his office to burn the midnight oil crafting his State of the Union speech. While dining at his desk in his underwear beside an open window that revealed a waning crescent moon, he kept smearing traces of fried chicken, coleslaw, and grits on his draft. The smudges made it difficult to read the text.

His eyes grew blurry from the strain. A piercing headache from the weight of his office and the constant repercussions of his contemptible behavior suddenly overwhelmed him. Little Big Hands collapsed in his chair with his head and neck resting on his State of the Union.

Ghost #35: John Kennedy

KENNEDY SPACE CENTER

Bullfrogs serenaded one another beneath Little Big Hands's open window. They croaked in cadence with his loud snores. Then POTUS awoke to rhythmic squeaks from a rocking chair in the corner of his bedroom. Wiping the drool off his face and manuscript, POTUS lifted his head to see a ghostly figure rocking back and forth. It looked a lot like the portrait of President John Kennedy in the White House.

The apparition shouted, "Ask no longah what you can do for yourself, but rathah what you haven't done for your country!"

POTUS cowered as Kennedy steadily rocked to relieve the constant pain that reminded him of the back injuries he earned playing football at Harvard—and when a Japanese destroyer sliced his torpedo boat in half. Even in the afterlife, some pains linger forever.

With great effort, Kennedy rose from the chair and stepped achingly toward POTUS. "Put some clothes on. Stretched out there in mustard-stained underwear isn't your most favorable profile in courage, Little Big Hands. We are about to visit a special place that is part of my legacy but that I have never personally seen. When I accepted this mission, I got to choose wherever I wanted to drag you along. As I am momentarily an unrestricted time traveler, I'd like to go to an event that followed my death.

"My colleagues who have come before me have registered how steep the escarpment is between you and us. So here I am, one more who will try to penetrate your empty soul and redirect you toward service to our beloved country."

POTUS perceived that the apparition was feeble and could not physically harm him, started to walk out of the room. In an instant, a force like a taser seized him in a paralyzing grip, and he passed out.

***

When he awoke from what he believed was another nightmare, Little Big Hands and Kennedy stood in a spectator area at the Kennedy Space Center in Cape Canaveral, Florida. Before them, the monstrous Saturn V rocket was poised to launch Neil Armstrong, Michael Collins, and Edwin Aldrin to the moon. The roar from Apollo 11 deafened the crowd as the ship belched a fog of gaseous mist over the site.

Kennedy's enthusiasm was beyond description. His assassination in 1963 cut short his dream to witness as an earthling the launch on July 16, 1969. Apollo 11 fulfilled a vision that he'd put in play while president. It continued to inspire America under the leadership of future presidents and Congresses.

Once Apollo 11 disappeared into the horizon, Kennedy said to POTUS, "Besides us observing my own thwahted destiny this morning, you probably wonder what the point is of us being here. While I explain, I'd like you to formulate in your mind your vision for America. Afterwards, I want to heah about it.

"Right or wrong, when I succeeded Eisenhower, I felt that his administration lacked imagination, vitality, and boldness. I realized later that I should have given him more credit for developing our nation's infrastructure and a national network of interstate highways. As much as that boosted the economy, you of all people know how hard it is to acknowledge your predecessor's accomplishments, especially if you represent the opposite party.

"Shortly after I won the presidency, I decided that America's indecision to embrace a full-fledged space effort represented everything that was wrong with the Eisenhower years. I came to the conviction that America needed to think and behave on a grand scale to boost its spirits after the Russians launched mankind's first spaceship Sputnik 1. I wanted to beat the Russians to the moon to invigorate the nation and gain an edge in the Cold War.

"I bet big that a lavish investment in space would unite our greatest assets: our people, government, industry, academia, and the press in a grand project to accelerate the pace of technological innovation. To win the race in space, the cost to the taxpayers swelled to over twenty-five billion dollars. To put that in perspective, in today's dollars that is over two hundred thirty billion dollars.

"Now that sum would make an advocate like yourself, in favah of shrinking government, go into convulsions at the thought of it all. Contrary to Neti Pot Wing's philosophy, our intense investment in space renewed the nation's spirit. All Americans were once again pioneers in the footsteps of Christopher Columbus, the Pilgrims, Lewis and Clark, and Dr. Livingston.

"And my God, man, it spurred the development of next-generation computer innovations, virtual reality, advanced satellite televisions, game-changing industrial medical imaging, kidney dialysis, enhanced meteorological forecasting apparatuses, nanotechnology, cordless power tools, bar coding, and other modern marvels. All things that you, Little Big Hands, take for granted. Think of how many businesses and jobs those innovations spawned.

"When the naysayers asked, Why go to the moon? I put my whole political career on the line. I responded, 'Why climb the highest mountain? Why, in 1927, attempt to fly nonstop across the Atlantic?' I told them, 'We choose to go to the moon not because it's easy, but because it's hahd. Because that goal will serve to organize and measure the best of our energies and skills. Like King Arthur, we became knights in space because to survive as a nation means being first in space.'

"Why are you cozying up to the Russians? They'll try to beat you like a drum when their national interests conflict with ours. And, they won't play fair. When Nikita Khrushchev sent missiles to Cuba, I stood him down. Our survival as a nation depended on him blinking and pulling out. You appear to be in bed with the Russians. I fear you might blink first now.

"I'll give you a bit of intelligence that I doubt you know of, since you have practically dismantled the CIA and foreign service: Watch your back in Latin America. The Russians are at it again, but this time they're even more devious and skilled at fake news. A pattern of antigovernment protests spreads like wildfire there. A rash of recent tweets fomented protests in Chile.

They originated with Twitter accounts linked to the Russians. They want to once again attempt to destabilize governments by trolling in Latin America. In Bolivia, their president resigned after tweets spiked to several thousand a day. And hear this: in Ecuador, Peru, Bolivia, Colombia, and Chile over a one-month period, the Russians posted a series of similar inflammatory messages within minutes of one another.

"Why haven't you questioned what's behind this outbreak? Would it be because the Russians perfected the same scheme to help get you elected as the lesser and weaker of two evils in their minds?" Not only have the Russians under Putin perfected poisoning the internet traffic, they have also literally poisoned prominent opposition to the Kremlin. Most recently activist Aleksey Navalny. Why haven't you expressed outrage?

POTUS either ignored or failed to comprehend Kennedy's dig about the Russians. He began to recite his big-picture plans for the nation. The more he talked, the more animated he became. In his enthusiasm, a foul drool leaked out of the side of his mouth.

"My vision for America begins with building a wall around the capital to keep vagrants and protestors out. Congressmen can't even go to lunch without getting their pockets picked or being robbed at gunpoint. Sitting at tables or in the restrooms, they are constantly being harangued by some left-wing splinter group.

"And you can't be sure if he is not a she, or she not a he! Bugs the hell out of me. I promised my conservative friends to stop this invasion and deprecation. The graffiti on the Mall is despicable. Just last week, the bastards violated the Lincoln Memorial. They suspended a banner from his right hand that said 'President Little Big Hands is an ignorant little prick. Impeach him!' That's slanderous, and disrespects my office—and Lincoln, too!"

Although Kennedy could not condone the graffiti and rioting, silently he thought Lincoln might have smiled at the rebel rousers' banner.

"I'm also fed up with banditry and murderous gangs and drug dealers in Central and South America. After I tame Venezuela, Colombia, Honduras, El Salvador, Nicaragua, and Guatemala, I'll turn them into resort paradises. Bring a lot of business. No more dope or immigrants headed north.

"There are the other things I have on my agenda to restore this great country. Exploit natural resources in national parks to fuel the nation. Appoint only judges who share the wisdom of my electorate. Protect American industry with more tariffs to spur innovation. Eliminate several cabinet positions and consolidate responsibilities to speed up decision-making. Tighten voter registration so only citizens who pass an English test are eligible. Remove all incentives to support the arts. That will eliminate a lot of bad art. End the popular vote, so we don't have any more election disparities. Pull out of NATO and the United Nations so no one tells us what to do anymore. Double the defense budget to scare the hell out of our enemies and give young people jobs. Cut civilian government employees by twenty percent to reduce the federal deficit. Eliminate food stamps and pare back Medicaid . . . to get those people back to work and to take responsibility for themselves. Make matters clear on right-to-life. Establish a mechanism to censor and punish the press for offenses against the government. Make each state responsible for maintaining and building its infrastructure to eliminate a costly and cumbersome federal standard for interstate transportation. Shut down the post office. And cut the inheritance tax to zero.

"When I die, my memorial tomb will be the greatest. It will shadow all others. It will glow like a year-round Christmas tree. Nothing like your little gas light in Arlington National Cemetery. I do admit, though, you have a great view.

"So, what do you think of my Really Big Plans for America?"

A long pause was interrupted by Kennedy's favorite ghost dog, Pushinka, who raised his leg and squirted POTUS's shoes.

A mixed-breed, Pushinka was a no-nonsense dog and a gift from Soviet Premier Nikita Khrushchev.

A slight, diplomatic smile came over Kennedy's face as he shook his head in disbelief at Little Big Hands's outrageous comments. He let out a sigh, and then said, "Want to know what Lyndon Johnson thought about the primary difference between Democrats and Republicans?"

When he got no response, Kennedy said, "I'll tell you anyway. We're for something and they are against everything. Furthermore, they hate all our presidents. By the way, Johnson will visit you next. He has something special in store for you.

"Those of us who came before you, while not always perfect, made at least some attempt to have a balanced and qualified judiciary. Why, even Eisenhower sometimes appointed liberal judges when they were better qualified to interpret the law than the alternatives. And I, a liberal, approved the nomination of some conservative judges that Ike recommended upon leaving office.

"The nation wept when I was assassinated. Unlike you, I had a seventy-percent approval rating, which only fell when I took a courageous stand on civil rights. That prompted Southern whites to defect. While I won both the popular and electoral vote, you only slipped into the presidency because of gerrymandering. Many of the things that would have benefited the country were well underway when I was murdered. You may have forgotten that Thomas Jefferson and Abraham Lincoln lost elections because of gerrymandering.

"My biggest regret is not pulling out of Vietnam. I knew we couldn't win. They all hated us. I also knew that if I pulled out before the election, I'd lose the vote. Woefully, my best intentions to pull out during my second term never materialized.

"Although these words may be wasted on a man of your intellect, our collective experiences teach that no one nation has the powah or the wisdom to solve all the problems of the world or manage its revolutionary tides. Those of us who pay attention to history have learned that extending our commitments does not always increase our security. That any initiative carries the risk of temporary defeat. That nuclear weapons cannot prevent subversion. That no free people can be kept free without will and energy of their own. And that no two nations or situations are exactly alike.

"Some think I committed a few lustful indiscretions with women, which I'll neither confirm nor deny. I at least attempted to keep my private life just that. And because I didn't berate the press, they exercised restraint and discretion. I did have a particular fondness for Marilyn Monroe. No one could sing 'Happy birthday, Mr. President' the way she could—or for that matter, light a candle. And out of respect, the press cooperated. You, sir, have made your despicable private life very public. You talk openly about what you like to do to young women who are powahless to stand up to you or desperate to make a living. Have you any thought about the example you set for our youth?

"I leave you now. Think hard about the warnings I bring. When your term ends, where will you go? How will you be remembered? How do you want to be remembered? There's a penance to pay. In perpetuity, mine is watching *Some Like It Hot*, starring Marilyn Monroe, every Saturday night.

"When you hear crickets chirp, expect another ball-busting visitor."

***

Frightened and at wits end, POTUS darted for the security of his bedroom. He shut the windows and doors, climbed into bed, and pulled the sheet over his head. Ready to run on a moment's notice, he wore his rumpled clothes and kept his shoes laced. He left the lights on and didn't have the energy to turn on Ferret News. No telling what Annie Oakely Remington, that sharpshooting reporter for Channel 6666, might have to say about him now.

Ghost #36: Lyndon Johnson

AT THE RANCH

Just as he began to ease into REM sleep, Little Big Hands dreamed that he could hear the scratchy sound of crickets crawling inside his ears. Then an image appeared in his mind of a gigantic man in cowboy boots, half-way dressed in red, white, and blue boxer shorts and a Resistol Open Road Western hat perched on his head.

"Dang you, Little Big Hands, when I got the callin' to come pay y'all a visit, I didn't even spare time to put my pants on. That's how eager I was to get my paws on you."

Giving POTUS a light kick in the butt, LBJ introduced himself. "You're a dew worm. I'd hang you out for bait. You brag about your leadership and political power, but you know nothin' other than how to distribute pork. Y'all let Congress squabble and second-guess your intentions, which you don't know either. You've been runnin' the White House by the seat of your pants, which is why I booted you.

"Get some clothes on while I fetch a pair of jeans. We are goin' to cactus country. Y'all and them have something in common— you're both green pricks!"

In the blink of an eye, Johnson transported POTUS to his beloved sanctuary, the LBJ Ranch near Stonewall, Texas, which was named after Stonewall Jackson. When POTUS learned this bit of local color, he shivered, remembering his torturous expedition with Andrew Jackson just a few days ago. He knew this encounter with Johnson meant double jeopardy.

"Climb into my little ol' convertible and I'll take you for a spin on the ranch. It's been almost fifty years since I've driven this darlin' blue-and-white cutie. Let's see if I still know my way around the property."

Johnson awkwardly engaged the clutch, grinding the stubborn four-speed manual transmission into fourth gear. With a belch of smoke and a lurch, the ancient convertible gathered speed on a narrow road that ran alongside the Pedernales River. On the other side of the bank, the Texas White House sat in the midst of a large lawn thick with Southern Live Oaks casting a canopy of shade up to the front porch. Along the way, Johnson commented on the prize cattle that grazed on the ranch.

"Little Big Hands, your daddy was too cheap to buy premium Texas beef for his meat markets. As I recall, there was a big to-do in the press about one of his nationwide butcher shops mixin' in expired beef with fresh ground hamburger. He must have paid a lot of bribes to avoid going to the slammer. You've got some pretty nasty prisons in Louisiana. How he got that butcher in Kansas City to take the blame must have cost him a fortune."

As Johnson turned his head to admire the house, the convertible suddenly plunged off the road as it followed his gaze. Out of control, the vehicle bounced down the bank, gained speed, and started rolling rapidly toward the water. Johnson shouted, "Dang, the brakes don't work. The brakes won't hold. We're goin' in. We're goin' under."

With a gigantic splash, they plummeted into a portion of the Pedernales that had been dammed up to create a lake. While Johnson smiled, POTUS screamed and swore that he wasn't immortal yet. He didn't know how to swim. He thought for sure he was about to get baptized into the underworld.

"Gotcha," Johnson said as he engaged the two propellers under the engine compartment of the German-made Amphicar. The wheels acted as stabilizers.

"The boys suggested I might be able to get your attention if I pulled one of mah favorite stunts. They said you don't listen well and have a short attention span. I argued if that's the case, then maybe I ought to just pick you up by the ears, like I did my beagles, Him and Her. So, listen up. I've got some things to tell you. Might do some good, as you seem to be sort of adrift right now—and in your presidency, too. Pardon the pun!

"I came into the presidency after Kennedy's murder. I perpetuated his legacy and I like to think that I got more out of Congress than he would have. I knew how to get things done, somethin' that seems to be missin' in your repertoire of skills. I passed unprecedented legislation to protect the land, air, water, wilderness, and the American people's quality of life. Also, I'm quite proud that I breathed new life into Roosevelt's New Deal, which included aid to education, Head Start, Medicare, and Medicaid. Let me point out that the latter commanded bipartisan support at the time…a time when there was less grand standin'.

"Imagine that, POTUS. Bipartisan support! Along with your uncompromisin', snarly, heartless Senate Majority Leader Ms. Billy Brickell, second-string cabinet, and castrated political advisers, bet none of ya can *say* bipartisan, let alone spell it. They'll kiss your ass, but the problem is y'all don't know where your ass is headed . . . other than these silly issues you concoct to make believe you're a president with big ideas. Ideas like a wall, separatin' children from their immigrant parents, swellin' the defense budget, bannin' athletes from comin' into the US from other countries, tossin' out trade agreements rather than makin' an effort to refine them, capriciously shuttin' down government, imposin' embargos, cuttin' taxes for the wealthy, and promotin' the merits of fattenin' fast food.

"Throughout my presidency, it was my dream to make life better for more people than even FDR thought possible. I'll admit that for a long time, civil rights were not a priority. Over time, I began to feel deep in my soul that the essence of government lay in ensurin' the dignity and innate integrity of life for every individual, regardless of color, creed, ancestry, sex, or age. I decided it must be our goal to assure that all Americans play by the same rules and all play against the same odds. Unlike your deaf ear, I heard our people cryin'. I had to act after John Lewis's marched for racial justice across the Edmund Pettus Bridge with 600 others in Selma, Alabama March 7, 1965. That day became known as 'Bloody Sunday. He and many others took a horrific beatin' from goons.'

"What did I do? I tore the glitterin' cellophane off our society and forced the nation to look at what lay underneath—poverty—injustice—illiteracy—sickness—and hunger. I was a big-picture guy who knew how to play Congress like a country fiddle. I was the man who held the bow, and they danced mostly to my tune. Like you, I was an alpha male and made a big deal about Jumbo. Sort of like, who is the biggest male dog peein' on the fire hydrant? I was that guy.

"However, you've let your dick do too much thinkin', and a lot of women now take you to task for your transgressions. I advise you to stop kowtowing' to your agin' wealthy political base and stand up like a man and represent all the American people. Your Make America Great slogan has pissed a lot of us ghosts off. Since when hasn't America been one of the greatest countries on earth? Sure, she's had her flaws, but she's always risen above them.

"I had my flaws, too. My zealous initiatives for the arts, the environment, antipoverty, racial justice, and workplace safety angered many economic and social conservatives. I moved too fast and became a target for white voters and tax revolters. I inherited that damn old crazy Asian war from Eisenhower and Kennedy. How was I to know that JFK planned to withdraw after he got reelected? He wouldn't speak up in advance because he was afraid he'd lose the election and then he got himself killed.

"I trusted the wrong generals and advisers. From what I've witnessed, your judgment is equally flawed. They kept promisin' me we could defeat the Vietcong. Secretary of Defense Robert McNamara took a statistical approach to measure success and kept askin' for more troops. Problem was, he measured the wrong damn thing. He didn't calculate the will of the Vietnamese people. I just wanted to create the Great Society. Sadly, the war distracted me from what I hoped to accomplish for the underprivileged.

"My main goals were to eliminate poverty and racial injustice, and I got sucked into eliminating' lives. The torment ruined my health and my drive. I got blamed for the war. Also like you, the press wouldn't leave me alone. If I had walked on water, they'd say it was because I couldn't swim. Gave me a heart attack. I found it too disturbin' to watch the ten-minute documentaries of myself that I used to enjoy so much. Similar to you, I was my biggest fan.

"I decided not to run for reelection, but I think I might have won. With one more term, I could have embarrassed those wrong-headed white voters and tax-revolters into doing the right thing. Somewhere in their hearts there's a soft spot for mankind. You've just got to paint the right economic picture for them with how their self-interest benefits, especially for the future of their children and generations to follow.

"I wish to be remembered for civil rights. Frankly, Little Big Hands, I'm quite annoyed with your position. The people you've hired in your administration reflect your racial biases and bigotry. Defendin' the Ku Klux Clan's right to protest reverses the nation's clock. Those folks deserve no quarter. And look at all those gangs of white supremacists who claim to be your fans. That's a real legacy to be proud of!

"Now that I've got the hang of being behind the wheel again, I want to show you what we called the Mexican school I taught in for a year over in Cotulla, Texas. When I was in Congress, I used to tell my colleagues that the students there were so poor that they went through the garbage piles searchin' for grapefruit rinds to suck out the juice. The children of Mexican Americans had been taught that the end of life was a beet row, or a spinach field, or a cotton patch. I lived and witnessed poverty firsthand. You, sir, with your privileged and insulated background, can't even begin to comprehend it.

"Damn you for cuttin' that three-billion-dollar aid package to Central American countries which Congress and the United Nations approved. That money was intended to reduce poverty and stem violence there. And it had some badly needed reforms and oversights tied to its administration."

Defensively, POTUS whimpered, "I'm only doing what my constituents voted me into office to do. Gotta keep them on my side. And if I've misinterpreted anything, I'll just buffalo them into believing that's what they wanted. Easy to do when just a few key issues drive them to vote the way they do. Like religion, taxes, abortion, minorities, guns, crime. You know as well as I do, if you cross them, deny everything. And never beg for forgiveness…it shows weakness."

Johnson responded, "Little Big Hands you've gone astray. I stepped down from office for exactly the opposite. I told the American people I regretted Vietnam and wished that things had been different. And then I owned up to my accountability, but not before tellin' em to soften their hearts for their fellow man.

"To teach you a lesson, again I'd like to pick you up by the ears and shake you. But I promised your earlier visitors not to pull that stunt.

"For me, every mornin' my penance in the afterlife is to awake to the newspapers reporting fifty-eight thousand lives lost in Vietnam and more wounded and permanently disabled.

"I think it's shaping up right now how you may be remembered, don't you? The annals of American history will label you dead weight. Years from now your biographers will document and record you and your administration as a pompous comedy of errors. My advice to you, Little Big Hands, is not to run for reelection.

"By the way, one of your most vocal critics, Congressmen John Lewis sends you his regards. We have welcomed him home. It's one more low water benchmark in your administration that amid an outpourin' of bipartisan tributes to the Congressmen's advancement of civil rights that you said so little other than a brief tweet upon his death.

"Expect another unearthly presence when the only sounds you detect are made by the cicadas. My best wish for you is that all your dreams haunt you. I am a vacatin' your head now."

***

Just before sunrise and as was his habit, Little Big Hands, half-asleep in a twilight zone, turned on Ferret News. He couldn't discern which state of mind he was in when he heard sharpshooting reporter Annie Oakely Remington for Channel 6666 say that the nation was deeply divided over President Daniel Hands's military takeover of a half dozen countries in Central and South America. White supremacists and Neti Pot members reportedly cheered him on. College students and AARP members across the country rioted in the streets and blockaded entrances and exits to the Capitol and Pentagon. Even Ferret News said that Little Big Hands's impulsive invasion without cabinet or congressional approval constituted grounds for impeachment. Annie Oakely drew nasty parallels between Vietnam, the Johnson administration, and POTUS's invasion of neighbors south of the border. Was this another dark nightmare or reality?

Day Four

AIR FORCE ONE

Little Big Hands struggled with his State of the Union Address. There had been too many distractions in his Belladonna retreat and country club. He dialed up Air Force One and ordered the crew to return him to the capital. Surely there were no creatures of the night around the White House like those that thrived here in the Louisiana wetlands. He was tired of the swamp.

As he climbed the ramp to Air Force One, POTUS felt a sense of calm and relief from the torments of the last two nights spent on his back porch and in his country club office. He had given up on scoring with Ms. Greensmith and had reluctantly left the golf course behind along with the lusty pleasures of the nineteenth hole with his curvaceous but not so young and innocent part time caddy and club hostess, Marjory Hickenbottom. Her only previous resumé experience was work at a string of New Orleans massage parlors owned by a wealthy Chinese lady who was a major campaign contributor. The ghostly images had sabotaged his game. Every shot he hit sliced, hooked, or chunked. Grass and roots clung to every club head.

The refrigerator system on Air Force One had just been replaced to the tune of thirty-five million to taxpayers. Although he had put on a show of disdain for government excesses when he campaigned for office, he felt he deserved this little indulgence. The system could support over three thousand meals. You never know when the proletariat might rebel and force him and his cronies to live, feast, and love in the clouds. Plenty of McDonald's hamburgers had been flash-frozen and stored in the cargo.

As he walked down the aisle to his private suite, none of the crew members looked him in the eye. They were ashamed to work for him. They worked out of respect for the country and for what the presidency once represented to the world. They all secretly prayed for a reincarnation.

POTUS wedged himself into a chair by a window. As he admired the red, white, and blue US coat of arms embroidered in the carpet, he noticed that cicadas began to emerge from the eagle's beak. They swarmed around his shoes and crawled up the inside of pantlegs. Their wings fluttered against his skin and their claws frantically gripped the fabric.

POTUS shot out of his seat. He did a square-dancing two step motion as he stomped on the invaders. He pulled off his pants, shook them free of cicadas and called for the stewards to come quickly. He stood there in his briefs, belittled the crew, and complained loudly that his beloved Air Force One had become infested. How could his staff be so incompetent? He thought to himself, just wait until we land—I'll replace them all. But upon inspection, no one but POTUS could see or hear any cicadas.

Ghost #37: Richard Nixon

DÉJÀ VU

Embarrassed after the incident with the cicadas, Little Big Hands requested a tumbler of Scotch to soothe himself and dull the insanity. He promptly retreated to his airborne office and locked the door. He swallowed a huge chug of whiskey, momentarily closed his eyes and savored the taste to shut out the encounter. He asked himself, "What was I thinking? Is it the antidepression medication? The alcohol? Or both?" His doctor had told him that alcohol is a depressant, but POTUS only heard what he wanted to hear.

As he drifted off from the self-medication, behind his eyelids appeared a caricature of a familiar political trickster. He thought, "Could that be President Richard Nixon? His framed portrait faces the lady's room in the White House and leers at them as they come and go. An inside joke."

"Little Big Hands," exclaimed Nixon, "A man I sympathize with. Some think we have a few things in common. But I want you to know, people view me as the better president. Not bragging, just saying. I groomed myself for the position and paid my dues to win the office. Unlike you, I expected to win, and had at the top levels a fully capable administration ready to immediately serve my presidency. And, not for personal financial gain.

"Some call you a lucky sperm who hawked meatloaf for a livelihood before you landed in the White House. Be honest. You really had little idea how government runs. Without a recipe to capture the nation's imagination, I am afraid your presidency has been more of a meat grinder. Easy to criticize from the outside looking in, isn't it?"

***

The next thing POTUS knew, he was in the White House cloak room. Nixon stared at the selection of overcoats and then said, "Here, put on this long black trench coat and hat so no one will recognize us. We're going incognito on an undercover mission. Aww, forget about it. What am I thinking? No one can see us. We're both invisible. Anyway, I have a place I'd like to take us. I've never been there before myself, but I feel like I know the structure inside out.

"Do you recognize this six-building complex here at Foggy Bottom? Ha! I like that name, Foggy Bottom! Sort of describes what we both do supremely well to keep things nice and murky for the press, our mutual enemies. Of course, some other presidents were good at covering their tracks, too. But we took the art of concealment to a new level for both the press and the American people.

"See those five fellas breaking into the Democratic National Committee headquarters? It's the evening of June 17, 1972. My dedicated, but amateur loyalists want to get the scoop on what Hubert Humphrey and those damn Democrats are up to. Watch their careless flashlights dance off the walls, cabinets, and furniture. The beams have alerted Watergate security. What fools! They bungled the assignment.

"They all got arrested and eventually confessed and went to jail. Unfortunately for me, one of them—a GOP security aide, I believe—received a twenty-five-thousand-dollar cashier's check earmarked for my campaign. See how hard it is to conceal a paper or electronic trail these days?

"You do believe me when I say that I had no idea these clowns intended to burglarize the Watergate complex? Perhaps I sent some careless message to one of my subordinates that it would be nice to know what the Democrats were up to. Unluckily for me, I couldn't 'foggy-bottom' that I tried to cover up the whole affair.

"My former White House counsel, John Dean, testified that I was deeply involved up to my neck in the Watergate cover-up, and also ran an illegal effort to obstruct justice. Another testified that during the election, I had requested that we plant a Secret Service agent in Robert Kennedy's security detail. And then that same guy said he heard me tell my chief of staff, HR Haldeman, that once we won reelection it would be more than ever a time for political vengeance. That we would nail those sons of bitches

. . . Democrats, the media, the antiwar movement, and any other perceived opponents.

"Before I knew it, Congressman Tom Railsback, a moderate Republican, broke with his party and helped draw up the articles of impeachment against me. He said he felt bad about what happened to me. After he heard the tapes, he felt all the evidence was damning and Congress had no choice but to impeach me. Then everything just spiraled downhill. The irony is that I even campaigned for Railsback in western Illinois! Who can you trust?

"Non-stop you've lambasted your enemies over their charges that the Russians helped you get elected. I couldn't have done better. Your involvement in the Ukraine affair to shape the next election is a little more problematic. It really is too bad you couldn't get your ambassador to shut up. You should have offered her a better job, and her boss too. In my case, the noose tightened around my neck rather than my enemies. The more I cried foul, the more suspicious the investigators became.

"I am not a crook! I said that not in response to Watergate, but to a journalist who asked whether I'd accurately reported my taxes. Turned out I hadn't, which resulted in the dubious honor of being the first sitting president ever audited by the congressional Joint Committee on Taxation. Fortunately for me, the IRS concluded I had not purposefully committed fraud. As the nation's number one and supposedly most exemplary taxpayer, I had to pay my own government another half million dollars.

"Did you know I was the first president to show my taxes as a matter of public record when I ran for office? I felt that was the honorable and moral thing to do. Since then, you are the only one who hasn't. Come on, you can tell me what you are hiding. I can't tattle on you now.

"On the other hand, maybe that was pretty clever of you not to reveal them. Too much information might have incriminated your campaign and revealed true character. Be careful you don't go down in history for deliberate tax evasion or, worse yet, criminal activity. It doesn't help your case that your long-time personal attorney claims you did. Don't let him out of jail or let him write a book. Keep a lid on it. Otherwise, you could dig a deep hole for yourself that would kill all chances for re-election and destroy the Neti Pot Wing. They have figurately and literally invested all their faith and dollars in you to carry the banner. Bad news would send all your loyal congressmen scurrying to the washroom to rid themselves of the stink and any association they had with you. My supporters fled as quickly as they could. History does repeat itself.

"I had a vision for government and let no one get in my way. I knew how to manipulate Congress and sway the American people. They loved that I opened up trade with China and ended the Vietnam War.

"By the way, how was Johnson? He claims that I worked behind the scenes with Vietnamese leaders to extend the war until I got elected. He also says he could have ended it before he left office except that I promised Hanoi to wait for a better deal. We'll let the historians be the judge of that.

"You know, President Johnson was very close to ending the Vietnam War. He had a deal in the works. Had he pulled it off, my opponent Hubert Humphrey might have gained an edge in the 1968 election. Fortunately, my enemies lacked proof that my campaign did anything to forestall a peace settlement. You don't believe I was capable of such shenanigans, do you?

POTUS answered, "He seemed pretty adamant that you undermined his presidency. But that's what you have to do sometimes to win. It's all about the winning. I admire you for that."

Nixon smiled and continued, "Although you and I are both accused of manipulating our elections, our enemies will never prove it. That business with the Russians planting fake news online really swung the election for you. Brilliant! Your invitation to them opened the door. Facebook and Twitter gave them a direct line to fire up several million gullible far-right-wing voters. What did the Russies get out of it? It's kind of funny how no voter believes they were duped by a foreign country. I ask you, what has accountability come to here in America?

"It seems we both had bad luck with our picks for the inner circle. Many of yours went to jail and they almost dragged you under. At least your vice president hasn't gone to jail yet. Mine went to the slammer because his numbers didn't add up. Tax evasion and corruption. I was caught off guard when prosecutors nailed him. Spiro Agnew really wasn't all that bad a guy. He was a good drinking buddy and liked the women. He could smooth-talk the tail off a donkey. But as the former governor of Maryland, he got greedy. Power does that to you, doesn't it? And like you, he was a real dealmaker extraordinaire. So, I had to settle for a Ford.

"Say, I never thought of Spiro as a poster boy for you and me. Those bribes he paid were not a deductible business expense. For that matter, neither are the ones you paid to those Go Club gals before your election to keep their mouths shut for those little dances under the sheets. No need for impeachment. No need for congressional action. That's a violation of election laws, and it could put you in a fast lane directly to jail. I'd be nervous about those prospects if I were you. I won't tell anyone though. You know, honor among...

"Watergate was a bit of mess for me. I thought I could bully the Department of Justice and the FBI into a corner. I fired the special prosecutor who was in the act of investigating the matter. The press called it the Saturday Night Massacre—as if I were a hit man in a gangster movie. Imagine that!

"I fought back and complained about all the lies my enemies told about me. Of course, that included the press. You really pushed the envelope when you tried to fire the special investigator snooping into Russian interference in your election.

"You dared to go where I could not have imagined. . . jury and sentence tampering. The public and press's reaction backfired on you when you attempted to smear the foreman of the jury. She was one of eleven who unanimously found your pal guilty of lying to Congress and tampering with witnesses himself. Ballsey of you to try to use your position of power to demand a new trial for your old friend and campaign manager, Paul McCavity. I must say you made me look like a Boy Scout... especially when you commuted his sentence. He was clearly a felon. That took guts! Anyone else, such action would have been political suicide.

"That's bold stuff...to meddle in due process and obstruct the findings of a legitimate jury that had been vetted by both the prosecution and defense attorneys. I should know. I was a lawyer. And it sends a frightening message to people who might serve as jurors on future cases near and dear to you. Now they know that if they dare cross you, your legions of lawyers will personally confront them and sully their reputations on a public stage. I can't imagine the size of your budget for lawyers. Say, where does all that money come from?

"Sometimes justice can be denied. In the long run, it looked like I was headed for impeachment and jail, so I became the first president to resign. If things get worse, you might think about that route. Good luck and keep a stiff upper lip.

"My finest hour as president was certainly when I established relations with the Chinese Communists. My announcement that we could be friends with China shook the world and the press. Overnight it transformed the structure of international politics. And I didn't hesitate to leverage it against the Russians. People were shocked that these two recent villains and backers of the North Vietnamese could be so transformed. The funny thing is, years after my resignation I started to regain some respectability because of what I accomplished with China. Trade blossomed with them and a lot of companies eventually shifted production there from the United States. I wrote a few books and was sought after to pontificate about foreign affairs.

"Listen carefully, Little Big Hands. Failure to follow this advice cost me the Oval Office. Always remember, some people may hate you, but they don't win unless you hate them back and act on that hatred. Then you destroy yourself. Your vocabulary in office and on the campaign trail indicates that you are consumed by hatred. You describe people with words like stupid, loser, moron, fake news, zero talent, enemies of the people. And then there are the words you use to describe women—horse face, fat, ugly, dog, pig, unhinged, crazed, lowlife . . . You get the drift. Perhaps you should enroll in a charm school class or maybe hire a tutor? It might save your presidency.

"One other thing. It seems to me that you try too hard to profit from your position while in office . . . feather your nest. Things like channeling meetings and events to your hotel and restaurants, rounds of golf on your multiple courses. Holding an unusual number of meetings on your commercial properties. People are beginning to notice. Little Big Hands, with great pride, I can tell you that during the five and a half years I sat in the Oval Office, no man or woman entered my administration and left with more of this world's goods than when she or he arrived. No man or woman ever gained financially at the public expense or the public till.

"It's is time to leave you now. I've said my piece, as instructed. Here's my penance. I am forced to watch the evening news every night and hear myself repeat "I'm not a crook!" And, three things haunt me. My hatred for real or perceived enemies. The damage that the threat of impeachment did to my name and legacy. And the additional lives lost in Vietnam up to my election."

***

Tormented, POTUS napped and twitched in his big chief chair on Air Force One. He dreamed that the IRS agent he had bribed to postpone any audits had found religion. To cleanse his guilty conscience, the agent provided his tax filings to Congress and Louisiana's Attorney General. POTUS could see himself facing a grand jury accused of income tax evasion.

Ghost #38: Gerald Ford

WHACKING THE BALL

Apersistent headache overwhelmed POTUS and clouded his thoughts. He wondered if the cabin pressure on Air Force One was defective or if the pilot meant him harm. His head throbbed. Next, he imagined a water moccasin, its reptilian tongue flicking in and out in his direction, coiled and poised to sink its fangs into his outstretched leg. Did the cabin crew have ill intentions? I can't trust anyone. He rubbed his temples to relieve the symptoms. As his vision cleared, his eyes focused on the image of President Gerald Ford dressed in a dusty, dark blue suit, frayed red necktie, and moldy black shoes.

"Little Big Hands," Ford said, "Come with me and bring your lucky seven iron. I want to show you my last few days in the White House." The next thing Little Big Hands knew, he was on the third floor of the White House. Under the circumstances, he questioned the need for a seven iron.

"The last night that Betty and I spent in the White House after my loss to President Carter, we invited Vice President Nelson Rockefeller and his wife, Happy, and their two young sons to have dinner and a sleepover. Over the years Nelson and I proudly served the country together, Betty and I had become very fond of him and his family. After dinner, Nelson and his two boys joined me right where we are on the third floor. Lots of cobwebs up here, and rumors of ghosts rattling the rafters. You probably don't get up here often, since you own several golf courses. I hear that you may yet break the record for most rounds played while in office on the taxpayers' payroll. By now you surely have discovered taxpayers don't give mulligans to presidents who whiff the ball on the job.

"Anyway, I had a date to play golf with Arnold Palmer at the Bing Crosby Tournament within a few days of leaving office. To tune my game and have some fun, Nelson and I erected a practice driving range in the hall. Like a pair of juvenile delinquents and truants, we laughed and whacked away at golf balls. Then we gave a club to Nelson's young son, who swung as hard as he could and shanked the ball. The little boy looked at his father and said, 'I wonder what President Ford thinks of me now?' 'Don't worry,' Nelson said, 'he understands all about missing shots.' Timing is everything in golf, as you know, and that was really pretty funny.

"You may ask what's the point? Well, I transported you here to talk about the shots you keep missing. I'd let you swing that seven iron, but I am afraid you'd damage even more government property.

"As Nixon's vice president, I got to observe the man up front and personal. He was a complicated, gifted, and flawed man. POTUS, you only possess one of those traits. Rather quickly, I realized he was controlled by neurosis and deep resentments and hatred of just about everybody at one time or another. Those resentments festered and never mellowed out. If you didn't agree with him, you were a violent leftist, a Communist, an enemy of the people, or worked for the goddamned press. And he could be ruthless."

Concerned that POTUS was still in a catatonic state, Ford shouted, "Are you getting my drift?"

Now fully awake, Little Big Hands's eyes bugged out. He wiped the drool off the side of his mouth and nodded, thinking, "God, I wish I hadn't chewed tobacco to win over those redneck voters. Will these nightmares ever end?"

"Okay, then, I'll continue," Ford said. "For example, Nixon sent a memo to his attorney general, Mitchell, that he wanted to go after the government's own eyewitness against teamsters president Jimmy Hoffa. Why? Because he wanted Hoffa to support him in his landslide reelection bid. Nixon even commuted his prison sentence. In that respect, you and Nixon are much alike. Neither of you hesitated to do business with shady characters if you could politically profit from it.

"Little Big Hands, if people aren't for you, they are against you. Black and white. And you may be just as cruel and vindictive as Nixon. Bad-mouthing the widow of a fallen warrior because she dared to question your policies was despicable. You have little capacity for empathy or kindness. You thrive on partisanship, dissension, and chaos to camouflage your incompetence."

Unabashedly POTUS pushed back on Ford's accusations, "You misunderstand and also underestimate me. I'm a businessman. I've come to believe that doing business *is* black and white. Win or lose. No quarter taken, none given, and no time-outs. My dad and grandfather taught me that's the only way to get to the top of the heap.

"The people who voted for me mandated that I eliminate nonsense in government, challenge fuzzy and unaffordable liberal do-gooder thinking, and shrink and run the budget like a business."

Ford frowned and asked himself, "Does Little Big Hands believe this line of crap he's feeding me? What an actor! He's more inhumane than I thought. How do I penetrate the corrosive armor that envelops his soul—if there is one?"

Ford took another shot at the task. "Little Big Hands, I took the oath of office during one of the darkest times in US history . . . amid the Watergate scandal. From possible collision with the Russians, refusal to release your tax information, and sordid affairs, you have now created a series of scandals that trumps Nixon!

"On a scale beyond Nixon's imagination, you have tampered with the courts, FBI, CIA, Department of Energy, Department of Health and Human Resources, the Post Office and other services to bend them to your perverse views of the world. The ultraconservative Neti Pot wing funds you in an attempt to preserve their archaic ways. You and they see only problems, while others see opportunities.

"Ever since the Kennedy assassination, the Vietnam War, Watergate, and the wars in Iraq and Afghanistan, the American people have wearied of politicians and government. Your administration feeds their cynicism. When I inherited the office, my most important task became the healing of the nation. Between their distrust of Johnson to end the Vietnam War, the distortion of truth and Nixon's lies, the American people had become disillusioned. I needed to try to nurture our country back to health. In my first speech, I said, 'Our long national nightmare is over. Our great republic is a government of laws, and not men.' It was met with universal applause.

"With that, I proceeded to close out the war in Vietnam and bring home our troops—the first time our nation ever lost a war in its history."

In the background, POTUS and Ford could hear the stairs that lead to the third-floor creak.

Ford said, "We are in big trouble now. That's Eleanor Roosevelt climbing the steps. I recognize her arthritic knees popping. Winter months really dry out her bones. On our last day here, she scolded Betty for dancing barefoot on the cabinet room table . . . something she always wanted to do before we left!

"Yes, other ghosts occupy this White House besides presidents. Eleanor ran a tight ship, protecting Franklin from Winston Churchill's late hours and propensity for alcohol. She gets easily annoyed and is kind of bossy when we practice golf on the third floor. She directs us to head to the attic or down to the basement for frivolities. The other first ladies get kind of grouchy too . . . don't like us boys having too much fun in the White House. But you, of all people, know the limerick about too much work and no play . . ."

"Let's scramble out of here. Before we leave, I invite you to think very hard and long about resigning from office before a second impeachment process begins. Don't take too long. You may not get a pardon; I don't think I could pardon you. Those Democrats in Congress have tested you. If they win the Senate, it's game over for you. Our nation does not welcome amnesty for those who commit criminal offenses against democracy, bypass the rule of law, and violate the checks and balances between the executive, legislative, and judicial branches.

"I made my mistakes. One of them may have been Nixon's pardon. I wanted to avoid a divisive impeachment process. I knew it would distract Congress from addressing our economic chaos. The enormous national debt from the protracted war in Vietnam was crushing. Pardoning Nixon, keeping some of his cabinet too long, first raising taxes to pay for the debt and fight inflation, and then later cutting taxes to head off a recession cost me a second term.

"It didn't help my image when Chevy Chase impersonated me every week on *Saturday Night Live* and President Johnson claimed I played too much football without a helmet. Stephen Colbert has made a career of working you over on *The Late Show. Saturday Night Live* is having a feast. And, just recently Jimmy Kimmel made the nation roar with laughter with his monologue on *The President's Back Out, COVID Sex Guidelines & NASCAR Flag Ban.* Your administration has been good for comedy. It's so funny that you appear such a comic figure since your niece wrote in her 'tell all' book about your family that you have no sense of humor.

"My penance is to second-guess every night before I rest whether I should have reprieved Nixon. I did what I thought best to restore public faith in government. In my farewell message, I told the American people I left them a more perfect union than when my stewardship began, and that I was proud of the role I had rebuilding confidence in the presidency. After my death, former presidents, senators, house members, governors of both parties, and even my critics noted my service, dedication, and likability. Little Big Hands, how do you think you will be remembered in textbooks and classrooms?"

***

POTUS fell back to sleep after Ford vaporized. In the depths of his mind, he pictured himself trying to hire a ghostwriter to do his biography and sanitize his legacy. Every freelancer refused his generous commission.

In his dream, he wondered, "If I am impeached again and resign, can I trust that self-serving VP Morebucks to be as magnanimous toward me as Ford was to Nixon? He just might decline to pardon me to whitewash himself. I know he'd like to be president. For that matter, so would Ms. Billy Brickell. Although she's the majority leader of the Senate, I know she thinks she is already running the show. They're both vultures waiting to feed on my carcass."

Days Five and Six

RETREAT TO CAMP DAVID

Upon landing at Joint Base Andrews in the Washington, D.C. area, President Little Big Hands requested that a doctor meet him at Camp David for consultation. The state of his mental condition disturbed him. He thought, "Perhaps it was that accident on the golf course. I spun out of control on the eighteenth hole ogling Ms. Josephine Greensmith. The seductive way she was dressed caused me to stumble and strike my head on the tee-box marker. I shouldn't have raised my head on the backswing." He decided to blame it all on Josephine. She shouldn't have distracted him. Decisively, he concluded, "I'm gonna cut her off the payroll."

POTUS wanted as much privacy as he could get . . . no need for more rumors, false or not. Camp David surely would provide the isolation he sought. Before deboarding, POTUS, ever the great dealmaker, swore his Air Force One crew to secrecy about his episode on the plane in return for not firing them.

Arriving at Camp David, Little Big Hands received an enthusiastic greeting from Wolf-gang, his muddy brown pit bull. The dog loyally licked his hands and jumped up on his chest, slobbering on his face. POTUS thought to himself, "This is the kind of respect I should be getting from the American people."

For now, he felt secure in the presence of Wolf-gang. With the fearsome dog at his side the next few days, he prayed there would be no more intruders. In bad need of a rest, the dark rings under his eyes revealed sleep deprivation. Little Big Hands ordered the Camp David staff to be very quiet. He told them he was about to take an overdue nap, and added, "No whistling in the hallways. I hate whistling."

Located in the wooded hills of Catoctin Mountain Park, Camp David can chill one to the bones during the winter months. Real or not, POTUS convinced himself that there would be no more apparitions appearing . . . especially since no swamp creatures could possibly thrive on the frozen grounds of Camp David.

Phantom #39: Jimmy Carter

HABITAT FOR HUMANITY

POTUS enjoyed having an aquarium on his nightstand. He gazed at the soft light, watched the rhythmic dance of marine plant life and tiny bubbles percolate to the top of the tank. Mesmerized and finally relaxed, his eyes drifted shut.

Beside him, Wolfgang snored and salivated on the pillow they shared.

Something stirred him. The goldfish were spooked. Several had leaped out of the tank and landed in bunches next to his pillow. In the throes of death, the fish flopped and thrashed in front of his nose. He clung to his pillow in alarm as if it provided a defensive barrier. Why didn't Wolfgang bark and lash out at the intruder Little Big Hands knew in his heart had arrived? "Damn," he thought, "I'll have to send Wolfgang to the dog pound next."

POTUS looked up at the humble man in jeans and a red and black plaid work shirt who stood over his bed, dispensing cracked shells on the sheets as he munched peanuts.

Good-naturedly, the man said, "Fear not, I mean you no harm."

Appreciating the moral character of the man who was now scratching his ears, Wolfgang remained submissive.

"Hello, I'm Jimmy Carter. Just call me Jimmy."

POTUS thought this can't be Carter. He's still alive. He wondered if his dreams had hijacked his mind. Could he no longer discern the living from the dead? The real from the unreal?

Carter realized Little Big Hands's confusion. He didn't want him to get distracted from the reason for his visit. "Let me set things straight for you. Contrary to the others, I am not a ghost. Rather, I'm Jimmy's metaphysical soul, or spirit. Just think of me as a phantom. You remember *Phantom of the Opera* don't you? The alive version of me has no awareness that his spirit has come here. But, if he were a ghost, I assure you that he would haven't missed the opportunity to confront you today. Those in the heavens have willed me to be here."

Then the spirt noticed a *Playboy* magazine on the nightstand. He picked it up and glanced at the pictures. "You know, I did a *Playboy* interview during the run-up to my election in 1976.

I confessed that I had lust in my heart because I had looked at a lot of women with lust. Just being honest. But I never grabbed them or embarrassed myself.

"That stuff about you paying off those hookers to silence them during your campaign was about as deceptive as it gets. If you hadn't bribed them, those sordid affairs would have exposed your lack of morality, shocked the electorate, and cost you the election. Your denials sure fooled a lot of people of religious faith. Or perhaps moral standards don't count anymore in politics. And what did you get for it? Another dozen or so women filing suit for sexual assault. I bet you silently twisted and squirmed when Roger Yikes, your personal attorney, provided the House of Representatives proof of the bribes, which among other things, led them to impeach you. Under Billy Brickell's badgering, the cowards in the Senate simply slapped your hand rather than vote to remove a lawless president from office."

POTUS could not restrain himself. He never took criticism lightly, admitted mistakes, or backed down. He learned as a child to perfect the art of obfuscation. "My attorney is a hack. Those girls all lied to get money out of me. He wanted a prominent position in my administration. When he didn't get it, he turned on me like a hyena. The whole thing amounts to extortion. Extortion, I tell you! And, that's a real crime!

"You can't tell me that Congressmen or other officials have never had affairs, a little fun between the sheets. Why look at that movie *Hamilton*. My press secretary Miss Josephine Greensmith practically forced me to watch it. She thought I might get some favorable press coverage if I mentioned that I had seen the film. Alexander Hamilton carried on with someone else's wife for four months. Awfully stupid of him to publish a tell-all pamphlet about the sordid details. That news destroyed his chances of becoming president.

Jimmy said "That's exactly my point!

"What's this world coming to? Even that fanatical Baptist minister in Louisiana publicly defended you and brushed off your character defects under the guise that we are all sinners and forgiven by Christ. What he left out is important to this conversation. Although we may be forgiven if we pray for it, that doesn't abdicate accountability for our actions, wash away the consequences, or open the door for repeated lapses in character.

"Looking back on it, my candid confession probably gave Gerald Ford a few more votes. I still won, and I have no regrets. But, we are wasting time here."

Carter, demanded rather than asked, "Little Big Hands, release that pillow and get out of bed. We have business to attend to. Aren't you the man, standing there shivering in your boxer shorts? Here, put these working-man overalls on. Don't worry, they'll fit. They've been tailored by angels."

POTUS had never worn a pair of bib overalls. He associated them with the helping hands working on the grounds of Belladonna or building his walls.

Carter laughed. "You're strapping them on backwards."

POTUS felt very unpresidential. Then Carter handed him a pair of work gloves and a hammer and said, "Let's go!"

***

In a flash, POTUS found himself at a Habitat for Humanity build site in a biracial neighborhood on the outskirts of New Orleans. African Americans, Latinos, Asians and a few undocumented immigrants hammered away next to him. The latter worked as hard as anybody. They were driven to pound their way into life better than the ones they left behind.

This was a new experience for Little Big Hands. But not for Jimmy, a champion of human rights who served up an ideal model of post-presidential relevance and philanthropy. He had pledged to work just as hard for the American people after he left the White House. Carter, now in his nineties, kept his promise.

POTUS felt ill at ease and awkward, both physically and emotionally. He was unaccustomed to laboring with his hands or working alongside people of different ethnic backgrounds.

In a just a few swings of the hammer, he managed to smash and bruise his left thumb and index finger. Both turned the color of ripening plums. Enjoying POTUS's dilemma, Carter chuckled and hammered away. Although they could not actually see or hear him in his state as a phantom, Carter pretended to comfortably kibitz with the work crew. The crew was building a home for a recently naturalized immigrant from Guatemala who had saved a synagogue from being burned down by a white supremacist.

Jimmy said, "I ran an honest administration and told the truth as I saw it. My integrity meant more to me than winning any election or kowtowing to special interest groups. I think history shows that I won my election on America's starved appetite for virtue and dutiful hard work. I faced challenges of epic proportions. So, do you. Are you up to the task?"

POTUS replied defensively, "Why else would the American people have elected me? At least I wasn't a peanut farmer, and I didn't hide underwater in a submarine to conceal myself from my enemies. The public knew what they were getting when they handed me the keys to the Oval Office. Couldn't be plainer. I'm a born opportunist and wheeler-dealer. And I don't carry a Bible to prove who I am!"

"Ouch. Guess I know where I stand with you." Ignoring POTUS's proclivity for cynicism, Jimmy continued. "Okay, I had a degree in nuclear engineering, and still struggled mightily to deal with Iran, Soviet aggression, the energy crisis, and most of all, a deep mistrust of leaders in political office and the military after the Johnson and Nixon administrations. The national psyche had been crushed by the assassination of a charismatic leader and the dirty lies that cost the lives of fifty-eight thousand of our nation's finest plus severely disabled another seventy-five thousand. And then the Watergate scandal sabotaged the rule of law.

"Although I hated war, I served the nation as commander of a nuclear submarine. We encountered so many high alerts and close calls with the Russians and the Chinese that I vowed to exhaust every effort at peaceful reconciliation. You know nothing of war.

"Little Big Hands, you flaunt your role as Commander in Chief. Your careless approach to diplomacy was evident in your handling of Iran. It was stupid of them to escalate efforts to become a Mideast imperial power after the nuclear treaty they signed with President Obama. It was equally imprudent of you to end that agreement without more efforts at diplomacy. Of course, you've burned quite a few bridges with many of our allies so maybe they would rather let you stew in your own mess.

"Instead, you ordered the assassination on Iraqi soil of Qasem Soleimani, Iran's top military leader and second to the Ayatollah in popularity. You instantly made the general a martyr and united hatred toward the United States in Iran and to large segments in Iraq. From our perspective, the general was deservedly a die-hard enemy. But your impulsive and premature actions triggered a chain of events. Sympathetically, the Iraqi parliament, former enemies of Iran, voted to evict the US! The dangerous gambit put our troops at risk. When Iran retaliated, many got severe concussions and permanent injuries. You ignited another nuclear arms race with Iran . . . further fueled by your threat to target Iranian cultural sights. That is an international war crime.

"Prior to your drone strike, past presidents and military leaders believed the risk of Iran killing one of our own presidents and generals was greater than the value of assassinating Soleimani. They had tracked him for many years but didn't want to trigger a wider confrontation. They realized that we could not afford to assassinate every bad guy who crosses us. Where does that lead? Suddenly, other countries take similar licenses. It gives open season to Vladimir Putin and other autocrats like him to do the same thing.

"Soleimani was a stupid man who wasted the lifting of sanctions that was part of the deal with Obama. By continuing to fight a proxy war against Americans in such places as Syria, Lebanon, Iraq, and Israel, he plunged his country into poverty. Sooner or later, Iranian citizens and their neighbors might well have come to realize he was the cause of their misery and perhaps forced domestic change.

"Granted Soleimani's behavior, with the backing of the Ayatollah, was crazy. Congratulations Little Big Hands, you have temporarily out-crazied and confused them. They don't know what to make of you. But this gains you nothing if you aren't smart enough to press hard now for a new nuclear deal while the iron is hot and to be prepared to make some compromises around the edges to get it done. Sadly, with all your personnel turnover, you are a bit weak in the state department to negotiate a deal and wrap this one up.

"Was killing Soleimani designed to take the attention off your impeachment and knock out the media's round-the-clock focus on your impending trial in the Senate? Afterward the assassination, your administration took over a week to get their story together to explain the event to Congress."

***

On another matter, "My principles may have cost me reelection. On my second day in office, I pardoned all Vietnam draft dodgers to help heal the nation's wounds. I championed a two-state solution for Israel. You have shown no objectivity in the matter. Worse yet, you've moved the American Embassy to Jerusalem, officially recognizing it as the capital of Israel during a particular tumultuous time for the region. You claimed it would promote peace. I don't see how.

"Rather than appease the energy czars to finance my political war chest like you did, I challenged them and pushed hard for alternative energy, technology, and conservation. Since then, substantial progress has been made in solar and wind energy. And now even electric cars.

"I opposed abortion rights but always remained empathetic to the needs of the poor and lame, as the Bible instructed. It does bother me that many people who object to abortion on religious grounds are unwilling to financially support poor children in the U.S. and the world whose mothers and fathers can't afford to care for them. And if they could see the squalor that some of these children are born into, they might rethink their values.

"Little Big Hands, you and the Neti Pot Wing are too callous to see that when you cut back welfare and education, you doomed many children to a lifetime of failure and underachievement. It's a pay-me-now or pay-me-later proposition. The cost at the other end to society far exceeds the upfront cost. Have you ever considered that your toxic presidency may be making people sick?

"Speaking of pro-life and pro-choice abortion issues, I could have respected you more had you stood your ground. You initially were pro-choice. I think you suspiciously changed your position on reproductive rights to woo conservative and fundamentalist Neti Pot voters.

"As head of the free world, I strove to be known as one of America's great moral leaders. To help restore faith in government, I imposed gift limits and a financial disclosure rule on appointees and increased the number of inspectors to root out fraud and mismanagement.

"After my retirement from political office, I traveled the world for humane purposes. I witnessed thousands of abandoned and starving children in third world countries. Had women been given access to birth control and better education, perhaps those children would not have been born into such horrible lives. With no job opportunities and little to live for, some young people become terrorists and anarchists. They have no real objective other than to vent their bitterness and disrupt the status quo. We have seen this in Africa, the Middle East, Asia, and North and South America.

"I am enjoying the longest post-presidency in American history and became the first president to receive the Nobel Peace Prize for orchestrating a long-lasting peace agreement between Egypt and Israel.

"Since my time in office, I have monitored a hundred and seven elections in thirty-nine countries. I never dreamed I should have monitored my own country's election. You and the Russians fooled a lot of voters. Ugly stuff, Little Big Hands, particularly in North Carolina where the State Board of Elections released hundreds of pages of documents showing evidence of ballot fraud directed by a Republican operative in your last election.

"Frankly, you and I couldn't be further apart. I adopted a presidential style as a peacemaker, and in an effort to de-imperialize the presidency, carried my own suitcase, sold the presidential yacht, and for a time, barred the playing of 'Hail to the Chief.'

"I only have one regret that haunts me every sunset. What more could I have done to institutionalize moral standards in government, establish checks and balances to prevent wackos from becoming president, and quickly purge malfeasance in office? I leave you now, Little Big Hands, but before I depart, we are going to pray.

"Is it true what your niece said that the only time you ever go to church is when the cameras are there? And that you have no principles? Well, no cameras here. Just the two of us. I doubt that we will ever meet again."

Grasping POTUS's hand, Jimmy said, "Bow your head."

Initially POTUS flinched. Jimmy's hand gripped his in a powerful vice and felt like dry ice to the touch. Jimmy began to pray:

"Dear Lord, I pray for your divine forgiveness for Little Big Hands. His transgressions have injured many. He has placed himself ahead of God and country. Many people seem indifferent to his bad behavior. He has methodically dumbed down the idea of morality in his administration. He has hired and fired a great number of people, many who now serve jail sentences rather than him. He has admitted to immoral actions in business and his relationships with women, about which he remains proud. His Twitter feed alone—with its habitual string of mischaracterizations, lies, and slanders—is a near-perfect illustration of a human being who is lost and confused.

"May you find worth in this man and salvage his soul. I pray that he may come to realize his sins and ask for your mercy. Restore him to clear thinking and fill his heart with compassion. He has not done all that he could with the powers and privileges of his elected office to promote peace and justice in our world. Nor has he loved his neighbors, let alone his enemies. Dear Lord, show him the light so that he may find eternal peace. Bless and protect America. And shield its institutions from corruption and its people from evil. Amen."

While Jimmy prayed for him, POTUS began to weep. Tears ran down his cheeks and he sobbed uncontrollably. Little Big Hands had been shaken to the core. Was he remorseful, or simply relieved that Jimmy was through with him?

***

Later that afternoon, a groggy Wolfgang and a weary President Little Big Hands met privately with Dr. Wots Themater, who found POTUS pale, exhausted, and stressed...bordering on psychotic. Noting the purple thumb and finger, he wondered what happened. Little Big Hands muttered something barely intelligible about spirits and phantoms.

After his diagnosis, Dr. Themater decided to increase the president's dosage of Valium. POTUS pleaded with Wots to keep his medical condition from reaching the ears of the press or his political adversaries, saying, "You know what that could do for those who wish me impeached again? And, by the way, your job?"

Along with the opioids that Wots had been steadily feeding him for the last couple of years, the higher dose of Valium further impaired the president's coordination, judgment, and memory. It also explained why Little Big Hands often missed the fairways on the golf course, buried his ball in the sand traps, struggled to get to the greens and yipped his putts.

Ghost #40: Ronald Reagan

THE BERLIN WALL

An hour later, Dr. Wots Themater decided to check up on his patient, who had retreated to the living room. He asked, "Why do you have all the curtains pulled open and every light switched on? In your condition, the brightness over stimulates sensory nerves and makes you anxious. With the meds I've given, your blood pressure could also soar." Themater then took Little Big Hands's blood pressure. He winced when it read 177/110 and pulse 133. "See what I told you! You've got to give the valium time to work. Calm down."

In contrast to the brightness in the room, Themater found the president's mind dark. Little Big Hands said, "Doc, just look at these lightning bugs flashing around the room. It's another bad omen. I was forewarned. Help me swat them." In the glow of the bugs playing in his head, Little Big Hands pointed. "Doc, do you see the man hidden in the corner beside the bookshelf, wearing a black leather bomber jacket with fur around the collar and the commander-in-chief patch over the breast? He's got my coat on. Help me catch the fucking thief!"

Baffled, Dr. Themater couldn't believe Little Big Hands's absurd behavior, nor could he see or hear anything in the room. Calmly, Wots did a full turn in the living room and then replied, "There's no one here, Mr. President. Trust me." Wots furiously took notes on his medical pad as POTUS continued to mumble and carry on some weird conversation with an invisible thing or character.

***

Frowning at POTUS, Ronald Reagan said, "I have learned that one of the most important rules in politics is poise, which means looking like an owl after you have behaved like a jackass. To the detriment of the American people, far too often you look and act like the latter. Get your gray trench coat. It might be raining in Berlin. But before we go, you wouldn't happen to have any jellybeans in that candy jar sitting on the coffee table? I can't get them anywhere in the afterworld."

A broad smile came over Reagan's face when he lifted the lid. "Ahh, licorice beans, my favorite—and my second favorite, blueberry." He exercised executive privilege and emptied the contents of the jar into his coat pockets. "Tell Treasury to send me the bill, if they can find my address."

POTUS observed Reagan's icy blue complexion. His last visitor's skin color had a warm, vibrant hue. He concluded that's the difference between a ghost and a phantom. Perhaps he hadn't totally lost his mind after all. The Gipper, as he was affectionately called ever since he had played Knute Rockne, an All-American football player, still possessed a full head of thick mid-night black, wavy hair. It contrasted with Little Big Hand's which resembled a thin layer of trampled straw.

The next thing POTUS knew, he and Reagan time warped to June 12, 1987, at the foot of the Brandenburg Gate.

***

"Let me show you how you talk to the Russians, rather than suck up to them. Watch this. That's me standing at a podium in front of two panes of bulletproof glass. Of course, I wouldn't need them now.

"I'm telling Mikhail Gorbachev, President and General Secretary of the Soviet Union, that there is 'one sign that the Soviets can make that would be unmistakable, that would advance dramatically the cause of freedom and peace.' I shout to Mr. Gorbachev, 'If you seek peace, if you seek prosperity for the Soviet Union and Eastern Europe, if you seek liberalization, come here to this gate and tear down this wall.' Nobody since President Kennedy had talked so tough to the Russians.

"Why haven't you made your own bold demands to the Russians to stop meddling in free elections around the world? Evidently, they've compromised you. What is it? Lewd pictures? Under the table loans? Other activity? A bailout your struggling businesses?

"No other president would have stood for them paying a bounty on the head of every American killed in Afghanistan. They would have retaliated with severe sanctions. Now the Russians are trying to steal the work our scientists are doing to come up with a vaccine for Covid-19. And there is evidence that they will attempt to meddle in the next election, like they did previously, to help you win. If that is the case, then here we go again! It explains why you do and say nothing.

"When Nixon occupied the White House, he thought I was a lightweight in foreign policy and a hawk because I wanted to go tough on communism, particularly the Soviet Union. He changed his tune after I got elected and then let it be known to his Soviet contacts that they should lobby me to appoint his buddy Alexander Haig secretary of state. Nixon hoped Haig and I might redeem his reputation in foreign affairs. Although I did help restore his reputation as a statesman, I never trusted him— for the same reasons I wouldn't trust you.

"I took the Bible literally and felt that we were approaching the point of Armageddon with the Soviets in the nuclear arms race. Although many Democrats and Republicans disagreed with my tough stance, I stood firm on a policy I had long and consistently articulated. It was no knee-jerk policy, like so many of your haphazard ones that lack substance, direction, vision, or personnel to execute them.

"I requested several meetings with Gorbachev. I sensed I could penetrate his Communist Party line, have a substantive conversation, and find he possessed a sense of humanity. At first he didn't believe me when I told him that if we could not reach an agreement on nuclear arms reduction, I would outspend the Soviets to establish military superiority and build a satellite system to protect America."

Pausing to chew another handful of jellybeans, Reagan smiled as he swallowed. "These are so good." Then he continued,

"When you hold the highest office in the land, you have to have the strength of your convictions, remain consistent, and stay firm. Creativity and humor help, too. Initially, I admit not much happened as a result of those first meetings. Every time we'd meet, I did my darndest to sweeten Gorbachev up. When we'd powwow, I'd always give him a blue gift box of jellybeans with the presidential seal embossed on the lid. I discovered he also really liked them. We started to call our meetings jellybean diplomacy, and that gave us some common ground. For obvious reasons, he feigned a preference for the red beans.

"The man had a good sense of humor. After his first helping, he looked at me with a grin and said perhaps he should give some of the beans to the Soviet Union Department of Agriculture. Their farming techniques were quite antiquated. As a result, food was in short supply, very expensive, and of poor quality. Left unsaid was the fact that if he could shift money from a wall to planting and harvesting more crops, all the Russian people could be better off.

"Because the world resents walls—particularly the kind you are building around the nation's capital and on the southern border with Mexico—I knew I could appeal to Gorbachev's sense of humanity. Together we tore down the Iron Curtain with words and big ideas, not missiles, bombs, and bullets. Next we reached an agreement on arms.

"And then a stranger thing happened: we actually became friends. He was even a guest at my California ranch. He sort of looked like a real cowboy when I gave him a ten-gallon Stetson hat. I didn't have the heart to tell him he put it on backwards.

"Gorbachev expected that I owned a palace like your Belladonna estate. He was surprised that I lived in a relatively modest ranch house. I told him we were experiencing the American dream, just like millions of others. Nancy and I left the lavish life to more pretentious and insecure people who needed to wrap fifteen thousand square feet of brick-and-mortar suits of confidence around themselves to project an artificial image of success and power. And, he understood when I said it's a small fraction who feel compelled to flaunt their wealth and project a false image of Americans. Gorbachev nodded his head in approval.

"He was frustrated with the oligarchs in Russia who rapidly accumulated wealth during privatization that followed the dissolution of the Soviet Union. I think Gorbachev knew he could trust me to be a man of my word. My instincts told me the same of him. It's called political capital, and it's built over a long reputation.

"The reason you will likely go down in history as one of our worst presidents is that, in the end, you lack political capital and good judgment. Like some of your business colleagues and even family members have said, you've told too many lies, screwed too many people and made too many mistakes. Nobody can work long for you before they discover how pompous, artificial and insincere you are. You never learned how to reach across party lines or compromise even when it's a win-win for everyone.

POTUS screamed "I object to your ill-informed contentions and biased conclusions! Fake news I tell you!" When he was on the wrong side of an action or allegation, Little Big Hands always doubled down on an opposing slant. His party loyalists always fell for it.

"I have political capital with President Vladimir Putin. More than you can ever imagine. We got to know one another at the 2013 Moscow Miss Universe Pageant. We both discovered we admired gorgeous young women, short skirts and bikinis, political and economic power, military strength, entrepreneurship, and fine wine. Why just yesterday, I announced at a press conference that I had just finished talking to my buddy Vladimir. Ha! That news made the press pucker, but none of them asked why. Would you believe we talked about coronavirus and arms control? I told him point blank that I hoped to avoid an expensive three-way arms race with China, Russia, and us. I've heard rumors that he had launched a satellite that could destroy others in space. He denied that as fake news and also denied that the Russians had paid a bounty on American lives in Afghanistan and Syria. I believe him. We look forward to the day when we can do a couple of real estate deals together and reminisce about all the beautiful women we've known."

Reagan just shook his head. "Your frame of reference about spending money on an expensive arm race rather than concern for lives bothers me. Does everything you do have to be about money? You've been seduced and duped.

"And, don't bull shit me about the press not asking you why you talked to Putin…as if it's every day casual news. Most of the reporters were from Ferret News and affiliates. And the ones you knew might ask, you didn't call on.

"Speaking of political capital, let me tell you another story. It's about Tip O'Neill. When I was president, he was the Democratic majority's speaker of the House. We disagreed on many important issues. He wanted higher taxes, more regulation, and more social programs. I wanted just the opposite. Between us we shut down the government over budgetary issues more than at any time in history. However, the durations were short, and not like the record-breaking and capricious shutdowns over your refusal to approve a budget unless Congress also funded your walls.

"To continue to build your wall on the Southern border, you diverted funds from the defense budget. The courts then decided that your action was illegal and subverted Congress's responsibilities and authority to specify where money is spent.

"How you could ever imagine building a wall around the nation's capital would attract workers and make politicians feel safer is beyond me. That wall symbolizes a shameful black mark on our country's history and the capital's landscape. Not since the Civil War has there been such a monstrosity. At that time, Washington was the most heavily defended city on earth. Thirty-seven miles of medieval-looking fortifications and trenches wrapped around the city. Did that really keep people out who were determined to enter the city? No. Nor will yours. Perpetrators will cut through it like it was made of butter, scale the heights, and tunnel under it. If you are not careful, your Washington wall will prove your demise. It'll be named after you.

"And as we stand here beside the Berlin Wall, I want to admonish you for suggesting that those people who try to climb over your wall around the capital should be shot in the legs or fed to alligators and snakes. That's pretty harsh and dangerous rhetoric. It invites trouble. You may have forgotten or never learned that over eighty people died trying to scale *this* wall. They were shot by East German border guards. Those killings symbolized everything that is wrong with the Soviet Union.

"With your government shutdown, you've put people out of work under the pretense of saving jobs taken by foreigners. Your action cost the nation billions of dollars in lost services. How in the hell do you explain that? You proudly and defiantly held the government and American people hostage over ill-conceived and selfish projects, when money was and still is needed to repair and improve the nation's infrastructure. Your better alternative was to spawn job-generating investments paying long-term dividends. The walls are a total waste of money that could be used to develop human capital.

"Prior to the Coronavirus, it was equally silly of you to keep immigrants out when the national unemployment was so low. The country needed their skill and eagerness to work. Instead, you've spread fear of a small minority of bad people.

"A little story about a big ship, a young sailor, and a refugee. Back in the early eighties, the carrier *Midway* patrolled the South China Sea and frequently encountered refugees from Indochina hoping to get to America. As the refugees slowly made their way in a tiny, leaky boat, one spotted a sailor from the *Midway* sent to rescue them. In the roiling sea, he stood up and shouted, 'Hello, American sailor. Hello, freedom man.'"

Impatiently, POTUS asked, "Why are you telling me about this story from almost forty years ago? Seems trivial in the course of human events."

"Ahh, perhaps it does to you. I agree, it was a small moment. But it signified a big meaning. Because that's what it was like to be an American then and until you. We stood for freedom. Seems you have forgotten, or never learned, that the vast majority of immigrants are driven to establish themselves and pay off any debts to society. They reinvigorate what this country has always stood for. Even your grandfather was an immigrant. All that seed money you inherited and wasted came from him and your father."

Reagan said, "Listen carefully. I was certainly an actor, but I earned my stripes as a politician, serving as a governor and then president. With vision and experience, I came into the office prepared to run the government. You are indeed just an actor posing as a president. Your only gift is your uncanny ability to fool people before they come to realize that you are the fool.

"I admit, we have a few things in common. We were both Washington outsiders, which appealed to voters who desperately wanted change. But my, how the changes you've wrought have surprised and disappointed your voters. The establishment attacked us both as being extreme and simplistic. Once in office, you remained simplistically extreme, vacillating from day to day over what you stood for. We were among the first presidents to have been divorced. I once and you twice. But I became a dedicated spouse to Nancy and, unlike you, didn't continue to break my wedding vows.

"We were also both Democrats and then became Republicans. But you changed parties for political advantage, not deep-seated beliefs in conservatism. Unlike you, I was not the captive of my political base, subject to their extreme whims and fancies, but its leader.

"The National Rifle Association lined your pockets. They spent millions of dollars to get you and several powerful senators elected. When I and my friend James Brady, White House press secretary, got shot, I supported the Brady Handgun Violence Act. You and your ultraconservative congressional colleagues, as well as a few liberals, have since whittled away at gun control legislation resulting in the slaughter of thousands of civilians and children in schools across the country. How can you live with that?

"I won favor and did my best to conduct the office of the presidency with a smile on my face and a generous heart. Although he and I disagreed and fought over policy, I never treated Tip O'Neill, Speaker of the House and my adversary, as an enemy, nor him me. We sought bipartisanship where we could. And many a time at the end of the day, we'd set our political differences aside and share a Scotch.

"As fellow Irishmen, we much enjoyed each other's humor and company. When it came to fundamental principles, we often tried to beat the other's head in on the political grid iron. But never with animosity. In fact, when I lay wounded in the hospital after the attempted assassination on my life, he came privately to my room. With tears in his eyes, he knelt and kissed my face. Together we recited the twenty-third psalm.

"On the other hand, you, Little Big Hands, treat not only your adversaries but also many of your former allies as enemies. You lack any political grace and forgiveness. Your life is black or white. If you can't buy someone, you belittle and embarrass them to gain the upper hand. It's a blood sport for you. Actions of a coward! And your Vice President Morebucks and Press Secretary Sweetlips grab at the chance to spread vicious rumors if they advance your and their misguided causes.

"It's no wonder parents turn off their TV screens to protect their children from you. Too much exposure to you could warp and distort the next generation's perception of decency and civility.

"Just as bad, you have let the Neti Pot Wing dictate your mandates because you don't have any of your own. Whoever is the last person to talk to you has the most influence. You are like a squid on a slippery rock, sliding from one agenda to the next with no real grasp of the situation.

"During my time in office I won a nickname: The Great Communicator. But I never thought that it was my style or words that made a difference. No, it was the content. I wasn't a great communicator, but I communicated great things. And unlike you, they didn't 'spring full bloom from my brow,' my ass or from—what do you call it, a tweet?—without careful consideration for the principles that had guided us for two centuries.

"Thanks to Congressman Charlie Wilson and my tacit support, we also broke the Russians in Afghanistan. But who could have foreseen that that victory would give birth to Al-Qaeda and then ISIS? Sometimes it may be better to leave your enemies alone, mired down in their own making. I think that's what Congress has decided to do with you . . . let you boil in your own broth.

"Gorbachev and I became allies for peace and reconciliation to the extent that we could. I always treated my former enemy with dignity and stayed away from name-calling. As a result, he and I signed the Intermediate-Range Nuclear Forces Treaty . . . a step in the right direction that brought sighs of relief around the world. Why you broke that nuclear deal with Iran, I will never understand. Now even the Russian deal looks precarious. If a previous agreement proves flawed, then pragmatic leaders renegotiate their building blocks to achieve peace, rather than box themselves into a corner.

"At the last Olympics, you refused to applaud athletes from the countries you call enemies. You misunderstood what the Olympics stood for and missed a golden opportunity—pardon the pun—to pin a medal of peace on the event and open dialogue with all nations. It reminds me of Adolf Hitler's behavior at the 1936 Olympics when he stormed off after our Jesse Owens defeated Germany's best.

"You may not recall, or for that matter ever realized, that former Prime Minister Margaret Thatcher and I were close friends. We belonged to a mutual respect and admiration society. I'd never dream of asking her to move the British Open to a golf course like the one you own in Scotland. The audacity of it all deeply offends me. Our ambassadors aren't paid by the American taxpayers to ask personal financial favors for their presidents. It's also against the Emoluments Clause of the U.S. Constitution, and, possibly grounds for removal from office if Congress weren't so gutless.

"I worked really hard to set a good example by how I treated women in politics. Frankly, many of them were a lot smarter than I. Why didn't you speak out against that Florida Republican Congressman who verbally accosted a female congresswoman, calling her a 'fucking bitch' on the Capitol steps? Oh, I know. She's the same woman who you said should go back to her country not realizing she was born in NYC like you. This fits your pattern of singling out female governors and mayors for special criticism when they object to your brand of politics.

"Your indelicate remarks tell me that you can't control yourself. You really shot yourself in the foot when you kept obsessing on Ferret News over how you aced a simple test to detect mental impairment. You should have kept your mouth shut when you said that simple test got progressively harder toward the end. Let me see, what were the five words you boasted you could remember in proper sequence? Oh, Person, Woman, Man,

Camera, TV.' The whole affair leaves the nation wondering why you took the test at all. I think I know. The gears in your head are beginning to lock up. The more you talk about something like that, the more suspect you become.

"Like your own dad, I died of Alzheimer's disease. I began to suffer some mental slippage toward the end of my last term. I had early signs of dementia and knew it. With the help of my wife and cabinet, I did my best to limit my exposure to the public and to pace myself. Ate well. Got plenty of sleep. Sometimes even in meetings!

"The fact that your speeches and tweets ramble on and your thoughts seem disjointed speak for themselves. Under these circumstances, it would be selfish of you to run again without getting a more complete mental wellness test and evaluation. Two years ago, thirty-five mental health professionals at a Yale School of Medicine conference signed an open letter saying that, in their opinion, your mental state makes you incapable of serving safely as president. They've observed that you have a strong tendency to distort reality to fit your personal myth of greatness, attack those who challenge you with facts, and lack empathy. Then in December 2019 another 350 health professionals signed a similar letter to Congress. And seven months later your own niece expressed the same fears for the country in her new book. She has a PhD in Psychology."

Little Big Hands, now drooling like a rabid dog, barked out "Those are all lies and distortions to make me look bad. They are politically motivated comments from a bunch of academic egg heads who couldn't hold a real job, like mine. As for my niece, she's just trying to ruin me because my dad disinherited my brother, her father. A simple family squabble. That's all."

"Well, Reagan shot back, I suggest you read the book. There's more to it than that.

***

"All my life, I loved to ride horses and mend fences, particularly after I retired. It gave me a sense of peace and an opportunity for reflection. When it's time for you to ride off into the sunset, how will you mend all your broken fences? Are you beginning to see your future?

"We all pay penance for something. Every day of my afterlife, I wake up with the Iran-Contra scandal on my mind. Yet I can live with it and decided to apologize to the nation for selling arms to Iran to secretly try to support resistance to the socialist government of Nicaragua and to free American hostages being held in Lebanon by Hezbollah. If you are likable enough, the people—and even Congress—forgive you for the error in your ways. I could have been impeached.

With a final gesture of farewell, Reagan offered POTUS all the yellow jellybeans and said, "When you think you hear the warble of nightingales, expect another unearthly presence."

***

While POTUS continued to babble on at some imaginary figure, Dr. Themater took emergency measures and administered a fast-acting sedative via injection to the president's arm.

As he drifted off, POTUS imagined he heard the news.

"Good evening. Annie Oakely Remington here, reporting the nation's news for Channel 6666. There's a massive evacuation in Washington, D.C. happening as I speak. A terrible tragedy has just occurred as the result of massive flooding along the banks of the Potomac. Miles of President Hands's half-finished multibillion-dollar wall circling the nation's capital have surrendered to the surging waters that have risen to record-shattering levels. Already political opposition blames the collapse on the president. They point to his bullheaded rejection of climate change and his refusal to take appropriate measures in concert with other nations."

Day Seven

MARINE ONE SANCTUARY

Temporarily shaking off the effects of the Valium and opioids, POTUS called for Marine One to evacuate him from Camp David as quickly as possible. Presidential security guards quickly surrounded him. With some showmanship, he proudly zipped up his flight jacket, which was similar to President Reagan's, with the presidential seal sewn on the breast. Then he straightened his spine and jutted his chin out as he shuffled as fast as he could to the copter pad.

The helicopter blades whirled above Little Big Hands and tugged at what little hair remained on the side of his head. The force created a miniature tornado that swept away the president's cherished *Make America Great Again* red baseball cap. It got chopped into red confetti. The guards had to suppress their smiles. Noting the urgency, the Marine One pilot greeted POTUS at the steps. He asked, "Sir, is this an emergency? Shall I call for fighter pilots to accompany us?"

"You bet! We are headed back to the White House ASAP. Get this bird off the ground full throttle now. We need security. This is an emergency. The enemy wants to brainwash the country."

As the door closed, Wolfgang tried to follow POTUS on board. Little Big Hands shouted, "Don't let that dog on the copter. He can't be trusted. He's no friend of mine." As the copter rose off the ground, Wolfgang whimpered in the blizzard of snow that blew over his muzzle and blinded his vision.

As they ascended, POTUS finally felt secure. He thought, "Certainly the military prowess of the marines will protect me from these incessant night-and-daymares. Those guys don't believe in ghosts; they just create them."

Dr. Wots Themater had declined to ride back to the White House with Little Big Hands. He had expediently decided to distance himself from the president. Wots feared that his questionable treatment protocol might come under closer scrutiny if he stuck around. Like many others who had served the president, Wots resigned on the spot. If lucky, he hoped to disappear into private practice and avoid implications of malpractice. He encouraged POTUS to see a psychiatrist when he returned to Washington. As he parted, Wots interjected his best recommendations in years. He cautioned Little Big Hands to keep his hands in his pockets at all times, to refrain from posting any new Facebook, Instagram or Twitter messages, and to absolutely avoid public appearances!

Ghost #41: George H. W. Bush

THE GREAT WALL OF CHINA

Aboard Marine One, POTUS requested privacy in the communications center. As the copter rose off the ground, he sat down with a sigh of relief in his thick leather commander-in-chief chair. Finally, he felt immune from the demons that had tormented him. As he gazed over the frozen tundra blanketed in fresh snow, he began to relax.

The expansive view gave him a renewed sense of power until he noticed a nightingale outside his window keeping pace with the helicopter. He wondered, "Where did that come from?" Then he heard it warble and it wasn't a vibration from the aircraft. "This is impossible! I'm losing my mind."

Out of nowhere, POTUS felt a cold hand press his shoulder. When the man removed his goggles, POTUS stared agog at George HW Bush, who was wearing a helmet, a military jumpsuit, and ankle boots. He had a parachute strapped to his back.

Bush stared down at the quivering Little Big Hands, who silently asked himself, "Why a parachute?" Distraught, POTUS wondered if everyone planned to bail out. "Is this how my life ends here on Marine One? An assassination labeled a mysterious helicopter crash. Coups like this have been known to happen. The military resents that I canned all those has-beens generals and admirals."

President Bush perceived POTUS's fear and said, "I mean you no physical harm. I took this route because I miss skydiving. As you slowly descend from the clouds, you can actually see the curvature of the earth, and from a different perspective, marvel at its immense beauty. Then when you land, you realize how interdependent we all are on this planet. I recommend you try it sometime.

"Speaking of interdependency, I'm here to take you on a journey. And along the way, you'll confront your soul. The Marine One crew will assume the physical you dozes off while you and I travel through a time warp to visit the Great Wall of China."

***

As Presidents Bush and Little Big Hands stood by the immense stone wall that ran for over a thousand miles, Bush, who had served as ambassador to China, gave POTUS the CliffsNotes on the reason for its construction.

He explained, "The wall was built at great expense to keep the hordes of invaders from overthrowing the dynasty. The architects thought the wall impenetrable. Ultimately, a series of invaders prevailed by going around, over, under, and through the wall. There were simply not enough imperial troops to defend its full length or anticipate where the conquerors might strike. Does this sound familiar to you back home?

"Actually, the wall attracted invaders, who considered it an insult. They were insightful enough to know that its cost depleted the dynasty's financial coffers necessary to maintain a powerful army. You should think about that. In some respects, the wall became the ruler's undoing. Decades from now, history may recall yours as *Hands' Folly*, the president who walled himself in!

"When you announced that you intended to build your own wall along the border with Mexico, immigration from there and all over Central and South America spiked to unprecedented levels. The irony of it all was that, before your presidency, it had been steadily falling for many years. The law of unintended consequences prevailed. Everybody wanted to cross the border before your wall went up. Singlehandedly, you created a national crisis, conned America, and now bleed the economy to pay for it.

"Many people who live along the border, including the mayor of El Paso, feel the wall is unnecessary. Until you strangled it, the city prospered from cross-border commerce. To make matters worse, you declared the need for an artificial border a national emergency! When Congress refused to fund the wall, you pouted and shut down the government . . . putting more people out of work than any jobs illegal immigrants might have taken from US citizens.

"To compound matters, you should never have undertaken building another wall around the nation's capital. Our country could hardly afford one, let alone two. To pay for the second one, you confiscated funds Congress had approved for national health and wellness. Now you have made it almost impossible for most minority groups and government employees to live anywhere close to the capital. In the process, you tore down historic buildings just to build a wall."

At this point, POTUS stuck out his chest and interrupted. "Wait just a minute! In this day and age, we don't need all those people in government. They're inefficient, bloated and overpaid... like the post office. Private companies, many my friends, can do the job better and cheaper. My people tell me we can soon employ more algorithms, technology, and game modeling in government to make better and faster decisions. It just takes one good man at the top to act on the information. Me!

"And something had to be done about those protestors and marchers who demonstrate in front of the Capital and other federal buildings all hours of the day and interrupt the business of government. A wall solves that problem. You've got the whole big idea wrong, Bush! You're past your prime, and so were those buildings we tore down."

Bush paused for a minute to digest POTUS's rebuttal. Then he responded, "You verify the imprudence of electing businessmen to the nation's highest office. You draw upon your narrow business experiences because that's the only thing you know. Then you try to overlay and apply it to government. Because you have never previously served in the public sector, you lack the foundation to understand how to get things done in that environment. Frustrated and impulsive, you resort to extreme autocratic behavior, more akin to your experiences as a captain of industry, an autocrat, and where few can challenge you short term. Those who do, you fire, for not sucking up to the boss.

"You malign the FBI, CIA, and Department of Justice and try to bend them to your whim and will. They are not your personal toys. I am familiar with the dedication of these pillars that protect our country from villains within and abroad. They suspect your actions and motives. These fine men and women have devoted themselves to the service of their country. Many have given their lives to the cause.

"For your own gain, you have callously and cruelly forced some of the finest out of service. On top of that, Little Big Hands, you demand their unwavering loyalty. That is something that cannot be requested. It must be earned. Simultaneously, you shame these revered institutions by casting aspersions upon them in the public eye. Such behavior from a president both saddens and disgusts me.

POTUS reacted condescendingly toward Bush. "Old timer, things have changed since you were around. If these same people went behind your back and started to investigate you, I rather doubt that you'd sit still for it. The folks you speak so lovingly of represent the deep state. They are trying to subvert my office and authority. They waste the taxpayer's money investigating areas of my life they have no business doing. It's irrelevant. If my voters don't care about my background, why should they? I don't care if these bureaucrats have all kinds of medals for valor, been wounded, lost friends in the line of duty, or admirably worked twenty or more years for several different presidents. People in my employ must demonstrate unconditional loyalty and accept that I have their best interests at heart, as well as the people they serve."

Bush thought to himself, this guy is not listening. He can't get beyond himself. A tough nut to crack. So stubbornly sure of himself. My predecessors warned me Little Big Hands is a narcissist. I'll try a different tactic…some intimidation. "If you could recall my background, you would feel even more terrified about my visit. I still have friends in government who admire my legacy. Even now, they make your political life very difficult because they neither trust nor respect you. In case you forgot, before becoming president, I headed the CIA. I don't believe in your silly conspiracy theories. You just throw that shit out because you know some people feed on it.

"I made tough calls and mistakes while in office, just like you. What president hasn't? None of us are saints. Even Jimmy Carter confessed to lust when an attractive woman passed him by. Each of us has flaws. We are simply human. But it's our strength of character that differentiates us.

"With your overly generous tax cuts to the wealthy and businesses, you have run the nation's deficit to new highs while starving essential human services that distinguish great nations from despotic ones. Great nations take great care to protect their weakest . . . the poor, elderly, ill, and young. Instead, you have slashed services to them. As a result of ultraconservative beliefs, states like Texas have some of the highest ratios of uninsured children in the country. Consequently, the public subsidizes the cost of this political folly by paying higher hospital and medical charges to cover emergency care for the poor.

"One other thing irks me about you, Little Big Hands. Both Reagan and Nixon made an important strategic decision to make friends with China. They worked hard to give a taste of capitalism. They recognized that in some respects, Communism and capitalism are antagonists. I continued the thrust to defuse the friction between China and the United States.

"To break down barriers, I'd invite Chinese diplomats to pitch horseshoes with me. I just loved that game and got good at it. Miss it in the afterlife. When they made a ringer, the Chinese got to tell me what they needed from us. And when I made a ringer, I told them what we expected. Kind of funny how a simple game can open up diplomatic relationships. I took the Chinese to baseball games whenever I could, for the same reason.

"As a result, over time our two economies became more interdependent and theirs more capitalistic. The technology explosion would have looked considerably different without the likes of Apple and other companies being able to source China's manufacturing capabilities, engineering knowledge and labor pool. Along the way it helped raise their peasants' standard of living.

"Through the years, Nixon, Reagan, and other presidents have exercised considerable diplomacy to bring China into the modern age and reduce the threat of nuclear confrontation. Then, you and your secretary of state…What is his name? You've had so many it's hard to keep score, Oh, Roger Oaks? The two of you must be out of your hard-headed minds to trigger a trade war with China. Together you are human wrecking balls, destroying in the blink of an eye what it took years to build.

I guess it never occurred to either of you that the people most likely to suffer are the American farmers, manufacturers, and consumers who either can't export their products or who find their disposable incomes shrinking as a result of your tariffs. Most Americans—and for that matter, many members on both sides of Congress—didn't want the script to play out the way it has.

Your thirty billion in subsidies to American farmers to compensate them for their losses from tariffs further strains the federal budget. And, that's just the tip of the iceberg. Many of them have gone bankrupt. To put things into perspective, your subsidy is over twice the size of the Obama administration's bailout to the auto industry during the recession of 2009! And they paid him back. How can you possibly call this folly a victory?

"And that's a ball buster to the Texas economy closing the Chinese Consulate in Houston. I helped bring it to my home city forty years ago. You just made it harder to keep Texas a red state. They helped bring a lot of business to Texas and boosted the economy.

"I have no doubt that the Chinese used the embassy to gather intelligence, just like we do there. If you caught them red handed trying to steal our technology and medical research, then I don't fault your singling them out. You should have done the same to the Russians. And rather than go full throttle, why didn't you force the Chinese to send half of their Houston embassy personnel home as a first step? Your timing and extent of your action just a little over three months before the election smacks of a pure political ploy...an act of desperation from a loser. I don't expect you to handle the fallout any better than you've handled the Coronavirus.

"With your trade policies, trade wars, and tariffs, you have transformed former friends into enemies. In your mind, trade is a win-or-lose proposition. How can you make America great or expect the world to want to do business with us without embracing a global view of a fast-paced, technologically savvy, and increasingly interdependent world?

"U.S. trade partners are more sophisticated and will not be bullied. They will enter into alliances with other nations, at a cost to us, if we continue to try to maximize gains at their expense. As a result of your actions, already you've driven the Chinese and Russian Foreign Ministers to set aside animosities. They've pledged to increase exchanges at all levels, cooperate on finding a cure for Covid-19, and strengthen coordination on major internal and regional affairs. Thanks to your political ineptness, Putin has a big grin on his face.

To solve trade and other disputes both sides need to compromise . . . but that's better done at the trade table than through public threats, counterproductive posturing, and the closing of consulates. Your approach only plays well to your loyal party followers and special interest groups who hardly understand the implications and repercussions of what you told them you'd do if elected.

"The fault with your tariffs is not that China shouldn't have been called to task for violating trade agreements and human rights issues, but rather how you've responded, pardon the pun, like a bull in a china shop. With China expanding their presence in the South China Sea, I give you some credit for calling a spade a spade. You could have reminded the Chinese what happened when Japan attempted to expand their presence in Asia. It led to WW2. They might have gotten the point, but you lacked the wits to pull it off.

"Worse yet, you have shorthanded yourself by churning all those cabinet members. You neutered much of your experienced diplomatic core in the process. Lacking much analytical ability and unwilling to read the diplomatic reports placed on your desk, you've blundered into a quagmire of our own making. Rather than warn the American people to prepare for a possible trade war and then progressively tighten the screws, you went full throttle. You hit China with a hammer, rather than alternating a carrot and a stick.

"When you pulled your stunt, did anybody bother to tell you that China was America's largest trading partner, with annual trade in goods and services worth about seven hundred billion dollars? Mexico was also a huge trading partner. And like China, you poked your thumb in their eye with threats to make them pay for the wall along the border. Guess who is paying for the wall? It really pissed Congress off that you redirected funds that they had approved for use by the military to a damn wall. In the process, you infringed on their Constitutional power of the purse.

"You know I wasn't much of a computer guy but let me put things in context for you in a way you might understand. 'Since you have come into office, the US and China have spent the past three years ripping out the software of their relationship. Now we are ripping out the hardware!'

"Little Big Hands, the American people will see through you, even if you're lucky enough to reach agreement with those countries you pushed into a trade war. More than likely, your trade opponents will hold out until the next election rather than negotiate with your administration. The public is wiser about your five-chapter playbook: 'take credit, exaggerate achievements, satisfy key stakeholders, divert attention and delay accountability.' You can't fool history. It has a long memory, and eventually the truth emerges.

***

"You have also made a mess of other foreign affairs. Why you didn't forcefully lean on the Russians after they meddled in our elections flabbergasts me. That's even more serious than the problem with China. Russia is messing with our democracy. The evidence shows they accepted a not-so-subtle invitation from you to dig up dirt on your opponent. Some would think that treasonous.

"There's a cyberwar going on . . . call it World War Three . . . and it, along with ransomware, threatens our institutions. Why didn't you react with the same swiftness and sense of urgency I did when Saddam Hussein invaded Kuwait and General Manuel Noriega crossed the line in Panama?

"Little Big Hands, a president has several obligations to the American people. He must speak for and to the nation. He must faithfully execute the law. And he must lead. But no function, in my opinion, is as important as his role as Commander in Chief. In that capacity, he must confront and make decisions that impact the lives of every American, as well as others around the world. Unfortunately, you have thus far failed to address the cyberwar or marshal significant resources and support to neutralize the perpetrators.

"My predecessor tripled the gross federal debt from nine hundred billion to $2.7 trillion. Your spending has taken that debt to about $23.7 trillion. Before he retired, even Reagan began to regret the deficit he'd generated. Conservatives used to be big on balancing the budget. What's happened to us?

"My biggest regret occurred during my campaign for the presidency. I told everyone to read my lips—that if I was elected, I would not increase taxes. I had to eat those words once I got in office and better understood the size of the deficit I inherited from Reagan. It cost me reelection. Your national debt will choke the life out of the next administration.

"For repentance in the afterlife, every evening at news time I hear again and again my famous quote—"Read my lips"—on television. How will you be remembered? What will you regret? I'm sure you've already carved out a long list in the eyes of the Beholder. Who, if anyone, will finance your presidential library? Moscow?

"All my life I was a very collegial guy. I liked people, and they liked me. When I assumed the office, I didn't make a spectacle of it like you do. I told my Secret Service, when we travel in a motorcade, no sirens going down the street. And, we halt at stoplights.

"Another thing I learned as a businessman, a civil servant, and a politician was to treat my employees with dignity and respect. I praised them publicly and criticized them privately. You, Mr. President, derive perverse pleasure from publicly torching your direct reports, civil servants, and military personnel. Then you wonder why 'Nobody likes Me' and answer the root cause, 'It must be my PERSONALITY!'

POTUS replied defensively, "I'm a living witness that my management style always worked for me, my dad, and his dad. We got the results we wanted, and few dared cross us. Same way you whip a horse, camel, or stubborn pack mule to get them to respond and obey. And those I called names deserved it. That's how you build a billion-dollar empire. Screw 'em before they screw you. In my business it was a dog eat dog world to get to the top of the pyramid. My TV show *The Art of Building a Better Burger* wasn't too far removed from how I ran my businesses."

Bush said, "That's interesting to know, Little Big Hands, and relevant to some decisions we ghosts will eventually need to make about you. Thank you for your candor. After I ascended to the afterlife, I founded a White House Club for Immortal Officeholders. We have some strict bylaws and standards for membership. Most former presidents have been invited to join. A few, like Andrew Johnson, James Buchanan, and Warren Harding, have been excluded for failing to safeguard the nation, to adequately lead during periods of crisis, or for tainting the office through scandal and incompetence. Don't count on an invitation."

Ominously, President Bush warned President Little Big Hands that he would not be his last visitor. Then, without further elaboration, he vanished right through the wall of the helicopter.

As Marine One returned to the White House, POTUS breathed a sigh of relief. He could see far in the distance the figure of a man with a parachute defying gravity and rising upward, headed to eternity.

***

As he dozed and slowly recovered from another ghastly encounter with ghosts, Little Big Hands dreamed that because of his policies, only third world countries would trade with the United States. Cyberwarfare had blocked his ability to tweet or use his phone, computer, remote controls, and wired devices. He had been electronically disconnected from the world. And, to top it off, all the Chinese restaurants refused to deliver carryout to the White House, to Belladonna, or to serve him in person.

Days Eight and Nine

RETURN TO THE WHITE HOUSE

Upset over his flight back to the White House, POTUS only managed to return a halfhearted salute to the military crew who'd delivered him safely there. He sensed their stone-faced salutes were an obligation to the office, not the man.

Little Big Hands dashed through the back door and headed straight to the Lincoln bedroom where he usually slept. As he climbed the steps, two at a time, he remembered rumors that past occupants haunted this room. He'd never believed those tales and deliberately chose the Lincoln bedroom to demonstrate his mettle.

With an about-face, Little Big Hands retreated to the Madison room to regain his composure. On the way, he thought with resolve, "Since these past presidents are coming sequentially, there can't be more than a few left. As far as I know, the rest are still alive. If they do come, the remainder will be phantoms, not scary blue-hued creatures from an unearthly dimension. Based on Jimmy Carter's visit, I'm afraid they can still act just as forcefully. What more can they exact from me? Old Ebenezer Scrooge had it pretty easy with just three ghosts haunting him." As he shed his clothes to take a shower, he glanced at the large antique mirror in the center hallway. He said to his reflection, "Why are they trying to paint me worse than that bad boy Scrooge? What will my grandchildren, their children, and generations to follow think of me?"

Phantom #42: Bill Clinton

HEARTBREAK HOTEL

Outside, a heavy downpour of sleet and rain splashed off the window, smeared the view, and dimmed what natural light remained. A man emerged from behind a chair in the shadows. He appeared a whole lot like the painting of #42 and he began to coax jazzy music from a tenor saxophone.

In a friendly overture Bill Clinton's phantom invited "Come on Little Big Hands. Get dried off and please join me. Climb into your tuxedo and pull up your suspenders. Hollywood beckons. Ahh, how appropriate . . . your bath towel has little red hearts embroidered on it. Which mistress gave you that?"

Once POTUS zipped up his pants, Clinton transported Little Big Hands back in time to June 7, 1992.

POTUS stood next to President Clinton's phantom as they watched from the sidelines *The Arsenio Hall Show*. On stage, a younger version of Clinton belted out an impressive version of "Heartbreak Hotel" on the sax. The cool factor helped improve his popularity with younger voters. Clinton had just clinched his party's nomination for the presidency, and everyone wanted to interview him. The event instantly gave Clinton a big boost in his faceoff with President Bush.

Clinton leaned over and whispered in POTUS's ear, "Listen up. That's how you reach the next generation. Unless you wake up to your situation, you don't stand much chance of winning reelection sticking to old horses. Have you noticed certain segments of your political base withering away? Look at their gray hair, plastic surgery, sagging waistlines, and bald heads. Even their cataract surgery doesn't alter their archaic view of a changing world.

"Speaking of Heartbreak Hotel, it's too bad the Belladonna chain of hotels seems headed to bankruptcy since you became president. Even before Coronavirus disrupted the industry, people began canceling their reservations in droves at your resorts, hotels, and restaurants. Now that they have taken a full measure of your presidency, few enterprises want to accept your advertising or sponsor an event out of fear of association with you. Few people want to identify with your brand as a guest, customer, employee, or affiliate.

"And my, how your lawsuits from disgruntled suppliers keep mounting. As a matter of routine, you underpay them and dispute and litigate their services. Investors have discovered that your business model screws others, and your profits are built on a shaky—no, shady—foundation."

Unable to constrain himself any longer, POTUS erupted, "That's bullshit. I'm only following my attorneys' counsel and doing what US law allows. All those contractors try to cheat you. It is just a game. They jack up their prices in their bids expecting to only get a fraction of it."

"Then, POTUS, how do you explain all your courtroom entanglements? Your number of lawsuits was unmatched when you began campaigning for office. You profit from loopholes in the legal system. New Yorkers have known for years what kind of man you are. It explains why you fled Manhattan and moved your primary residence back to Louisiana. You are no longer welcomed in the Big Apple." Clinton chuckled. "Ha! If you were a fish, they'd call you a bottom-feeder!

"I feel sorry for your voters and your investors. You keep telling them you're a genius and that no one knows the art of the deal like you. Well, they'll find out that you gave them a raw deal. You certainly don't represent what they expected or thought they signed up for. Only the very wealthy and large corporations benefit from your tax cuts. Those mega corporations and special interest groups that pay no taxes disgust younger voters trying to make ends meet and retirees living on a fixed income. They're bitter. You're like Nero, fiddling in his toga while Rome burned. That probably went over your head, though, since you lack any grasp of history.

"Worse yet, history repeats itself. All those falsely projected savings from your tax cuts a year ago have been offset by tariffs. Jobs are being lost and farmers are losing their land. You play with farmers' lives like poker chips. The taxpayer, on average, pays over a thousand dollars in tariffs. That cuts deeply into their disposable income. And the national debt has broken new records. The subsidies to farmers and other losers in your trade wars with Mexico, Canada, Japan, China, and India are costing the country dearly. Our nation, on a per capita basis, is poorer than it has been in decades as a result of your capricious policies.

"Vice President Morebucks doesn't help matters either. I mean, come on. Do you really believe him when he says smoking doesn't kill, condoms don't protect, and the best way to curb an epidemic is through prayer?

"Those spineless politicians in Congress who supported your policies are probably now burying their heads like ostriches, hoping you'll just go away."

***

Clinton limbered up his bony fingers, caught a second wind, and played a few more notes of "Heartbreak Hotel" for POTUS's listening pleasure. When the music stopped, he gave him a sly smile.

"That was really something about your affairs with Ms. Knockwurst in New York City. The special prosecutor will sniff out that your company's human resource manager paid her a quarter of a million dollars to do a television ad and to keep her mouth shut. He's not going to buy the story that her clumsy thirty-second spot promoting the health and safety of your meat markets during the presidential campaign was anything more than a bribe, a quid pro quo!

"Don't you think it's kind of ironic how she butchered the name of your brand? Bellaboner rather than Belladonna? Shortly afterwards the ad got recalled. You were even bolder, inviting Ms. Lily Knockers—oops, I mean Knockwurst—to make a brief campaign appearance at the Republican Convention. Do you remember all the whistles and lecherous smiles from the old guys there? My, how they admired you! How you glowed with pride.

"Let's you and I step into another room, another time and place. Ahh! Here we are at the 2013 Moscow Miss Universe Pageant." Swirling around them were sparsely clad young ladies from around the world parading lots of cleavage.

Clinton said, "I thought this might cheer you up." In a moment of weakness, POTUS reached out to give Ms. Costa Rica an encouraging pat on the bottom as she slithered by in passion-pink bikini with a tropical green bow attached to her derriere that jiggled with each step in her high heels. Although no one other than POTUS could hear him, Clinton roared, "Hey, I saw that! Didn't I say no touching? You've been down that troublesome road before! Stop it!

"POTUS, your criterion for selecting these beautiful women was fascinating. None of them had to possess much talent to participate in Miss Universe. They just needed other incredible virtues. You made sure of that when you purchased the right to own and host the event from 1996 to 2015. Astute move to jettison it right before you ran for president. Why your opponents didn't have a field day with that investment is beyond me. I guess they were playing by a different set of rules and decorum than you.

"One of your great joys in life was flirting and circulating among the contestants while they rehearsed a day or two before the pageant began. I hear rumors that sometimes you got lucky. Most of the ambitious contestants weren't naïve. They knew as owner that you reserved the right to inspect the merchandise. Over time you made sure that the bathing suits got smaller and the heels higher. Although you retained a cadre of qualified judges, you reserved the right to pick nine of the top fifteen finalists out of the original eighty-six contestants. Those who came from cities and countries where you had other business interests had an advantage. And your little secret: Those countries where Miss Universe had strong television ratings helped shape the finalists."

Failing to detect the cynicism in Clinton's voice, Little Big Hands beamed with pride at his comments. Sticking out his chest, he bragged "Each of my businesses mutually reinforced and complemented all the other Belladonna products—from hotels to steak, vodka, women, clothing, and golf resorts.

"Prudently, if I do say so myself, I sold the contest, just as you observed to launch a serious run for president. Like all my deals, I made a killing on the price.

"You and I know it's all about the art of the deal. In your own way, you can't tell me that you weren't also master of the spin and superbly in control of your own brand."

With a cunning smile of self-satisfaction, POTUS continued: "Here's my secret. Even though American viewers fell from twelve million when I bought the pageant to fewer than four million by the time of the Moscow event, I had a grander and more profitable goal in mind. For decades, what I really desired was a large luxury hotel across the street from the Kremlin in partnership with the Soviet government. I could see the opportunity to make billions of dollars off those people.

"By 2013, my prospects in Russia began to look more positive. But I regret that my brother Bubba told that golf sportswriter that we don't rely on American banks. We have all the funding we need out of Russia. Stupid, stupid, stupid! Bubba eventually denied that remark on Twitter. Twitter is a wonderful political tool. Greatest ever. You can keep remarks short, sweet, and ambiguous. Don't need to explain much . . . just dribble enough out there that your followers can swallow. Patiently let them read into it their own biases and conclusions. Then you've got 'em hooked. They've joined the *All Hands On For America* movement."

After a long pause to digest all that Little Big Hands had just dished out, Clinton responded; "If I were in your shoes, I think I'd consider resigning before I got impeached again—or worse yet, went to jail as the first sitting president in history to take a tumble. I had my own close call.

"Who knows where the investigations into the sordid allegations of Jeffery Epstein's sex trafficking will lead? He may have committed suicide but his enabler, Ms. Maxwell, still lives. I bet she has a long memory.

"Poor Prince Andrew, the Duke of York, can't explain why there is a picture of him with his arm around that bare waisted minor. Others are scrambling to distance themselves from any past connections with Epstein. You famously called him a 'terrific guy' and Fox News had to apologize for inadvertently cropping you out of a photo with Epstein and Maxwell. And none of us are untouched. I praised his 'intellect and philanthropic efforts.' Is that why you have come up with another one of your weird, unfounded conspiracy theories that I was somehow involved in his death while he was locked up in a Federal jail under your jurisdiction as president? Believe me, once Natasha Hands gets wind of all the details, you might go down in infamy as the First Divorcé while occupying the Oval Office."

POTUS responded "Natasha is already trying to take me to the cleaners. What's one more divorce settlement? But you know my little conspiracy theory meant no harm…just trying to help the tabloids survive and sell news. Given the opportunity, wouldn't you do the same?"

***

"Little Big Hands, I'm not going to stoop to your last comment. I think it speaks for itself what kind of man you are. I was a good old boy. Unlike you, most people liked me, found me charming, with the exception of some Republicans. Most voters forgave me for a few wrong turns because they felt I identified with them.

It didn't hurt that I could articulate my policies in a manner that most people could understand.

"They also rather approved of my accomplishments, including a balanced budget. On that matter, you, Sir, have exploded the deficit to meet your selfish agenda to make the wealthy even wealthier.

"POTUS, as leader of the largest nation in the free world, you are derelict in your duty to the American people. Sir, why haven't you paddled the behinds of corporate heads who paid themselves big salaries and bonuses for cutting costs, slashing jobs, and pairing back research and development in lieu of making America great? Why haven't you employed the bully pulpit to tell them to use those tax cuts you laid in their laps to reinvigorate the country?

"And you sure have made a mess of the North American Free Trade Agreement, which was ratified under my leadership. How embarrassing that both Canada and Mexico now ask you to build a wall on their borders and pay for it.

"After I left office, I shifted my appetite to a plant-based diet. At the time, it was mostly for cardiopulmonary reasons. However, Little Big Hands your corrupt family businesses would be reason enough for me to stop eating meat!

"I think a measure of your character rests in your refusal to attend the annual White House Correspondents' Dinner. Honestly, they haven't missed you. And why not? You have put their lives at risk around the world. You abuse and label them enemies of the people. That's an old tactic from dictators and despots who can't tolerate the truth. When you declined the invitation to share in the frivolities, you broke a long chain of participating presidents with less-fragile egos than yours. Really, it's just as well you didn't go. The event would have been a bust. Those journalistic piranhas would have eaten you alive over your sick, caustic humor designed to destroy reputations. People who can't laugh at themselves should not be taken seriously. At my inaugural ball, I played the sax to the tune of 'Your Mama Don't Dance.' I was reaching out to a new generation of voters, and I wanted to convey an optimistic future, full of potential.

"At my last White House Correspondents' Dinner, I played a faux farewell video of me wandering around the White House. It included a press report to an audience of one, me washing the presidential limo, answering the phone for the White House receptionist, bicycling through the hallways, wearing my pajama bottoms for a cabinet meeting, mowing the lawn, watching cartoons, and making a to-go sandwich for Hillary.

"I left in the good graces of many in both political parties, despite the noise over an impeachment vote, because they knew my intentions to improve the lives of others were sincere. Little Big Hands, you just don't know how to be likable. Your impeachment dragged on for months and made mine seem like a misdemeanor. At least my administration continued to function and get things done in a more bipartisan way. What did you do? You announced that during impeachment proceedings you wouldn't work with Congress on fixing infrastructure, or anything else of substance. Meanwhile bridges collapse, highways buckle, and dams break. You set back the interests of the entire country including, of course, those who elected you and who would have benefited from the resulting job creation.

"Honestly, I owe you a debt of gratitude. With all your tawdry affairs out in public and the bribes to your mistresses, you make me look like a choirboy.

"For vastly different reasons than yours, I feel I never really had a honeymoon with the press. I was often amazed how I could be condensed into a two-dimensional cartoon character. Unlike you, I never called the press an enemy of the people. You don't seem to understand the important role the fourth estate plays in perpetuating our democracy.

***

"Looking back on it, I am quite proud of my service to my country. I intervened to help end the civil war and ethnic conflict in the Balkan Peninsula. The outcome saved thousands of lives and set the stage for that criminal regime to go to jail.

"I endorsed the Brady Bill enforcing background checks on handgun buyers and a ban on assault weapons. The crime rate fell to its lowest level in a generation. You continue to kiss the ass of the NRA and its rich and powerful members. As a result, the mass slaughter of innocents rolls on. In front of the public's eyes, this group continues to shoot themselves in the foot.

"Your cozy gun-lobby buddies obscure where donations go, enrich themselves, and siphon off hundreds of millions of dollars for top NRA executives and vendors. Congressional investigators have uncovered an extraordinary trail of red flags. Their findings laid bare a workplace mired in secrecy, self-dealing, and greed. The discovery revealed that the NRA encouraged disastrous ventures and questionable partnerships while marginalizing those who objected.

"Little Big Hands, prepare to lose one of your biggest campaign contributors. For good reason, the IRS will sooner or later revoke the NRA's tax-exempt status. What a huge effect that will have on you and your loyal members in Congress who have fed out of the NRA trough for years.

"In my 1999 State of the Union Address, I said the previous year was the hottest year ever recorded. I warned that our most fateful new challenge will come from global warming. Recent heat waves, floods, and storms just hint at what future generations may endure. Twenty years later, you and your supporters continue to ignore the evidence and cut back regulations on the environment to appease your base of nonbelievers and benefactors. Recently the worst conflagrations in history happened in Brazil, Australia, and California. Yet your administration shows little concern, does little to help, and refuses to understand the root causes of these environmental catastrophes.

"Some of these fires proved manmade, set accidentally or deliberately—some by extremists trying to prove a point. Nature's lightning bolts caused others. No matter the cause of it, the extent of the damage has been amplified by the driest conditions in recorded history. Sooner than you think we will be witnessing fires raging out of control in the Southeast, Southwest, far West, and Northwest. The burning prairies will wipe out half of the livestock on those acreages. Don't think that won't rob the cradle of America's breadbasket! And if the nation continues to lose its forests, Americans will be living in mud homes like those in rural Africa.

"How do you justify ignoring what's happening to these vital lifelines? Don't you care about the welfare of your grandchildren, and theirs? Climate-denying Neti Pot politicians are no different than lung-cancer patients who continue to smoke until their last wheeze. Who are you going to blame, Little Big Hands, as all these catastrophic wildfires show the planet the road to hell?

"I have a few regrets to atone for every day. One of them involves explaining every morning to Hillary what I meant when I said I did not have sex with that woman. You know she's a lawyer. With her, one must carefully choose one's words. Semantics matter.

"I've got another gig to go to with my sax. I can assure you that the saints won't be marching in when your time comes."

***

Fatigued, Little Big Hands nodded off. He experienced another bizarre dream. Performing in a comedy club, he couldn't remember the lines and got the timing all wrong. Seated in the audience, Jimmy Carter threw peanuts at him, Ronald Reagan tossed yellow jellybeans, and George HW Bush threw up.

Phantom #43: George W. Bush

THE INTERVIEW

After his traumatic encounter with Clinton's phantom, POTUS concluded that even the Madison room was no longer a safe haven from those who wished to confront his past. He beat a hasty retreat to Franklin Roosevelt's former World War II Map Room on the ground floor.

POTUS usually referred to the Madison Room as the Situation Room. There was no doubt in his mind that he had a serious situation. Or was all this just a disorder in his scrambled mind, just a long series of illusions and nightmares? He could no longer discern or recall which of his predecessors were alive or dead. He prayed this secure space could insulate him from all his torment and buy time to restore his sanity.

Little Big Hands would not have chosen the Situation room if he had remembered that it was the same one where President Garfield lay dying from a gunshot wound which a quack physician failed to treat correctly. A strong gust of wind rattled a nearby window. As the pane quivered, another phantom slipped seamlessly through the glass, wearing a Texas Rangers baseball team windbreaker and tan slacks. He carried a bat in his right hand. The closer he got to POTUS, the more the intimidating figure looked familiar.

Bush broke the spell with a "howdy" and gently tapped POTUS on the backside with his bat. "I see you've been corn-fed." Prodding him to get moving, Bush herded Little Big Hands like a steer toward the exit.

"Giddy up, we're goin' to Dallas. Since you probably will never get anyone to fundraise a presidential museum, I'm takin' you to mine on the Southern Methodist campus. That's a university, not a church."

POTUS was not eager to return to any university; he'd barely graduated in six years.

"Say, I noticed that upon running for president, your lawyer immediately sent the registrar's office a demand not to reveal your grades to the press or anyone else. And then as part of presidential privilege, he sent a follow-up letter that prohibited anyone from revealin' your academic performance for life. That's rather odd behavior for a fellow who claims to be the second smartest president ever. One who often refers to himself in the third person as a genius. Somethin' doesn't add up.'"

***

In a warp-speed *Star Wars* moment, they stepped back in time to July 13, 2017. They found themselves among a large crowd gathered to watch David Rubenstein interview on stage Bill Clinton and George W. Bush at the George W. Bush Presidential Library. Both former presidents sat at ease, one a Republican and the other a Democrat, side by side as friends on matching plush red leather armchairs.

Bush quietly explained to POTUS some background information. He said: "I think you may know, as a self-proclaimed financial wizard yourself, that Rubenstein cofounded *The Carlyle Group*, one of the largest private equity funds in the world. What you might not know was that he also had served in President Carter's administration. As a side note, Rubenstein apologized for the high interest rates at the time. More importantly, he has become a world-class philanthropist and hosts a televised show called 'Peer to Peer.'

"Having paid the winning bid of $21.5 million at a Sotheby's auction, Rubenstein acquired the only available original copy of the thirteenth-century Magna Carta not secured in a British institution. *The Perot Foundation* in Plano, Texas put it up for auction. Rubenstein feared one of the most important documents in Western civilization might never again be available for citizens to see on American soil. The National Archives lacked the funds to make the purchase. Shortly after takin' ownership, Rubenstein put it on display at the National Archives in Washington, D.C. so Americans could view the document that inspired the Constitution.

"I'm rather disappointed that Perot, a fella Texan, was willing to sell the document at auction rather than do his patriotic duty. It took a big city easterner from Maryland to do the right thing."

"My god," POTUS interjected. "That's a lot of dough!" I would have just photocopied it and spent the rest on developing my golf courses for the American people."

Bush could see that POTUS's ability to process information had already waned. Everything seemed to be about him. To get POTUS to focus, he tapped him firmly on the foot with the head of the bat. When he got an 'ouch' he continued.

"Rubenstein felt deeply disturbed that many Americans could not name the three branches of government, that less than fifty percent voted, and that civics and American history had been deemphasized in public schools due to lack of funds. Sometimes Little Big Hands, I think you fail to remember that we have three branches of government. We'll get to that later.

"Rubenstein told me that when citizens forget the sacrifices made to make America a truly great nation, democracy falters. By not bothering to vote, they forfeit their responsibility to shape government at the polls. Eventually a person with dictatorial leanings becomes the leader of the land. He then begins to progressively suppress our independence and self-governance. At the very least, the loss of our history makes Americans more vulnerable to the appeal of simplistic slogans, polarizin' statements, and extremist views.

"Having discovered that many Congressmen and women lack a firm grasp of the country's history and guiding principles, Rubenstein also hosts a popular program for them. To elevate their knowledge, once a quarter he interviews a famous historian. That person talks about our heritage and the sacrifices made to create the largest democracy in the world. These sessions are always well attended by members from the House and the

Senate." Bush looked at Little Big Hands and frowned "Too bad he didn't send you an invitation."

***

Bush shifted gears. "So here we are Little Big Hands. I want you to witness two men, who often put the good of their country ahead of their political parties, engage in a civil conversation. I think you'll discover that these patriots disdain the rigid ideology that it's my way or no way . . . the sort that creates gridlock in government, harms Americans, and earns disrespect for politicians. As they talk, I want you to think about how ungraciously you grabbed the presidential baton from your predecessor."

Keeping his doubts to himself, the phantom Bush said, "Listen carefully, Little Big Hands, you might learn something in this interview. Better yet, I am fixin' to interpret what each said in response to Rubenstein's questions about the transition of power from one president to another to make sure you get it. So, here is the gist of it. I'm going to ad lib a bit for the sake of relevance and brevity.

"First, President Clinton began by sayin' I told George W that when he assumed the office of the presidency I would never embarrass him in public or call him names. I had too much respect for him, his father, and the demands of the office to second-guess him. I sincerely wanted him to succeed . . . even though he was a Republican.

"In turn, I stated that Bill was humble in victory. When he beat my father at the polls, he was respectful and went out of his way to be kind to my dad. He did not disparage his reputation or achievements. As a result, all three of us became friends and together continued to serve humanity after leaving office. We appreciate and value that respect, trust, and integrity is all about an individual's character.

"Then Clinton chimed in, and I'm paraphrasin', that 'If you disagree with a person, that doesn't mean you don't like him or her.' He said that 'regrettably, people today separate themselves into like-minded communities. They don't want to be around others who may have different perspectives and viewpoints.' He observed that 'some politicians, special interest groups, and even religions facilitate this ugliness. People get their news from insular sources.

"Now this is really important Little Big Hands. Listen up! Clinton emphasized that in a complex world characterized by environmental and commercial interdependence, leaders with access to diverse groups and opinions make better decisions.

"In a sign of the times, Clinton went on to say that many on the far left and far right feel that to get elected, they have to create sound-bites that weave people into beliefs and cocoons of right and wrong. Once insulated inside those cocoons, they close their minds, ears, and hearts. Sometimes none of these soundbites are based on facts, they just feed raw emotions."

Bush observed "Now we see how the Russians and others sowed discord and manipulated the public's viewpoints on Facebook, Instagram, Twitter, and other social media."

POTUS scowled, "Are you suggesting that's how I got elected? Everybody knows that's fake news. I won the election the old-fashioned way." Then he grinned, "I bet neither you nor Clinton would have been smart enough to use Twitter and Facebook to your advantage. Nor make bold, controversial statements of the sort that helped the press sell news. I got plenty of free publicity that way and saved a ton of money on campaign expenses. Pretty clever, don't you think?"

Ignoring Little Big Hand's senseless response, Bush plowed forward. "Clinton observed that no one will ever acknowledge or recognize that their votes were founded on falsifications because the claims confirmed their beliefs and prejudices about their chosen candidate. Comfortable with their own interpretation, they remained unwilling to question or fact-check their conclusions.

"Let's move on to another question Rubenstein asked during the interview. I think you might find this more interesting. He wanted to know what qualities Clinton and I felt are most important to serve as president? Was it hard work, luck, intelligence, optimism? What do you think he said?"

POTUS whispered under his breath, "Intelligence and balls." But the actual response made him flinch.

"You got that all wrong, Little Big Hands. What Clinton said was if you want to be president, it's your obligation to come into the job with an agenda and realize that the role is about the people, not about you. It's not about brayin' like a jackass about all the people you beat or belittling those you defeated. Time in office flies by quickly. At the end, he said you want to be remembered for how many lives you improved, how you gave kids a better future, and how you made the world a better place. I added that humility is also an essential virtue."

POTUS interrupted and shook his head. "No. Humility is a sign of weakness."

Ignoring him, Bush continued. "In the interview, I went on to explain that it's important for a president to know what you don't know and listen to those who know what you don't know."

Of course, POTUS either didn't care much about what he didn't know or assumed he did know. He relied on his prejudices, his business instincts, and his whims of the moment to make his decisions in political office...over-riding his cabinet and professional advisors. For better or worse, those decisions had already affected millions of lives.

Reading POTUS's mind, Bush interjected, "Hush up! You don't know how to manage. You've never been a truly successful businessperson. Even your niece says as much...all those bankruptcies! You're just a real-estate hawker and hamburger promoter who inherited and squandered a lot of money!

"Your antics pull the country apart. If we are to give the nation a future, we must pull it together, not divide it. Just look at how polarizin' some of the things are that you've done.

"For example, decisions like implementing tariffs, shutting down government for the wall, switching TSA employees from their jobs at airports to protect the capital from imaginary invaders, shrinking regulations that protect the environment, castigating NATO and other allies, limiting women's rights, makin' generalizations about Muslims and minorities, befriending dictators and despots, subordinating the roles of cabinet members, and tryin' to bend the justice department to your will.

"I could continue. These are but a few examples, Little Big Hands, of you blurrin' the lines of your authority and demonstrating lack of expertise."

After the Rubenstein interview, the Bush phantom bluntly told POTUS "It's regrettable that the American electorate couldn't see your lack of fitness for the office before they went to the polls. Otherwise they would have known that you fall short on the virtues that defined your peers.

"But I've got to give you some credit. You were masterful at disguisin' the truth from the public until you took office. Then the real you emerged. Like other notorious autocrats, your litany of divisive communications spewed hatred and resentment. I can't imagine what President Franklin Roosevelt would think of you! His inspiring, comforting, and informative fireside chats united Americans, givin' them the courage to make it through the Depression and World War Two. Your tweets foster insecurity and sow confusion! You lack the skills and heart to guide the nation through the darkness of the war that the pandemic has brought to our shores.

"My friend and Dad's, Ronald Reagan, sensed someone like you might come along when he once said, 'Freedom is never more than one generation away from extinction. We didn't pass it on to our children in our bloodstream. It must be protected and handed on for them to do the same, or else we will spend our sunset years telling generations to follow what it was once like in the United States where men and women were free.'

"Do you remember George Washington takin' you to the *Temple of Virtue*? His concerns about you have been borne out. As much as you may deny and lie about it, your actions speak much louder than words.

POTUS responded "That episode no longer remains very clear in my mind. Kind of foggy; there have been so many intrusions." Sarcastically, he added "You know the old saying, fish and visitors stink after a few days."

Bush replied, "How about I give you some frames of references. Most dictators and autocrats fancy themselves coy and clever. In reality they are anythin' but. And, their intentions soon become apparent.

"Little Big Hands, you have left an incriminatin' trail of sound-bites, video, tweets, film, quotes, paper trails and speeches that expose you for what you are. Aspiring despots like yourself serve only the best interests of themselves with little regard for the consequences to others.

"How else can you explain your suggestion that the November presidential election be postponed? That's never happened in the history of our country and smacks of seizin' control of the government for your benefit. That could be another impeachable offense.

"Without an invitation and often unannounced, how about the way you've sent masked, camouflaged federal law enforcers wearing no insignia or other identification into states and cities run by the opposing party? And then arrestin' innocent demonstrators with no charges? Or, clearing Lafayette Square of peaceful demonstrators for a photo op of you holding a Bible in your hand at St. John's Episcopal Church?

"How do you explain overridin' the rule of law by pardoning convicted felons? Then to prevent your personal attorney from writing a book about you, you kept him under lock and key. To stop investigations into your scurrilous past, you remove attorneys from office and recall ambassadors and embassy personnel. And to top it off, you install people in the FBI, CIA, Homeland Security, and Courts that you think you can control.

On a roll, Bush became even more animated and incensed. "What about featherin' your own nest by channeling campaign money to your private businesses…restaurants, hotels, and golf courses? Shamelessly, you have promoted your own businesses even though it's a clear conflict of interest while president! To prevent the public from making an informed decision about whether to vote for you, you refuse to reveal tax information.

"You hand-pick a political ally to take charge of the postal system on the pretense of expense control. Your real motive… interfere with and limit voting by mail…perhaps by slowing down delivery of ballots and implementing unreasonable deadlines for submissions during a pandemic. To facilitate that, your Postmaster ordered the removal of over 600 high speed processing machines and then eliminated overtime right before the election. You and he know all but seven states allow anybody to submit a mail in ballot. This is your way of obstructin' the will of the people. And to incite alarm, without a sliver of evidence, you speculate that there will be massive voter fraud in the coming election because of mail in votes.

"You further add to the toxic mix when you claim Black Lives Matter are infiltrated by communists and contend that it's mostly thugs and vandals who are fomentin' demonstrations. Your behavior smacks of fascism."

Bush added, "You hint at limiting freedom of speech, particularly if the press speaks out against you. You remind me of our second President, John Adams. He orchestrated a sedition law, makin' it illegal to criticize his government. When someone called him a fat ass, he locked the poor bastard up. Fortunately, Jefferson had the good sense to get that law rescinded. He recognized that our country was built on demonstrations and dissent, beginning with the Boston Tea Party."

"Some of the things I'm most proud of are my responses to the terrorist attacks on the World Trade Center and the Pentagon. I assured Americans that we would seek justice. I authorized aggressive military action in Afghanistan and Iraq. However, I underestimated what it would take to restore stability and reform in both countries."

"That reminds me, how dare you insinuate that my Dad was a 'loser' for getting shot down in World War II and then inferrin' that he and I were 'suckers,' along with all others for serving in the military! You said the same thing about my friend Senator John McCain. I take that personally and deeply resent it...you draft dodger.

As he swung the bat, George said, "Missed! No one can predict what's coming at you. Sometimes when you hold the office, the president is forced to react to events when he would rather shape them.

"I promised voters that I would function as a compassionate conservative and continue to give them much of what Clinton had done, only better. Along the way I said I would commit myself to shrink government and cut taxes. And yes, I inherited a federal budget surplus. But the enormous cost of fighting two wars, makin' broad tax cuts, and going into America's worst financial crisis since the Great Depression resulted in annual deficits from 2002 onward. Not what I had planned.

"As president, I had the honor of eulogizin' Gerald Ford and Ronald Reagan. Once regarded as the worst mistakes in presidential history, Ford's pardon of Richard Nixon is now looked upon as a selfless act of leadership. And those who once denounced President Reagan as a dunce and a warmonger now talk about how the Great Communicator won the Cold War.

"Who doesn't have regrets? I believe every president who's visited you thus far shared his with you. I wish we had been able to better document weapons of mass destruction in Iraq. But it is still too early to say conclusively how my decisions will turn out. I hope I will be recognized as a president who recognized the pivotal issues of our time and kept my vow to keep our country safe.

"Be very careful about engagin' in military action in Central and South America, North Korea, China and Iran. Don't you dare use these manageable conflicts as an excuse to divert attention from the fact that you are losing in the polls.

"Evidently, you don't see, believe, or understand it, but you have a cyberwar on multiple fronts. You're pointing your weapons of mass destruction in the wrong direction and underfundin' the high-tech civil service and military personnel you need to defend the American way of life. Can you imagine a world where all cell phones, computers, landlines, radios, televisions, robots, radar, artificial intelligence, and traffic controllers are disabled? Imagine your life if you couldn't tweet all hours of the day and night?

"One other thing, not so little: I noticed the empty bottle of Scotch on your desk. Simple question for you. Can you remember the last day you didn't have a drink? Your compulsive consumption effects your judgment, perceptions and energy. Worse yet, it makes you a threat to yourself and more importantly the nation.

"Quittin' drinking was one of the toughest decisions I ever made. I rationalized my drinking habit was nowhere as bad as some of my friends'. I didn't drink at work, and I exercised. Then Laura helped me realize that alcohol had become my god. Quittin' saved my marriage, my family, my career, and my self-esteem. It put me back on course to achieve my potential. When I quit, not drinking became a habit of its own, and I was better off. If you have the fortitude to quit drinking, and many presidents didn't, it might change how you go down in history. But until then, if I were you, I'd write my own eulogy and record it.

"So that's my counsel to you, Little Big Hands. I wish I could change your contemptable character, but it looks like the American people are stuck with it. We phantoms have limited powers of influence."

***

After George W left, Little Big Hands ignored his advice, threw down four large jiggers of Scotch and drifted into a stupor. In his head he kept hearing, "This is Annie Oakely Remington for Channel 6666. A terrifying cyberwar permeates the country from all sides. Is it coming from Russia, China, Iran, Venezuela, and Pakistan, the radical left, the far right? Who knows? We're unsure how much longer Ferret News will be able to bring you bull's-eye reporting. Here's the latest: Walmart and Costco say they have run out of batteries. There's a great risk your credit cards won't work, and any electronic record of your assets could be erased. Take action now."

Phantom #44: Barack Obama

LIES, AND DAMN LIES

The thunder from the freakish winter rainstorm penetrated the thickly insulated White House walls, rattled the bulletproof windows, and pierced the ears of its occupants.

Hands in his pockets, POTUS aimlessly wandered the carpet in the Oval Office and pondered the nightmares and daymares that incessantly tormented him. He had become a nervous wreck and could find no refuge. He kept asking the same questions. Was all this the powerful hand of dark forces at work, the sort that the extreme right-wing cult group QAnon imagines? He had always tried to maintain a tough-guy James Cagney demeanor. Now he worried that his long list of enemies, in some mysterious way, had collaborated to ravish his mind and body. Throughout life, he specialized in conjuring up a lot of conspiracy theories. His false and sensational accusations and wild speculations accumulated ever more enemies.

POTUS sensed the new presence in the room before hearing it. Out of nowhere appeared an image of the nation's first black president. He rapidly dribbled a basketball while doing a jazzy two-step and singing Otis Redding's famous soul tune hit *A Change Is Gonna Come*.

Making a spin move, the phantom of Harvard-educated President Obama suddenly bounced the ball off the wall, jarring loose POTUS's favorite portrait of himself. The treasured picture crashed to the floor. Its glass shattered in all directions and sliced through POTUS's image.

Little Big Hands gingerly stepped over the tattered remnants of his profile and bolted for the door. As he frantically tugged on the handle, it resisted with the force of a locked bank vault. POTUS feared for his life and started to hyperventilate. Obama's soothing voice said, "I am not here to cash you out. I am here to talk about your bad debts to society.

"Before we do that, I've got a personal score to settle with you. Put on that pink and orange flowered Tommy Bahama shirt. You will blend right in where we are going.

***

The next thing POTUS knew, they had entered the Kapiolani Maternity and Gynecological Hospital in Honolulu, Hawaii. It was a beehive of activity, with overly pregnant women anxiously checking in at the counter and proud moms leaving the lobby with their new additions to their families.

Obama directed Little Big Hands to the nursery. Once inside, he pointed to a newly born milk-chocolate American baby boy cuddled against the breast of his beaming Caucasian mother. "See that sign on the doorway? It says Barack Obama, born August 4, 1961. Parents: Barack Obama Sr. and Ann Dunham.

"You were only playing to one kind of audience when you made your false accusations about my origins. And since your shallow campaign platform lacked substance, you resorted to divisive comments and side show entertainment. You knew I was born in the US, yet you persisted with these lies over many months and challenged my legitimacy. Your cheap shots and inferences spewed hatred and tried to suck the air out of any meaningful debate and dialogue that could help voters make wise choices between you and Hillary Clinton."

POTUS knew he had been ferreted out of a hole that he had personally dug. He meekly began back tracking: "Obama, I was just trying to have a little fun with the campaign. You know... add some showmanship and entertainment to otherwise dull political rallies around the country. I can assure you that the American people always realized I was only kidding. And, you know I eventually publicly conceded that you weren't born in Kenya."

Obama just shook his head as he stared at a man with miniscule conscience and compassion. Then he gathered his thoughts, "Since you like to talk about origins, let's talk about yours. I'm not going to dwell on the seedy whorehouse your ancestor ran in New Orleans as he began to build the family fortune that you eventually inherited. But I've got a few things to say about the man, a fixer by trade, who tutored you in the game of politics . . . the one you frequently say shaped you the most politically. It's catastrophic for the American people that you fell under Roy Cohn's influence and became his alter ego."

"Cohn was Wisconsin senator Joe McCarthy's right-hand man during the early 1950's when they trumped up all kinds of false charges about the enemy within. His unproven and ruthless allocations that somebody might be a communist resulted in a trail of fear, prison sentences, and ruined careers for hundreds. After the American people realized that McCarthy was a fraud, somehow your pal escaped punishment. Over the ensuing years Cohn became the premier practitioner of hardball deal-making and inside fixes. One lawyer who knew him well said that 'When in Roy Cohn's presence, you were in the presence of pure evil.' That's the man who taught you to intimidate potential adversaries with hollow threats and spurious lawsuits.

"Toward the end of his life, Cohn was 'disbarred for dishonesty, fraud, deceit, and misrepresentation.' He knew you well enough to say that 'you pissed ice water.' And the day after you were elected, you told Cliff T. Parsons, that convicted felon, 'Wouldn't Roy love to see this moment? Boy do we miss him.'

"Employing Cohn's charm school tactics, you turned your last campaign into a vaudeville act. Afterwards, you contended, without one iota of proof that if the polls hadn't been fraudulent, you would have won the popular vote by several million ballots. After that, your lies just keep rolling over the next four years as you built momentum toward the next election.

"I wonder why you never reminded voters that you were indebted to three states for your victory in the electoral college? I believe it's fair to say that seventy-seven thousand votes out of more than one hundred thirty-six million cast decided the election and 'trumped' the popular vote. You spent a lot of jet fuel romancing Michigan, Wisconsin, and Pennsylvania.

Taking that as a compliment, POTUS smiled and said "We were pretty smart concentrating on those three states to win their electoral college votes. The popular vote and the so called will of the people means nothing. To win today, you've got to exercise power where it counts…pull the strings that are available to you."

Obama responded "Well, right now your poll ratings are slipping in all three states. You could get lucky again. Only time will tell whether events will catch up to you like they did Cohn.

"Kind of funny how your ex ally Wesley Smith, the former Republican Speaker of the U.S. House of Representatives from Pennsylvania, made a joke during your last campaign about you being paid by Russian President Vladimir Putin. That got caught on tape. Turned out not to be so funny and then relationships between the two of you got testy.

"Gotta hand it to him, though. He was one of the first in a long line to resign from your once loyal cadre. Explaining himself, Smith courageously said in an interview that he was an old Jack-Kemp guy who strongly believed in inclusive, aspirational politics that brought people together rather than divided them. He concluded, no thanks to you, your cronies, and some on the other side of the aisle, that polarization has made it difficult to achieve political goodwill in America.

POTUS interrupted "The people who leave my administration are the ones I want to leave. With encouragement, I help them out the door. It's my job to make crystal clear the difference between Republicans and Democrats and what is at stake for the future of America. I keep it very simple."

"Say, that reminds me," Obama said. "I know you have never heard *Of Thee I Sing*. It's a Gershwin musical that ran for over four hundred performances on Broadway. It won the Pulitzer for drama and was FDR's favorite musical. It was a biting satire on American politics and the public's attitude toward it. The protagonist, Wintergreen, was elected president on a campaign of nonsense . . . just like you, Little Big Hands.

"Wintergreen ultimately resigned for love. Love of country proved the reason you got impeached. And then there's the irony that two songs are still relevant today! One about impeachment and another about a woman wronged who makes her case public. Juicy stuff, don't you think?

"Now let's talk about more damn lies regarding the deficit and taxes. One of the many chiefs of staff you ousted, Michael Micky, confessed to Ferret News that the Republican Congress never wanted to pass laws when I was president. To facilitate that position, they engaged in a continuous stream of conspiracy theories that had been conclusively debunked. He even admitted that during the Teapot Party wave in 2011, the last thing they were interested in was giving me any legislative successes. Ms. Billy Brickell, the Senate majority leader and her Republican lackeys didn't really care about the deficit. They manufactured it to feed a different agenda. It was to force me to reduce popular domestic spending programs that were helping the country recover from the greatest recession since the 1930s. Why? So they could cut taxes for the affluent.

"Since neither cutting retirement programs nor reducing taxes for the rich were popular, Brickell framed her policy as deficit reduction. She even boasted that she pressured Republicans to refuse to compromise with any of my administration's priorities because she believed the only way Americans would know that a great debate was going on was if my measures were perceived as lacking bipartisan support. Brickell held the country hostage over ideology . . . just like when you shut down the government over your agendas.

"You know, even Nixon and Clinton when they were going through impeachment proceedings never stopped the business of government. On the other hand, POTUS, you told Democratic leaders that you wouldn't work with them on shared priorities, such as bringing down the cost of prescription drugs, unless they stopped investigating you. Man, that's disgraceful and right out of Roy Cohn's playbook.

"You pulled another similar stunt. You refused to discuss action on the next budget unless Congress approved your agenda for a wall around the capital and your request to increase military expenditures in Central and South America. That's despicable! Your decisions affected millions of Americans. Many couldn't afford medical treatment, let alone food, since you cut back the food stamp program.

"Now, another reverberation. Recently more than fifteen hundred former federal prosecutors signed a statement that in their professional judgment, based on the facts described in the special counsel's report on the nefarious circumstances of your election, you should have been criminally charged with obstruction of justice. This outcry from such a large number of prosecutors who once served both Republican and Democratic presidents is unprecedented.

"Little Big Hands, you're an inveterate, shameless, and boldfaced liar. Some claim you are an artist at it. You distort facts and circumstances to create your alternative view of the world and to manipulate those who believe in and trust you.

"How can you boast that there has never been, ever before, an administration that's been so open and transparent when in your first eight hundred sixty-nine days as president, you said ten thousand, seven hundred ninety-six things that were either misleading or outright false—an average of twelve untrue utterances a day. Your constant misrepresentations force people around you to become complicit, or at least sheepish bystanders. By association with you, these untruths taint the careers of others.

"For example, your Attorney General Tony Bark insisted that he had read the Millert Report before releasing a redacted version to the public. He declared that the report cleared you of collaborating with the Russians to influence the previous election. Special Counsel Craig Millert immediately said Bark's conclusions and redactions distorted the actual findings. Millert protested Bark's misinterpretation and added that if the evidence had cleared Little Big Hands of obstruction, he would have said so. Bark's statements compromised his integrity and that of the Department of Justice. Rather than acting objectively on the evidence, he prostrated himself to represent you rather than the best interests of the American people."

Little Big Hands immediately protested Obama's insinuations and defended his political friend. "You're wrong! Since I appointed my attorney general, he works for me. And since the American people elected the president, the attorney general, by serving me, serves the people. Same for the United States Department of Justice. They work for me, and by doing my bidding, also work for the people."

"Could your mind be going? You forget that the Senate had to approve your recommendation for the job. And since when did the Senate work for you, rather than the people? Hmm, I can see why some people might think otherwise. But perhaps you forget the attorney general and the DOJ's job is to enforce federal law, not laws you make up or bend.

"Your frequent lies, distortions, and disclaimers make me wonder if you might have hardening of the arteries, Alzheimer's, or some other form of dementia like your father. You should get tested fast, before you further harm the nation, injure someone or yourself, or disgrace your family.

"Most politicians have some sense of shame in dissembling, misrepresenting, spinning, prevaricating, and masking the truth. Or at least they fear getting caught. But you have learned from your mentor Cohn to lie without distress or regret. It turns out no matter how much crap you throw on the wall, somebody is gullible enough to believe you.

***

"That gets me to your mishandling of the Coronavirus. Our country has almost 25% of the world's cases and deaths yet only about 5% of the population. Something doesn't compute. We have historically been viewed as one of the most advanced countries on the globe with exceptional medical care for those who can afford it. So, I ask myself what makes us different? The only answer I can come up with is YOU, your administration, and the ultra-conservative governors who support you.

"Little Big Hands, you set the stage for the Coronavirus to run rampant in this country when you tried to defund the Center for Disease Control and Prevention and reduce investment in our pandemic response infrastructure. Your proposed cuts revealed your attitude toward the organization. You began two years earlier leaving positions vacant responsible for managing pandemics."

In his own defense, POTUS muttered, "I didn't cut funds for pandemic response to save a buck. I just felt these matters are better privatized."

Obama shot back, "I think you mean commercialized.

"Once the virus reached our shores, you down-played its seriousness. With great confidence, you assured the American people that it would soon dissipate. When it started to rapidly spread, you refused to accept that it was your responsibility to give central leadership to combat the problem. You made no sustained effort to assure a consistent and badly needed supply chain of masks, personnel, and other medical necessities across the country. What's the result? Fifty different states and thousands of cities competing to find cures and essential medications and supplies. By failing to lead, you forced them to go their separate ways, duplicate expenses, and repeat mistakes. All the while you pass the blame, fight with your chief medical advisor on infectious diseases, and advocate idiotic cures.

"With the disease having its way, you set a bad example in public for several months by never wearing a mask yourself to protect others. Then your fanatical followers start mirroring your bad behavior. And you continue to hold political rallies, like the one in Tulsa, where many attendees take your defiant lead and selfishly don't wear a mask...all in the name of freedom of choice, irrespective of harm to others. Sadly, one of your best and most prominent African American advocates at the rally got Covid-19 eleven days later and died. Shortly afterwards, the virus accelerated in Tulsa and the rest of Oklahoma.

"After abdicating your responsibility to lead to win the war on the virus, you finally decided to assert your position and push schools to reopen all across America for the fall semester. If they don't, you attempt to bully them into submission with a threat to withhold school subsidies from the federal government. Ironically, it was about the same week you canceled the Republican National Convention in Jacksonville because of the severity of the virus in Florida.

"How do you reconcile pushing kids to go to school there when it's too risky for your devotees to attend the convention? Seems to me your administration has a double standard, and that's being polite.

"You probably haven't heard what Dr. Joseph Varon, chief of critical care at Houston's United Memorial Medical Center, said yesterday about the virus you claim only kills a small percentage of the population. He stated that in the last week in July, he signed more death certificates than in his entire career. He added that 'It's a war against Covid-19 and stupidity.'

"When Dr. Varon was asked if the governor of Texas called him up to say he'd really like to reopen schools but wants to know if your hospital can handle it locally, what would you say? Varon replied 'Absolutely not. No hospital can handle the surge. One individual can infect up to 52 persons an hour.'

"I believe historians will see you as the direct cause of deaths of tens of thousands of American Citizens by not acting soon enough and responsibly enough to save them. Almost three times as many have died in all the years we were engaged in the Vietnam War. The body count continues to grow. You will share that pedestal with President Wilson, who ignored the Spanish Flu until he caught it and died shortly thereafter.

"Thanks to your paralysis, the virus has wiped out five years of economic growth. It's the worst three-month collapse in our nation's history. Of course, you took credit for the growth, which was well underway when I left office. I am sure you will find a way to blame the Chinese and others for the fall. At election time next November, I rather doubt that voters will forget that the extraordinary degree of our plummet, compared to others, is because the U.S. failed to get the virus under control the way other countries have. The buck stops with you.

"By rebuffing the truths of science about our planet and diseases, you've accelerated the collapse of the economy. Even worse, you've compromised and perverted science with partisan dogma, so people only trust scientific 'evidence' based on their political beliefs. The Coronavirus respects no political boundaries.

"Like your buddy Cohn and your one-time pal Epstein, whom you called a really a terrific guy, your days of believing that you can do whatever you want and no one can stop you are coming to an end.

"I am proud of the Paris Climate Agreement, the Affordable Care Act, my election as the first black president, disposing of Osama bin Laden, and setting the nation on a path to economic recovery. Unlike yours, POTUS, my administration was scandal-free and run with dignity.

"I have regrets, some about Syria. Perhaps I should have intervened sooner. Another is about the leadership of the Republican Party declaring that their highest priority, more important than the public good, was to ensure that I didn't get reelected. I wish we could have reached more common ground with them to better serve America. Their rhetoric had unintended consequences. It unleashed a racial and ethnic backlash that our country hadn't seen for several generations.

"Ask yourself, Little Big Hands: Where are you going after botching this job? What regrets will you have? There are no do-overs. My assessment is that 'you haven't grown in your capacity as president because you can't. You've turned your presidency into one more sad reality show.' How will you go down in history? What future burdens will the Hands family have to bear because of your legacy? They may well change their name to distance themselves from you.

"The arc of the moral universe is long, but it bends toward justice. Eventually, Little Big Hands, you will be taken to task to pay your dues. Democracy thrives in the light of truth."

President #00: Daniel Hands

A FINAL RECKONING –
TWO SCENARIOS

His reckoning with ghosts and phantoms of presidents past over, President Daniel Hands hibernated in the Oval Office. His hair, what little he possessed, lay disheveled, sweaty, and matted. He twitched the way a hound does when it dreams it's in pursuit of a squirrel or chased by a dogcatcher. With his chin collapsed on his chest, he snoozed at his desk. The American eagle in the painting overhead looked alarmed and ready to take flight.

POTUS awoke, dripping with perspiration, from a bad dream that he had been subpoenaed by Congress for tax evasion and falsified documents submitted to banks, insurance companies, and the IRS. Nancy Pilar, the Democrat Speaker of the U.S. House of Representatives, and her colleagues had sliced and diced him and his administration like a Thanksgiving turkey. He felt nauseous.

As POTUS dashed for the bathroom, he still wore his rumpled pink and orange flowered Tommy Bahama shirt. He urgently needed to heave up all his memories of the past week or so. He flung the door open and knocked poor Henry Noxolo, who had been polishing the marbled floor, to his knees.

Without even an apology, POTUS embraced the sink and released one great heave of relief. Wiping his jowls with his sleeve, Little Big Hands looked down and sarcastically said, "Are you still here? I thought I ordered someone to fire you."

Henry smiled up at him. "I'm still one of the few. Sir, you may not have noticed, but most of your staff is gone now. Your Secret Service let them go. They lacked security clearances.

Don't concern yourself about me, though. This is my last day. Since you built your wall around the Capital, my commute to work has risen to two hours and twenty minutes each way. I do have some good news. My son Timothy has been accepted to the Nelson Mandela University of South Africa with a full scholarship in computer science. The president of the university has reached out his hand and offered me a job as head of campus sanitation. With me gone and the White House shorthanded, you may have to clean up after yourself. South Africa welcomes talented immigrants, and I already have my green card. Here, take this mop and clean up after yourself."

***

Over the next week, President Little Big Hands pondered his future. He wondered if his series of nightmares and hallucinations might have been triggered by overindulgence... too much food and Jack Daniels mixed with too many meds? Or, was it the stress of the job? Or, that he was getting so little love back from the majority of American people in return for his efforts? Did he believe in spirits? Even if he did, he wondered what was the point of their messages? Repent? Resign? Reform? Confess?

POTUS began to take stock of his last forty-two months in office and as he did, mentally give himself a report card. He thought to himself he could have had a lot easier presidency doing nothing.

His mind wandered back to the early days when he was on the campaign trail and went forward from there. What follows is his stream of consciousness as he talked to himself.

"At first I didn't think I had a prayer of sitting in this Oval office swivel chair. On the side, I quietly hedged my bets and continued to work on my plan to build a classy Belladonna Hotel in Moscow Square. I knew the campaign over the ensuing six months would enhance my brand, no matter whether I won or lost.

"One small regret... I wish that Russian businessman Joseph Borsch with ties to the mob and who drew up a proposal to license the Belladonna name to an office tower in Moscow hadn't sent an email to my personal lawyer, Roger Yikes. Stupid! He wrote, 'I will get Putin on this program and we will get Hands elected . . . he can become president of the USA and we can engineer it. I will get all of Putin's team to buy in on this.' That little leak caused me nothing but grief.

"Looking back on my campaign, I give myself an A++. Not since my hero Andrew Jackson swept the election back in the 1800's, when he did a great job, has anyone run a campaign like mine. They say mine was even better than his. I stormed the Republican Party like that actor in the movie Attila the Hun. Then I scaled the Capitol before they knew what hit 'em. Honestly, I couldn't believe how easily all my opposition scattered and fell by the wayside - like bowling pins.

"A few things worked in my favor. Thanks to Billy Brickell's work behind the scenes, the American people were tired of government grid lock under Obama. Smart woman to back me. She knew I could just as easily have run as a democrat.

"Music to her ears, I told her I would self-finance my campaign. Told the public the same thing. I made as much mileage as I could from free TV, radio and news-print coverage. I knew that if I could create enough disruption and outlandish statements, they would have to give me free airtime. It was a win-win situation. Their viewer ratings soared. Eventually, the big-ticket Republican donors stepped up to assure my victory and more in the Senate. And, thanks to Citizens United's 2010 Supreme Court decision, money from wealthy donors and corporations poured into my campaign in record amounts.

"Hmm, how would I rate myself on the first few years on the job? Probably a B+.

"I was a little new to the job, a little new to the profession, and we had a little disappointment for the first year and a half. People that should have stepped up did not step up. They didn't step up, and they should have. So things were a little chaotic. Great leaders are hard for underlings to understand sometimes.

"In my first year, it's definitely fake news that the Wall Street Journal claimed my administration suffered an unprecedented level of key staff turnover in the modern era, with a rate of turnover twice as high as any other presidency in the past 40 years. And those guys at Forensic News don't know how to add. They claimed that in my first 1,095 days in office, 489 top officials left their positions. Whatever the real number, that one is an exaggeration. They were all losers. And many we didn't need anyway, so why bother to replace them? I don't get enough credit for saving the government a lot of money.

"Awkwardly for me, a lot of my supporters got indicted and some went to jail. Who knew that it was illegal for foreign nations to contribute to American campaigns, including opposition research? If I had to do it again, I would accept foreign intelligence on a candidate opposing me. Gotta get useful intelligence wherever you can discover or fabricate it. That's what made that Machiavelli guy so successful.

"When I heard illegal immigration had cost the nation as much as $275 billion when you add in incarceration, border security, welfare, black-market income, and all that jazz, I knew I had a campaign platform. Can you believe that? No wonder my beautifully cultivated slogans played so well: 'Drain the Swamp, Make America Great Again and Lock Her Up' played well to a lot of ears. People could read into it whatever they wanted. Pissed off a lot of liberals who tried to turn down the noise with claims like 'When hasn't America been great?' A harder sell.

"Ok, let's examine my domestic policies. I think I'd give myself an A-.

"I'm particularly proud that President Hands—pardon me, I like to refer to myself in the third person—created the President's Commission on Combating Drug Addiction and the Opioid Crisis and requested twenty-seven point eight billion in drug-control efforts. Believe it or not, I got bipartisan support on that one! I also took the drug manufacturers behind the woodshed for a good spanking.

"Shameful how the doctors let prescription of opioids lead to more than a hundred and thirty deaths per day in the United States. That's more lives than we lost in the Middle East conflicts, and about as many citizens who lose their lives in motor vehicle crashes. So, it was about time the nation realized it had an internal war at home to fight against the medical industry and their lobbyists.

"My handling of the virus, one of the largest global outbreaks in over one hundred years, was stellar given the circumstances. I boldly challenged the individual states and local medical communities to do what was right to save the lives of their citizens. They know better than the federal government where and when to lock down the population. And, it's just fake news that had I acted sooner, over 30,000 lives could have been saved. The Democrats can't point the blame on me. Blame it on the Chinese.

"I finally accomplished the greatest tax reform ever. Much, much bigger, much better than anybody. In their excitement, the Republican Party wet their pants. I could do no wrong as long as I protected their wallets and private industry, like FedEx. My tax cuts put one point five billion dollars to FedEx's bottom line in the sweep of a pen! Now that's political power and a lot of good will with the people who count. Movers and shakers. I gave the American people the greatest tax cuts ever, and they loved me. Nobody's seen anything like it. My tax action should preserve some congressional seat votes for my friends and Electoral College votes for the party:

"Only George Washington appointed more Supreme Court judges than me. I truly made my people happy by packing the federal courts with conservatives.

"I've made lifetime friends with the right to lifers. No president has ever done what I have done for evangelicals or religion itself. It's not even close! If you take care of that evangelical base, they will take good care of you. Why, even my good friend, Art Pigeon, the former Texas governor and then U.S. Secretary of Energy, told me that I was the chosen one. I'm not bragging. I'm sure I don't have to tell any of my voters the implications of his gracious comment. Many in QAnon agree with Pigeon. God, I love 'em.

"I will go down in history for so many fine things, particularly my use of technology. FDR was the first to use the radio for his fireside chats. Kennedy was the first to wow the electorate over television. And I will be remembered as a professional at technology and the Luke Skywalker of the internet, the first to win the Oval Office with a blitzkrieg of tweets. My people loved them because they didn't want details or facts to get in the way of the message. Until I came along, Reagan was viewed as the Great Communicator. Made him look like a freshman.

"Republican Congress is thrilled with my unheralded brashness. Billy Brickell just hand delivered a bottle of Jack for ending the Population Census early. That action should also help save some congressional seats and set back the Dems. If I had let the Census drag on, it would have counted more of the estimated 40% who have yet to respond or be contacted, a good share of them minorities...no doubt screaming liberals.

"Nobody, but nobody, has done more for black Americans than me. They tried to push me into a corner because I didn't attend Congressman John Lewis's funeral or visit him when he lay in state in the Rotunda. But he didn't come to my inauguration.

"My contributions to the balance of trade are unequaled. I still can't figure out why Ferret and Opossum News had the audacity to report that I made false claims about the effect of the U.S. tariffs I've put into effect without checking with me first. I thought those people had more sense and were on my side. I'll get my people to straighten their people out on the details of our achievements.

"I have two major regrets. Some people claimed that President Hands failed to use his words carefully regarding immigrants and Latin Americans. After the anti-Hispanic manifesto of a shooter who killed twenty-two people and wounded another two dozen in El Paso, the press and Democrats pinned the blame on me. Some nerve they had the to say I inflamed racial division and encouraged white supremacists. I can tell you that's definitely fake news!

"Another piece of fake news contended that research showed that counties that hosted a Hands rally saw a two hundred and twenty-six-percent increase in hate crimes. How could that be? They can't fool me. I know how figures lie and liars figure.

"Then word started to circulate that I was in bed with Senate majority leader Moscow Billy who repeatedly blocked discussion of major gun-control legislation and prevented a vote on the Senate floor. On the same weekend as the El Paso shooting, my good buddy Billy tweeted an image of a tombstone bearing her opponent's name in the senate primary race in West Virginia. Talk about bad timing . . . you just can't make this shit up! Tweeting has the same effect as drinking too much alcohol. Some people can't handle it. Poor Billy. And shortly afterwards she tripped on her own patio and broke a shoulder.

"Undeservedly, my West Virginia sidekick and I were cast in history as the two trigger-happy politicians who didn't do enough to stop mayhem and slaughter. Opponents asserted that we were protecting the NRA. How was I to know they would spend $55 million on elections, including $30 million to support me? They alleged Billy received more than $1.3 million over her lifetime. Of course, this can't be true.

"I do have recurring nightmares that I am inside Walmart looking down the barrel of a white supremacist who mistakes me for a Latino. Then I take comfort that my blessed Secret Service watches over me. I always wave at them. I never seen so many guys with machine guns in my life. Nicest machine guns I've ever seen. Secret Service and military, these are great people, and they don't play games. They don't like waves; they don't even smile. Just like me, they take their job seriously. They do a nice job of protecting President Hands from anarchy.

"I've got one more assessment to make…foreign affairs. Hmm. I think I earn a solid A.

"I mean no other president has had the balls to fly to North Korea and meet with Kim Jong-un to resume peace talks. I wonder when the little bastard will come to his senses. My wall on the border sends a loud message to those countries south of the border who encourage their worst elements to come to the U.S. None of my predecessors had the moxie to tell NATO members they weren't paying their fair share. Or, to pull out of the U.N. climate change agreement. Not since Reagan has any other president reached out to the Russians with an olive branch. And they were all afraid to put America first ahead of the rest of the world. I fixed that!

As Little Big Hands admired his report card on his first term as Commander in Chief, he basked in the glory of his amazing station in life, holder of the highest office in the land. He asked himself, should I run for a second term? Trusting his instincts above all others' advice and counsel, he called for a press conference.

Since his press secretary had been forced to resign for committing perjury under oath at a congressional hearing, President Hands stood before a room filled with carefully vetted and supportive reporters from Ferret and Opossum News. With smiling faces, lights glaring, and cameras focused, they eagerly awaited his pronouncements.

True to form, his recall of the past presidents' visits had become blurred and sketchy. In the pit of his stomach, he couldn't shake nagging feelings that their business with him remained unfinished.

Holding the dual office of president and press secretary, Little Big Hands began, "I am pleased to inform you that President Daniel Hands will run for reelection. No one has accomplished as much as Hands in the last few years. His people frequently tell him that he may be the greatest president since George Washington. But Washington was flawed—he decided not to run again after his term expired. Although Lincoln is also to be admired, he put himself in jeopardy by going to that damn theater. Poor judgment, in my opinion.

"I have even bigger plans for this great country. Soon I will be telling you more about them. And whatever the other news networks might have said about my absence the last couple of weeks, remember, my good friends, they are enemies of the people. I'm here to assure you that their wildly absurd speculations about my state of mind are pure rubbish."

Then POTUS fell back on his familiar campaign format . . . a vitriol of hatred and divisiveness, bullying the weak, poor, and people of color, and passing the blame for his inadequacies on others. He employed a racist vocabulary that he knew appealed to a small segment of an aging, conservative, white population and resonated with an aimless younger generation.

One reporter remarked to a companion that the last time he saw a performance like this was in an old newsreel of Adolf Hitler rallying ugly crowds in the Nuremberg stadium.

On the campaign trail, POTUS trumpeted his hatred of minorities and people who opposed him. He singled out six new congressmen and women who he claimed were critical of America. In a stadium in Atlanta, he suggested that if they didn't like it here, they should go back to their own country. Then, with a glow of satisfaction and a smug smile, he orchestrated the crowd into chants of "Send them back" and "Lock them up."

He'd failed to do his homework. Five of the six newly minted congressmen were born in the U.S. Although he unwittingly patronized a small base of his electorate—white nationalists and neo-Nazi thugs—what he really meant was "If you don't like *me*, you should leave the country." Two days later, he recanted that he approved the crowd's nasty behavior. He even tried to reinvent history by saying he'd tried to stop them. Of course, the evidence proved otherwise.

Desperate to win, POTUS scrambled to contrive new last-minute initiatives that might sway some voters. Most of his past ones succumbed to the law of unintended consequences, like his tax cut that had sent the federal deficit soaring. The deficit left the atmosphere when the government, out of necessity, started dispensing subsidies to those out of work because of Covid-19.

One last minute initiative had some real possibilities and might be a really big deal. A major foreign policy victory. Both sides of the aisle sung praises. Even the liberal press. He had pressured and brokered a peace initiative between Israel and the United Arab Emirates. The potential for such an agreement could reduce conflict and perhaps pave the way to eventual peace in the Middle East. It deservedly turned a lot of heads. But it was only an agreement in principal. The devil would certainly be in the details. Skeptics doubted he had the skilled diplomats remaining in his administration to bring it to fruition. His escapades with North Korea had little to show for it. But optimists remained enthusiastic and encouraged.

In his next big undertaking, Little Big Hands startled the nation when he eliminated over-time work at the post office and announced his decision to hold back their resources. To say grace over the whole sordid affair, he appointed Shane Dickens Postmaster General and Chief Executive Officer over the world's largest postal organization.

Neither understood the intricacies of the federal post office nor that it was a public service that was never intended to make a profit. But then again, Dickens knew who buttered his bread and fired capable managers who did understand how the Post Office functions. In a blatant attempt to disenfranchise voters, he reduced post office hours. Next he hauled off hundreds of high-speed mail sorting machines and even more stand-alone blue postal boxes that been entrenched in plazas and neighborhoods for decades. Dickens, more oligarch than manager, began to run the post office like a private enterprise for profit. Questions of conflict of interest appeared as a result of his connections to a post office contractor. Then disaster struck. Delivery of the mail backlogged. Medical prescriptions for seniors and veterans ran late. Social Security checks and stock dividends were delayed. And invoices arrived after their due dates.

In a not so subtle attempt to impair mail-in ballots, POTUS's timing could not have been more consequential or move visible. Nancy Pilar, Speaker of the U.S. House called all members back from August vacation to address the calamity caused by the choke hold POTUS and his minion had placed on the U.S. postal system. Cornered, Dickens vowed not to make any more changes to the post office until after the election. But the scars remained because a number of those high-speed sorting machines had been deliberately destroyed. In August, just three months away from election day, Dickens also raised the cost of postage to cities and states for mail in ballots. Dickens was called to testify before the House and Senate and twenty state attorneys general said they would file lawsuits.

As the campaign drew to a close, the nation sensed a bad moon on the rise. Another term for Little Big Hands would take the country down a path the Founding Fathers had tried to prevent with a system of checks and balances when they framed the Constitution.

Little Big Hands seemed invincible. He was now being called the Teflon president by his admirers because no matter what offenses he was accused of—bribery, rape, racial hatred, bigotry, campaign interference, a long record of outright lies, and perjury . . . nothing seemed to stick.

The Netis, the populist, ultraconservative group that splintered off the Tea Party and had marshaled enough electoral college votes to get Little Big Hands elected the first time, backed his reelection with hardly a second thought. They were about winning at all costs and preserving political power, however abusive, malignant, and corrupt.

Bravely putting the nation ahead of their party affiliations, only a handful of Neti Pot congresspeople spoke out against him.

And those who did were punished by the Senate majority leader. Billy Brickell pledged that she would use all the PAC money at her disposal to unseat them when it came time for them to run again for office. She also revoked their seats on various committees. It raised questions. To what extent can democracy be bought? And is democracy for sale?

To gain power, both parties spent desperately and with abandon for the opportunity to govern the country. Newspapers, magazines, broadcast, and adverting industries happily harvested the crop of campaign dollars. Never in the history of the country had so many funds been thrown at an election.

But things began to crumble for President Little Big Hands when a former US senator and Neti Pot Wing founder broke from the ranks. Now William Rankels, the host of a popular conservative weekly talk show broadcast throughout the South on politics, race, and religion, had this to say about Little Big Hands, his former friend and political crony:

"I've examined my soul and repent the hateful rhetoric I've spewed in the past about President Daniel Hands's political opponents. Now I recognize that he is a racial arsonist who cleverly supports bigotry and hatred of foreigners to gain election at any expense.

"Hands is careless on fiscal matters. He doesn't understand the complexity of border issues. He circumvents the rule of law; he's ill-informed on international trade; and he misinterprets and misapplies his executive powers.

"To end the division and derision, we require a candidate who can look Little Big Hands squarely in the eye and say, we've had enough of your indecency. We are through with your lies, bullying, and cruelty. We cannot tolerate your insults, your daily drama, your incitement. You place this country in jeopardy every single day. All this has to end. The country cannot endure four more years of you."

How would the vote turn out? Would party loyalists and the independents who could swing the vote discredit Rankels's remarks as just another disgruntled politician who didn't get a cabinet seat?

Would entrenched supporters, bent on winning at all costs, ignore the evidence and still find Little Big Hands fit for office to accomplish their limited agenda? Would the twenty-first century spell the end of history's greatest democracy? Would the motto on the Great Seal of the United States, *E Pluribus Unum*, fall like an ancient monument crumbling in the parched desert of what was once a fertile land?

SCENARIO ONE

There was nothing POTUS liked better than a good fight. He and the faithful enthusiastically set out to discredit William Rankels, the political commentator and disparage Eileen Choy Springer, of Asian American heritage, his opposition for the presidency. She was backed by the new Centralist Coalition Party made up of Republicans and Democrats who were compassionate conservatives.

Eileen grew up in Mississippi. She played volleyball and graduated from Ole Miss. Gifted, she spoke six languages fluently, including Chinese, Russian, Spanish, Arabic, and French. While at Ole Miss, she was recruited for the Olympic team because of her leadership on the court, her hustle, and her outsized ability to spike the ball.

At the head of her class, Eileen took a law degree at Georgetown University and then clerked for Ruther Bader Ginsburg, an associate justice of the Supreme Court. While working for a law firm, she defended Planned Parenthood in a renewed attack from the Neti Pot Wing that went all the way to the Supreme Court. Her victory in the case secured a woman's right to choose and propelled her to national prominence.

Exhibiting a head for business and executing an odd twist in her career, she rose to Chief Legal Counsel for Caterpillar Inc., a large multinational corporation. How that happened defies understanding. It must have had something to do with her language skills and the need to diversify the executive offices.

During a primary debate while running for the US Senate, Springer said, "While at Caterpillar I lobbied for more women to be appointed senior managers, to join the board of directors, and to become Caterpillar dealer principals. History shows that corporate stocks perform better with more women in responsible positions." That experience in diversity and leadership became a springboard to winning a US Senate seat from Illinois.

The Centralist Coalition's message during the presidential campaign conveyed a balanced perspective that acknowledged the strongest and wealthiest in the nation have an obligation to care for the weakest but must not be taxed so excessively that they become weakened, nor lose their entrepreneurial incentives. The Coalition spent most of their time and money to explain what they stood for and how they would mend the nation's problems and build a bridge to a brighter future. They pledged to not run a negative campaign and, for the most part adhered to that pledge. They were content to let POTUS shoot himself in the foot with his ugly rhetoric, antics, distortions and lies that he spread on the campaign trail. Spewing one incomprehensible tweet after another, he singled handedly ran a negative campaign against himself.

For his part, Little Big Hands and Billy Brickell pursued the same strategy and tactics that helped them win in the last time. Destroy Springer's reputation and that of others who stood in his way. Sling as much mud as possible at the opposition. They believed that the public loved the mudslinging arena and game show mentality because that currency livened up the contest and held their constituents' limited attention spans.

Little Big Hands started his campaign run with his usual dosage of innuendos. He pursued the same old dirty tactics with the hackneyed line "Some people say…" His most recent, "Some people say that Springer is ineligible to run for office because her parents were immigrants." For Hands and Brickell capturing a second term was about the win and ego rather than morality.

POTUS and many of his allies had long ago concluded that morality in government no longer existed and that truth was rarely a politician's objective. Power is the grand prize.

The leaders of the Neti Pot Wing used the familiar instruments of power mastered by dictators around the globe who clung to their office for years. This was their creed:

"Your message doesn't have to be true—only believable.

"When unfortunate or negative truth arises about you, blanket it with disinformation.

"To hold on to power, cultivate a mob-loyalty mentality among staff and subordinates, including the military.

"Whenever possible, consolidate your power by denigrating and eliminating opposing voices. Attack the press.

"Protect your political base by manipulating voting through intimidation and restrictions directed at minorities and dissenters."

To splinter the Democratic ticket and in effect peel votes away from Springer, POTUS and company arranged to get divisive candidates on the ballot to run in swing states as independents. Ones, like a popular but mentally ill performer, that might sway minority voters inclined to be more liberal. In truth, this insidious maneuver revealed the Neti Pot Wing's disrespect for the intelligence of minorities. With mixed success, they also tried to purge the polls of registered voters to suppress eligible minorities and naturalized immigrants. Infamously, Texas removed ninety-five thousand registered voters in 2019.

Judges ruled that the Texas Secretary of State's shenanigans were deceptive and partisan. Subsequently, Texas was forced to reinstate tens of thousands eligible voters.

The timing of Madison Treacher's suspension as the head of Liberty University, a Christian focused campus, was unfortunate. Treacher had endorsed Little Big Hands during his last campaign. He fervently supported POTUS and compared him to Jesus, excusing any un-Christian behavior. His endorsement became instrumental in bringing other evangelical Christians on board. A sordid and embarrassing tryst had gone public. He also foolishly posted a video of himself with an arm around a woman with both of their pants unzipped. Some evangelicals began to wonder about a double standard. If Treacher was fired over an amorous liaison, perhaps Little Big Hands should have been removed from office for the bribe he paid to silence a sexual escapade before his previous election.

During the week of the Republican National Convention to nominate POTUS for a second term, an unheralded natural disaster occurred in the Gulf of Mexico. Two overlapping hurricanes appeared is if to make a plea for climate control to protect the environment. Laura, whose winds gusted up to 132 miles per hour, sent a half million people scrambling for shelter. In the process it knocked down a tall monument to Confederate soldiers in Calcasieu Parish, La.

Simultaneously, some of the worst fires in California raged throughout the state. San Francisco was blanketed in smoke. As clearly as possible, Mother Nature had sent her apocalyptic message to the American people. Was she sending a warning about the consequences of re-electing POTUS?

The last night of the Convention, Little Big Hands violated all propriety by accepting the nomination on the White House grounds. The whole spectacle looked like a carnival, complete with fireworks on the Mall. He turned the People's House into a political site, a clear violation of the Hatch Act. Understanding its symbolism, no other president in modern history had stooped to using it for blatant personal gain. Worse yet, he spoke to over a thousand people seated close together on the lawn, most not wearing masks and ignoring the threat of Covid-19.

Just weeks before the election, Little Big Hands's campaign crew staged a big indoor rally for him in Nevada. His ally, Ms. Annie Oakely Remington at Ferret News attended. She was horrified to witness an event that mocked social distancing in the heart of the pandemic. Thousands of the party faithful were packed close together in a corporate owned warehouse. Most followed their leader who disdained wearing a mask.

Afterwards, she cornered POTUS and asked him "Why aren't you subject to Nevada's fifty person gathering cap?" In true dictator form, he answered "I don't think the rule applies to the President. And, their Democratic Governor deliberately suppressed the will of the people by forbidding us to hold an outdoor rally."

Remington continued to press POTUS. She said "There's new information that you knew about the severity of Covid-19 in late January yet played it down to the American people. Can you explain why you put us all at risk and did nothing?"

Unabashedly, Little Big Hand's reaffirmed he did know more than he let on. He said "I didn't want to panic the country. In that regard, I compare myself to Churchill. You know…a cheerleader."

That evening, POTUS's former ally, Remington, broadcast this live across America: "President Daniel Hands just showed us his true character. He put politics before medical science. Hundreds of those in attendance may come down with Covid-19 and become too sick to vote. When they go home, they will spread the misery around. This man does not care. He has turned the party faithful into sacrificial lambs to gain a second term.

"The President tells me that he believes his primary role is that of a cheer leader during our war against a global virus. He says he models himself after Winston Churchill during the blitz of London during WWII. Well I've got news for him!

Churchill was far more than a cheerleader. He took action. He applied leadership to establish bunkers throughout London and elsewhere and oversaw the creation of elaborate early warning and defense systems.

"During his rally today, Hands suggested that if he wins, he will try to negotiate with Congress and the American people a third term. Our President thinks he may be entitled on the basis of his phenomenal record. Ladies and Gentlemen, I've sadly concluded that Hands isn't even qualified for a second term. I am resigning from Ferret News. I can no longer support my employer's propaganda. Good Night and Good Luck. God Bless America."

Finally Little Big Hands's reckless disregard of protective masks during his re-election campaign caught up with him. At an exclusive reception for a newly minted Supreme Court Justice in the Rose Garden, POTUS's anointed elite sat elbow to elbow to worship their leader's success in purging the courts of liberals and moderates. Most believed they were impervious in the presence of their leader. Their house of cards came tumbling down as Covid-19 claimed victims. A little over three weeks before the final debate, Little Big Hands caught the virus along with family members and others in his inner circle. A flurry of news media speculated that Little Big Hands knew he had contracted the virus and continued to expose others while promoting and glorifying himself. World class medical treatment, including some costly drugs not available to his minions, enabled the president to recover in time to contest Springer on the national stage.

On the day of the election, the Neti Pot Wing attempted to close the polls early wherever they could, particularly in red states. Except for Florida, they challenged mail in ballots, claiming fraud and ballot stuffing. Little evidence existed that such foul play occurred. Bar coded ballots made it difficult to cheat. The Neti Pot Wing sought injunctions and demanded recounts. The popular vote showed Springer had won by several million votes, but the electoral college only slightly favored her. The resulting political gridlock threw the whole election into disarray. Riots cropped up around the country, flamed by extremists from both parties.

Clearly the election was going to take months to determine a winner. POTUS and the Senate advocated that he serve as president until the mess could be sorted out. Of course, the House called foul. The Supreme Court stepped in.

The Court determined that Little Big Hands and his VP could no longer serve in office beyond noon on January 20th. because that was when their term of office expired. The only solution the judges could come up with was that if the president and vice president couldn't serve, then during the interim the U.S. Constitution calls for Nancy Pilar, Speaker of the House to assume office. The court ruled that another election must be held within three months. It's too early to speculate on whether POTUS would prevail or new leadership.

SCENARIO TWO

During the campaign, Little Big Hands employed every trick in his political play book to distract the American people from condemning him for one of the worst economies in American history. It produced the greatest decline in GDP and over 200,000 Americans died in a pandemic. POTUS said, "It is, what it is." He surrendered rather than fight the virus which proved beyond his wherewithal. To appeal to his now dwindling white evangelical base, he beat the drums as loud as he could on immigration, trade war, the second amendment, and the enemies from within: Muslims, civil right protestors, right to lifers, ballot stuffing and mail in voting. He used scare tactics and warned his constituents that social despots would control their lives and rob their children's inheritance.

Why Little Big Hands had remained popular with a lot of polite Southerners for so long defied understanding. Historically the South resented anyone who lacked manners, disrespected women, feigned religion, lacked sensitivity and refinement, and valued money over all else. Perhaps POTUS's reputation as a fighter appealed to a "Southern Scotch-Irish" element that loved a good fight and admired anyone who told the establishment 'Screw You!' Now his administration had become the establishment tainted by inflated promises, corruption, and incompetence.

The people had become fed up with his conspiracy theories that had begun with President Obama having been born in

Kenya. His most recent…a massive explosion of volatile ammonia nitrates recklessly stored in a warehouse for years in Beirut had been caused by terrorists. None of his intelligence officers supported his sensational speculation.

The Lincoln Project, a group of dedicated Americans who held accountable those who violated their oath to the Constitution and put others before Americans, endorsed Democratic candidate Springer for president. The irony is that most of the influential, wealthy and vocal membership were registered Republicans. They pledged to defeat President Hands and put an end to heavy "Handism." Their endorsement precipitated a chain reaction of compassionate conservatives bent on casting their ballots for Springer. For many, this was the first time they had ever voted for a Democrat! They had just had enough!

To deflect any criticism that might tie directly to him, Little Big Hands announced in one of his many campaign rallies that if he got re-elected, he might replace his whole cabinet. Essentially he tried to infer that if deficiencies existed in his government, others were to blame. This news shocked discerning voters. It sent a loud message that the job was too big for POTUS. He lacked the ability to select, manage, and retain talented people in his administration.

During the fall campaign, Vice President Warbucks, aka Morebucks, finally got indicted for accepting bribes while serving as governor of Louisiana. Shortly afterwards, the Louisiana State Attorney who had been investigating Little Big Hands for tax fraud announced that he might be facing criminal charges based on bank records and other documents the court just allowed to be released. Then Timothy Justin Fannon, who served POTUS as chief architect in charge of his bid for president in his first campaign and later as White House Chief strategist, was charged with fraud in the Let's Build A Wall Campaign. He was accused in a scheme to use funds designated for construction for personal expenses. The high living, flamboyant bad boy was seized on board a $35 million yacht which belonged to an exiled Chinese businessman. Fannon, who aligned himself with a loose network of groups who promote white identity, joined a long list of associates charged with federal crimes. The Swamp continued to leak from the White House.

Little Big Hands found himself on a political roller coaster with no peaks. It was downhill all the way from there. Facebook removed or restricted QAnon accounts and other far right groups from its social network. Next, it labeled dangerous individuals and organizations that threatened democracy by shutting down more than 1,000 pages and groups for militia activity and encouraging riots and mayhem. Instagram followed suit. These actions were taken shortly after POTUS had said on national TV that if QAnon liked him, then he liked them. He had followed it with a disclaimer that he didn't know much about the group even though it been had been spreading misinformation for several years related to what members called a "deep state" conspiracy against him. The cult like group also claimed that government insiders were involved in child sex trafficking and cannibalism.

Meanwhile comedians mercilessly haunted POTUS every evening during the campaign. One quipped "What will Little Big Hands's presidential library contain after he's booted from office? Answer: A putting green, recipes for chocolate cake, a live Twitter feed for visitors to post on, and a little black book with phone numbers of porn stars." The nation desperately needed a laugh because four years of POTUS had left a trail of tears.

Judicial Watch, a conservative tax-exempt group, published that POTUS's golf outings had topped a $110 million after thirty months into his presidency. To his ire, they pointed out that was more than President Obama spent over his first two full terms on travel!

The roller coaster POTUS rode continued on its plunge when Twitter and Facebook removed his posts because of a potentially deadly and misleading claim he made concerning children and Covid-19.

Just as chilling, a bipartisan Senate report shocked skeptics. Over the last four years, there had been few things Republicans and Democrats agreed upon. The report confirmed that personnel on Little Big Hands's previous campaign did have contacts with the Russians. The findings supported the Millert Report and added new information about communications between Little Big Hands's associates and Russian officials during and after the campaign.

Just a few weeks ahead of the election, Roger Yikes, Little Big Hands's private attorney, released a new tell all book. The details, events, and behaviors shocked the American people. The explicit portrait of Little Big Hands as a reprobate caused a lot of Neti Pot Wing members to wonder just what kind of man they had put in office and what the consequences might be of reelecting the occupant of 1600 Pennsylvania Avenue. As expected, the more cynical came to POTUS's defense, contending the attorney was just trying to even the score because Little Big Hands didn't grant him a parole.

POTUS's campaign took another punch when a secretly recorded audio tape made headline news. Penelope Hands could clearly be heard to say in a conversation that her younger brother lacked principles and that he was cruel and a liar.

The cruelness factor got magnified when Little Big Hands called those who died in military action 'losers' and those who served 'suckers.' When he was in Paris he declined to visit the nearby Aisne-Marine American Cemetery. Eighteen hundred legendary Marines and their Allies were buried there. They had sacrificed their lives in Belleau Woods halting the advance of German troops on Paris in WWI. Suggesting that it wasn't worth his time to honor them, he labeled them 'losers' for getting killed. He even wondered "Who were the good guys in this war?" In the pivotal moment his unseemly utterances became public knowledge during the heart of his reelection campaign, POTUS lost support from the majority of outraged veterans and active military. No other president in the history of the United States had ever spoken despairingly about military honor and duty.

On the matter of the mysterious taxes that POTUS refused to divulge, the New York times reported they had received information on good authority that Little Big Hands had paid no federal taxes in ten of the last fifteen years prior to the last election. And only $750 in the year he had won election and the same the following year. Disenchanted voters quickly noted that Little Big Hands had paid his mistress far more money that he had paid Uncle Sam for services rendered.

Although still quite confident he would win, Little Big Hands contrived with Senate Majority Leader Billy Brickell a secret contingency plan to steal the election in the event they lost the electoral college vote. Without a speck of evidence, they decided to shamelessly lie to sympathetic ears that the election was rigged against them. After all, they knew all the ins and outs of manipulating elections from their success in 2016. POTUS and Brickell thought that if they could cast enough suspicion and salt on America's democratic election processes dating back to 1798, they could persuade state leaders to throw out the will of the people and cast electoral college votes in their favor. Both were desperate. If returned to private life, they feared a long series of criminal charges that threatened to put them behind bars wearing one piece orange suits.

***

Eileen Springer's talent, and thus her victory, lay in her ability to unite rather than divide the American people. Unlike Little Big Hands, who spewed out the message that America was a mess, she talked about what was good and possible. Her vision for what could be accomplished during her term in office focused on shared values and what made us similar as a people rather than different.

More importantly, she campaigned on a history of integrity and truthfulness. In a final debate with Little Big Hands, she had plenty of ammunition to keep him ducking and dancing. But what really won it for her was her honesty and the importance she put on having lost and won, just like Lincoln, several different political offices during her rise to the top. She said, "Frankly, without those losses, I never would have learned what it takes to become successful and genuine."

With a daring sense of humor during the last debate, Senator Springer looked POTUS in the face and said, "President Pinocchio, you have a documented history of lying to suit your purposes and those of your special interest groups. It's time for you to leave the public and political arena. Don't stumble on the way out!" Then, looking straight out at the audience, she touched her hand to her nose and drew it straight out, to roars of laughter. That gesture resonated in the voters' minds. In the campaign posters it spawned, POTUS was portrayed as a Pinocchio cartoon. They were immediately sought after by collectors of political memorabilia.

She pledged that she would not play Russian roulette with the Coronavirus like her adversary, Little Big Hands. She chastised him for entertaining a 'herd immunity' solution that could conceivably claim over two million lives. Springer condemned him for listening to a neuroradiologist from Stanford's conservative Hoover Institution who advocated this solution. It resonated with the American people when she said, "You wouldn't go to a radiologist to replace a hip, why would you listen to one to solve an epidemic rather than an infectious disease expert?

"If elected your kids will not be asked to go back into school classrooms until we can make them safe from Covid-19. Somehow, someway we will find a way to take care of you if you can't work because you need to help your child with home schooling. Of course, we can't rob Peter to pay Paul forever. But, I think when we can get back to something close to pre-Coronavirus employment, the economy will accelerate our recovery. I may have to raise taxes but I think you will understand. If we are lucky, my ambitious plans to overhaul our nation's aging infrastructure may help generate many years of full employment that helps bring down the national debt to a tolerable level."

POTUS scrambled to save his political life and centered his campaign on quelling the riots occurring throughout the summer and into the fall. Throwing red meat to his political base, he blamed the rise in crime on democratically controlled cities like Detroit, Chicago, and Portland. He had the audacity to suggest that a young white man with an AR-15 style rifle who killed two unarmed people and injured a third in a protest march against police brutality in Kenosha, Wisconsin, might be an action in self- defense. Others wondered how a seventeen-year-old got his hands on an automatic rifle and how was he raised. Springer countered that Little Big Hands was the one to blame for fomenting the riots with his policies and tweets and that he was using these scare tactics to unite his party.

In truth, Springer's beliefs were more those of a moderate Republican. She had the common sense to know that the nation could do more to help the poor, but that the poor also needed to help themselves by taking advantage of programs that offered opportunities to improve themselves. As a senator, she had blocked a push by the extreme left wing to pass a bill for universal basic income like that of many Scandinavian countries. The plans in northern Europe had destroyed economic incentives to innovate and invest in the future.

In a rare and daring move for a political candidate, Springer identified during the campaign those she would invite to serve in her cabinet. A talent pool of experienced and nationally recognized professionals across a variety of fields stepped up to her clarion call to duty. Some were Hispanic, African Americans, and other skilled minorities.

All revealed their tax records in advance of the election. Most were seasoned enough to understand how to get things done in government. By boldly identifying ahead of time who she would like to have serve in her cabinet, the voters knew exactly who they'd get to help right side a sinking ship.

Once again, Little Big Hands campaign was badly wounded when the CIA caught the Russians's fingers in the election cookie jar. The proof was overwhelming. Even the Senate dared not deny it for fear of repercussions on their own reelections. Of course, POTUS disclaimed fore knowledge and did nothing to prevent it.

***

Little Big Hands challenged the outcome of the electoral votes. He claimed voter fraud and boldly declared himself the true winner. His demented mind refused to accept that he had lost re-election. Over the years, POTUS morphed into thinking himself a born winner. Evidence of five bankruptcies, multiple divorces, charges of sexual assault, myriads of failed lawsuits, and despicable allies suggested otherwise.

What happened next became one of the most bizarre and tragic times recorded in American history.

If one believes something hard enough and long enough and keeps repeating the delusion to others, isn't it true? Certainly his followers thought so. They wanted to believe POTUS. If he said he had been cheated out of winning, then they swallowed the bait like a large-mouth bass. His cadre of lawyers forced a recount of all the votes in seven key states. The results mirrored the original outcome. POTUS and his co-conspirators filed over fifty lawsuits. They were all denied for lack of credible evidence of voter tampering.

If there is any humor to be found, President Springer won the election three times in Georgia after forced computer and hand recounts. Not to be denied, Little Big Hands pushed the issue to the Supreme Court where he felt assured that the three new judges he appointed would be beholden to him. The highest court in the land wasted no time booting his unfounded claims out the door.

So, what alternative did that leave a would be dictator, tyrant and supreme ruler? The despot pursued the only avenue open to him. Little Big Hands incited a mob to riot the same day as Congress convened to bear final witness to the outcome of the election. Following two misfit senators last stand at contending the election in the congressional gathering, shortly afterwards hundreds of POTUS's loyal insurrectionists bashed down doors and broke windows to lay siege to the Capitol Building. They posed provocatively in the sanctuary of democracy. The proud boys, white supremists, and far right wing bandits exuded smiles of victory. They were sure, acting on POTUS's encouragement, they had overthrown the government and were now in control. Lives were lost.

But democracy prevailed. The National Guard helped secure the Capitol Building and surrounding grounds. Ignorantly revealing their identity, many of the invaders smugly took cell phone photos and videos which ended up on social media. With the help of video cams on the Capitol Building and reporters on the scene, hundreds were captured on film, which led to arrests and jail time for crimes against the nation.

Congressional leaders and citizens across the U.S. called for Little Big Hands to step down. He refused, and his Vice President declined to exercise the 25th Amendment. His crime committed against the most revered democracy in the world begged retribution. Wasting little time, the U.S. House of Representatives impeached him again, thus branding Little Big Hands in infamy as the foulest president in American history and the first ever to get impeached twice, all in one term.

Next, the U.S. Senate met to try Little Big Hands for high crimes and misdemeanors. This time they found him guilty. The trial's judgment was harsh. Consequently, POTUS lost his $200,000 annual pension, his $1 million a year travel allowance, his lifetime secret service protection, and his ability to ever run for president again.

As Annie Oakley Remington, the Anchor for Ferret and Opossum News, observed following the turmoil: "No one can make such outrageous stuff up. It's beyond belief!"

The six foot portrait of himself, that Little Big Hands infamously spent $20,000 dollars from his own charity to own, now hung despondently in the Oval Office. Like Oscar Wilde's villain in the book, *The Picture of Dorian Gray*, the once glamorous painting began to wither and age right in front of him. The portrait's face hardened. Its skin yellowed and wrinkled on the canvass. Its eyes squinted and became vacant. Its mouth formed a sinister smile. Its hair thinned. Its jowls on the once proud chin sagged. And, tobacco juice drizzled down from the corner of the portrait's lips.

***

Audaciously, President Springer, age fifty-five at the time of her inaugural address, told the nation, "We have been experiencing under President Daniel Hands's previous administration an epidemic of myopic, partisan ignorance. Our beloved country has been the worse for it. I believe you can be passionately pro-choice and not necessarily be pro-abortion. You can feel outraged at seeing toddlers torn from their parents and confined in cages and not support unrestricted borders. And you can call for gun laws that acknowledge the modern age, not eighteenth- and nineteenth-century times, and yet support the Second Amendment."

Many formerly divisive heads began to nod in agreement.

During her inaugural address, President Springer said, "The vaccine for ridding the nation of another kind of malady—Little Big Hands—was found at the ballot box. I want to thank the American people for immunizing themselves from another four years of his chaotic administration and giving me the opportunity to serve. I promise you I can do better. But I won't mislead you. He was a disease that destroyed bridges and created a lot of ill will here and around the world. Please give me time to restore the nation's vitality and relationships."

The Republican Party and their Neti Pot Wing retained only eleven percent of their seats in the House and seventeen percent in the Senate. The Free Ticket Wing on the far left retained even fewer seats. This was only the second time in the history of the United States that an independent had won the election. George Washington was the first, and eventually became known as a Federalist. There was no disputing that Eileen easily won both the electoral and popular votes.

Was this extreme revulsion and rejection of POTUS, the Neti Pot Wing, and the Senate Majority Leader from West Virginia a final cleansing of a morally defective regime and one without compromise? Only time will tell.

***

By the way, Ms. Billy Brickell, the Senate Majority Leader and a close ally of POTUS, fled the country rather than stand trial before a jury of her peers on charges of conflicts of interest and perjury. While she led the senate, her husband's frequent dealings with China raised serious concerns. Brickell went down in infamy as a conspirator in President Hands's administration.

Just a few weeks before the election, Brickell's duplicity and hypocrisy in accelerating the process for Ruth Bader Ginsburg's replacement on the Supreme Court symbolized everything wrong with politics. Many people remembered toward the end of the Obama administration Brickell had blocked an appointment. She pompously declared then that no "Supreme Court Justice should be voted upon in the Senate until after we have installed a new president. Let the will of the people decide at the polls."

Brickell's replacement for the Senate seat, Val Antrom, was quoted as saying that everything wrong in Washington began with the Republican Senate Majority Leader from Georgia decades ago. Antrom added that it continued with Brickell, who blindly emulated him.

Drawing upon a quote from Winston Churchill about one of his own adversaries, Antrom said, "President Daniel Hands and Ms. Billy Brickell were united by their desire to hold office at all costs without regard to their own reputations or their country's fortunes." For obvious reasons, both were longtime foes of tougher restrictions on campaign donations. PAC money had enabled them to secure office and win the electoral vote while losing the popular vote.

Oh, what became of Vice President Warbucks, aka Morebucks? Although Little Big Hands swore that he was a fantastic person, Morebucks changed his favorite blue pinstripe suit for a penitentiary version. He got sent to the big house for thirty-five years with no possibility of parole for child molestation and rape in Palm Beach, Florida, and corruption while governor of Louisiana.

As a result of their decadent conduct in and out of office, Little Big Hands's administration would go down in history as the Marquis de Sade of the nation's capital. The new president and her husband, upon moving in, steam-cleaned and repainted the revered White House, inside and out.

***

Under Springer's leadership, a cultural change blossomed in America called the Civic Renaissance. It spawned thousands of new community organizations. They focused on healing political divides, combating homelessness, sponsoring immigrants, encouraging social mobility and fashioning new communities. These organizations stayed agile, local and tuned to those they served.

During her time in office Springer, took every opportunity she could, by word and example, to remind those serving in her administration, Congress and the American people that rudeness and kindness trickle down from above. She said "Rudeness does not have to inhabit the DNA of politics. It need not be a blood sport."

Using Little Big Hands as an example, she had plenty of illustrations to show how degrading language had divided the nation, crippled productivity and morale, increased employee turnover and fostered rudeness and hostilities toward one another.

Springer stepped into office facing a monumental task created by Little Big Hands's administration and a Senate that had forgotten how to deliberate and legislate. Under Brickell's leadership, all they had accomplished the previous four years was to advance, with any longevity, her list of preferred nominees for lifetime appointments to the federal bench.

She invited the Senate to 'swing back to the old days of more bipartisanship' and offered an olive branch to achieve reconciliation. There was plenty of work for them all to do: Reel in exploding deficits and gut-wrenching unemployment. Solve the coronavirus crisis. Fix a health care system that had gotten weaker. Address unprecedented climate change. And repair damaged international relations.

Although Utopia was never achieved, slowly President Springer transformed the political culture and the nation's children were healthier for it. Throughout her presidency and at great risk to her political career, she began to discuss candidly that Democrat and Republican political leaders rigged our political system to ensure those with power keep it...no matter what voters think.

She contended that the situation is so bad that that only about 40% of Americans trust elections. Springer, leading by example, joined the *Represent Us* movement (@represent.us) and advocated membership in this bi-partisan organization, or one like it.

She used her bully pulpit to educate citizens that if real change in government were to ever occur, it would come by passing and implementing, state by state, The American Anti-Corruption Act. If enough states took action, then she expressed confidence that the Federal government would inevitably follow suit. The aims would be to end partisan gerrymandering, ban lobbyist gifts, stop special interest groups from funding elections, put reasonable term limits on elected officials, implement Ranked Choice Voting to eliminate the spoiler effect, and realize secure voter registration.

Her efforts brought conservatives, moderates, and progressives together to fix a broken political system and preserve democracy well through the twenty first century. Following her Presidency, Springer would be remembered for her legacy as the iron lady who had the guts to change what was wrong with America at the institutional level.

Rumor has it that although the ghosts who visited President Daniel Hands couldn't agree on all these measures, every Fourth of July they light up the sky with their overall approval.

POSTSCRIPT – VISITORS'
FINAL WORDS
(January 20, 2021)

In his final act on his final full day in office, President Daniel Hands completed his pardon of over 200 individuals. While he had always framed himself as a law and order President, POTUS effectively replenished the swamp by pardoning many who obstructed justice and who were convicted of public corruption. His actions spoke loudly about himself…a man who championed weak regulation. He deemed laws an inconvenience and worked around them anyway he could. It did not occur to him that some people pardoned had not yet been charged with crimes. His pardon tainted their reputations and made them de facto above the law in the eyes of the general public.

As was his habit, during his last night in the White House, POTUS woke up at 3 am. To his admirers, he claimed that he always functioned on little sleep. The truth of the matter was that over the years a troubled mind gave him no rest. And now banned from Twitter, he fretted restlessly in bed, wondering if there was anybody else he should pardon before his term expired at noon.

Sour and bitter as ever, Little Big Hand's had defiantly declared to his loyal followers that he would not attend Springer's inauguration. After all these years, she quipped that they finally agree on something! This would be the first time in nearly 152 years that the outgoing president has not attended the inaugural of his successor.

His thoughts about who else to anoint with a pardon were suddenly interrupted by the shuffle of shoes that broke the silence in his gloomy, darkened world. The twenty-three ghosts and phantoms, who had previously visited him, formed an inescapable ring that glowed around his bed. Each had one final message for POTUS.

George Washington spoke first. "I warned you about the consequences of your despotic behavior."

Thomas Jefferson, "I counseled you not to pervert the Justice Department nor mess with the Supreme Court."

Andrew Jackson, "I shared a story with you about Aaron Burr's treasonous conduct and you didn't listen. He viewed his time in government as a sport, rather than a dedicated undertaking."

Abraham Lincoln, "I encouraged you to treat political opponents with dignity and respect."

Ulysses Grant, "I shared with you that I crushed the Ku Klux Klan and expressed concern you were opening the door for white supremacists to suppress minorities."

James Garfield, "I warned you about the perils of disputing medical science."

Teddy Roosevelt, "I showed you how your decisions about our environment would scar and spoil the earth."

Woodrow Wilson, "I gave you an opportunity to lead the nation to wellness from the Covid-19 virus. Your inactions led to the loss of tens of thousands of lives."

Calvin Coolidge, "I warned you about corruption, scandals, and fooling the public with smoke and mirrors."

Herbert Hoover, "I forewarned you about the repercussions of sparking a trade war."

Franklin Roosevelt, "I counseled you to treat the press with respect and to get them on your side to benefit the country."

Harry Truman, "I advised you not to pull out of the United Nations Human Rights Counsel and the World Health Organization. Ignorantly, you removed our UN Ambassador from serving on your cabinet. You have alienated longtime allies who fought beside us to end tyranny."

Dwight Eisenhower, "I talked to you about leadership and command. The importance of listening to your professional advisors. Instead, you cost the nation dearly by following your flawed instincts. I also shared by example how to transfer power gracefully to the next president."

John Kennedy, "I told you about the importance of a vision for the future that unites people rather than divides them. You ignored me. You ran for reelection without a platform."

Lyndon Johnson, "I shared with you my human right initiatives and caring for the poor. Your tax cuts and other actions favored the rich and privileged."

Richard Nixon, "I counseled you about bad behavior that might get you impeached. You didn't listen and became the first president in U.S. history to get impeached twice. That makes me a choir boy!"

Gerald Ford, "I warned you about the ill effects of tampering with the courts, the FBI, CIA, Department of Energy, Department of

Health and Human Services, and the Justice Departments. You've driven talented and devoted people out of government service."

Jimmy Carter, "I warned you about character, principles and putting the American people ahead of yourself."

Ronald Reagan, "I cautioned you not to get in bed with the Russians. I warned you not to continue building walls. They never last."

George H.W. Bush, "I showed you what diplomacy can do to break down hostilities and build bridges that lead to prosperity. You made a decision to become president of a political party rather than the American people."

Bill Clinton, "I warned you about your prospects for impeachment. I shared with you that if the American people believe you are truly trying to improve their lives, they extend you a measure of forgiveness. I also advised you to balance the budget."

George W. Bush, "I warned you about your lack of knowledge of American and World history. We are but one generation from losing the Republic to those who ignore history. I also advised you to treat your predecessors in office with respect, as well as those who serve you."

Barack Obama, "I admonished you for your filthy and manipulative lies. Now you have become the first president to foment and incite an insurrection. Lives have been lost. You and your allies will go down in history as swamp creatures that tried to devour our democracy. For the rest of your life, I want you to ask yourself the same question every day. If you could have glimpsed the future before you ran for office, would you have chosen to become president? Endure two impeachments, the ruin to your family and brand names, poor approval ratings, devastating lawsuits, financial losses, the avoidable deaths to Covid-19, constant ridicule from the press and nightly comedic political parodies dished out by talk show hosts Stephen Colbert, Jimmy Kimmel, Jimmy Fallon, and Seth Meyers."

After a vote among equals in the exclusive Presidents Hereafter Club, Little Big Hands was declared an outlier whose characteristics and actions serve as a stark warning for the future. In the words of Sir Winston Churchill, who was half American, they noted, "Those who fail to learn from history are destined to repeat it."

EPILOGUE

Charles Dickens wrote *A Christmas Carol* in December 1843 to enthrall his readers and creatively remind them of the importance of sensitivity, awareness, and responsiveness to the lives of those around them. In particular, he was appalled by poverty and its effect on children. He believed the only way to raise them out of the depths of despair was to ensure that they got a decent education.

The author of *Ghosts of Presidents Past: A Reckoning* drew upon aspects of Dickens's format to draw attention to how some distinguished past presidents might confront a dysfunctional one with a pathetic moral foundation, compromised integrity, and weak character. Of course, opinions vary on the matter, and none of the visitors was without flaws. Each was selected because his mark on history offered the opportunity to make a point.

Following the tradition in England, our Founding Fathers rolled out barrels of spirits on courthouse lawns and squares to attract voters to the polls on Election Day. George Washington was the first president to reward his voters. Candidates paid for votes with intoxicating beverages up to the time of Prohibition. How easy it was to buy voters then. The day after, some people might not have any recollection for whom they'd cast their ballots—and maybe they didn't care.

In *Ghosts of Presidents Past*, we have a fictional character, President Daniel Hands, who even after he has won office, never stops running. He continues to serve up another kind of liquor to woo voters. His intoxicating brew of words, ample libations of exaggerated claims, outright lies, and negative attacks cloud voters' judgments and provide cheap entertainment.

Because truth is stranger than fiction, it became relatively easy to visualize President Daniel Hands, aka Little Big Hands and POTUS, the fictional President of the United States. Can you imagine a similar character? A president who performed his job like no other could or would. Who had little grasp of the Constitution: invited the Russians to dig up dirt on his political opponent; arbitrarily imposed tariffs; broke up long-established alliances; alienated and insulted long-time allies; tore up treaties signed by his predecessor; declared a national emergency to build a wall along the Mexican border; shut down the government; overrode his admirals' and generals' traditional line of authority and expertise; concealed his taxes; divided the country with his ugly and polarizing rhetoric; held back support to the Ukraine for a political favor; muzzled members of his administration from testifying before Congress; churned over his cabinet and other key government officials at an alarming rate while claiming himself a skillful manager of people; exhibited racist tendencies; possessed a short attention span in addition to being a poor listener; assumed he was smarter than anyone else; and, worst of all, offered a poor role model for the nation's youth.

Contrast President Little Big Hands's actions with Abraham Lincoln, who knew and respected the sacrament on which our nation was conceived: the Constitution. When Lincoln became convinced that the entire democratic foundation was about to implode, he assumed unprecedented authority to wage war against the South to maintain the Union. Declaring a true national emergency, he suspended habeas corpus, created military courts to try civilians, and used his sweeping powers to justify the Emancipation Proclamation.

But as author Michael Beschloss says, "Throughout the war, Lincoln made clear that his expansion of presidential authority was intended merely for the duration of the conflict and should not be taken as a precedent either by himself in peacetime or by later presidents." Unlike President Little Big Hands, Lincoln exercised his power as Commander in Chief within the democratic process. He did not seek power for himself to satisfy any ego or clandestine purpose.

Beschloss adds, "Lincoln's leadership illustrates the overwhelming importance of political skill and preparation to hold the highest office in the land. While president, he applied his parliamentary skills to relate to Congress and to consult members when strong differences of opinion emerged. He built coalitions with Congress to help invent strategies that would restore the Union."

Here's another important contrast with our fictional president. Lincoln did not trick or lie to Congress and the American people to suit his purposes. He earnestly tried to inform and educate Americans about his actions. "His sublime abilities as a thinker and writer, his legal background, his Bible reading, and his self-acquired knowledge of history enabled him to connect his to Americans' shared historical memory, their understanding of the Constitution and their sense of morality."

Then we have our antagonist, President Little Big Hands, and presidents like John Adams, who reveal aristocratic tendencies. Thomas Jefferson and John Adams disagreed on no other issue more than the question of monarchism. "Jefferson feared that the American president yielded too much power. He also resisted the temptation to magnify the pomp and power of the office."

To safeguard their freedoms, Americans must not forget that "German Chancellor Adolf Hitler and French statesman and military leader Napoleon Bonaparte rose to power in republics whose elective powers they usurped. They lulled their power bases into complacency with trickery, false promises, and bent the established laws of the land." To gain footage, these autocrats criticized the free press and then suppressed them from telling the truth. Alarmingly, a similar beat goes on in over fifty countries today run by dictators and autocrats, including China, Cuba, Egypt, Iran, North Korea, Pakistan, Russia, Turkey, and Venezuela.

One way to safeguard our freedoms is to renew and fund the teaching of both American civics and history in the classroom. Such education will equip young people to become active, discriminating, and responsible voters. It will give them a sense of their heritage and a deep-rooted understanding of what distinguishes this great country - the sacrifices that were made by their predecessors to give them a democratic form of government.

Character is a central theme in *Ghosts of President Past* and *A Christmas Carol*. How much does character matter in the selection of a president, and how do we define, measure, and judge it? To get some answers, Jim Lehrer, an icon in the broadcasting world and host of twelve presidential debates, moderated a classic discussion titled "Character Above All" in 1996. Among the panelists were nine prominent historians, writers, and commentators, including Ben Bradlee, David McCullough, Stephen Ambrose, Michael Beschloss, Robert Dallek, James Cannon, Hendrik Hertzberg, Peggy Noonan, and Tom Wicker. Some measures they focused on included the company a person keeps, how truthful he is, how he treats others, a sense of fair play, and acceptance of personal responsibility and blame. One conclusion: a leader of inferior character can't conceal it very long.

Another way to get a glimpse of character is reflected in a new survey the military began using in 2020 to promote officers to battalion commanders. Perhaps something like this should be used for presidents too. Those who have served the candidate are asked:

Should this person be a commander? Yes/No

How well does this leader display appropriate trust in others' judgment and capabilities, giving them the latitude to exercise authority over their work?

How well does this leader confront and correct unethical behavior that does not align with the Army Values?

How well does this leader energize others by communicating clear vision and purpose for his/her mission activities?

How often does this leader lose their temper at the slightest provocation?

How often does this leader adopt a bullying style, influencing others through threat and intimidation?

How often does this leader behave in a way that makes you try or think about physically avoiding them?

***

In the spirit of free speech, not everyone will agree with all the ideas expressed in *Ghosts of Presidents Past – A Reckoning*. Whatever the reader may have taken away from this book, the author invites you to absorb and ponder these last two thoughts. One from a world-famous German author and scholar whose books were systematically burned as he was driven into exile in 1934. The other from an honored warrior and statesman who, himself, is now a significant figure in our national journey and memory. Within these two brief quotes may lie the parameters of a more united future:

> *"I have seen the great mass of ideologies grow and spread before my eyes – Fascism in Italy, National Socialism in Germany, Bolshevism in Russia, and above all else that pestilence of pestilences, nationalism, which has poisoned the flower of our European culture."* —Stephan Zweig, author of *The World of Yesterday 1941.*

"We weaken our greatness when we confuse our patriotism with tribal rivalries that have sown resentment and hatred and violence in all the corners of the globe. We weaken it when we hide behind walls, rather than tear them down, when we doubt the power of our ideals, rather than trust them to be the great force for change they have always been." —Senator John McCain, 2018.

BIBLIOGRAPHY

Abutaleb, Yasmeen. Dawsey, Josh. Trump advisor pushing 'herd immunity,' Houston Chronicle, September 1, 2020.

Adwar, Corey. Lyndon Johnson Liked Taking His Advisors Out For Joyrides That Ended With This Terrifying Prank, Business Insider, August 27, 2014.

A&E Television Networks. Lincoln-Douglas Debates, https://www.history.com/topics/19th-century/lincoln-douglas-debates, August 21, 2018.

AKC Staff, 14 Presidents and Their Pups, akc.org.

Alesse, Liz. Did Trump try to cut the CDC's budget as Democrats claim? Analysis, abcnew.go.com, February 28, 2020.

Alfaro, Marian. Donald Trump Avoided the Military Draft 5 Times, Business Insider, Dec. 26, 2018.

American Experience. Legacy of the Clinton Administration, www.pbs.org, 2012.Andrew, Scottie. The US has 4% of the world's population but 25% of its coronavirus cases, CNNhealth, www.cnn.com , June 30,2020.

Anirudh.10 Major Accomplishments by Andrew Jackson, https://learnodo-newtonic.com/andrew-jackson-accomplishments, June 22, 2016.

Appelbaum, Yoni. How America Ends, The Atlantic, December 2019.

Ashford, Grace. Michael Cohen Says Trump Told Him to Threaten Schools not to Release Grades, The New York Times, Feb 27, 2019.

Ax, Joseph and Chung, Andrew. Electoral map bias may worsen as U.S. gerrymandering battle shifts to states, Reuters, June 29, 2019.

Baker, Kevin. The Doctors Who Killed a President, New York Times, Oct 2, 2011.

Baker, Peter and Karnie, Annie. Trump Accuses Democrats of Outbreak Hoax, New York Times, February 29, 2020.

BBC, Four questions about Trump's tower in Moscow that never was, bbc.com, January 18, 2019.

BBC. Belarus election: Opposition leader Tikhanovskaya fled for sake of her children, bbc.com, Aug 12, 2020.

BBC NEWS, Israel and UAE strike historic deal to normalize relations, www.bbc.com, August 13, 2020.

Bedard, Paul. George Washington Plied Voters with Booze, U.S. New and World Report, Nov. 8, 2011.

Paul Bedard, Exclusive: Falwell says Fatal Attraction threat led to depression, Washington Examiner, August 23, 2020.

Bender, Michael C. Trump Welcomes a Senate Impeachment Trial, Defends Giuliani's Moves in Ukraine, WSJ.com, Nov 22, 2019.

Bersin, Alan. Bruggeman, Nate. Rohrbaugh, Ben. Yes There's a Crisis on the Border. And It's Trump's Fault, PoliticoMagazine, April 05, 2019.

Berwick, Ben and Parker, Kristy. President Trump argues he Is above the law. A thousand prosecutors say he's wrong, Los Angeles Times, May 30, 2019.

Berzon, Alexandra. Donald Trump's Business Plan Left a Trail of Unpaid Bills, wsj.com, June 9, 2016.

Beschloss, Michael. Presidents of War, Crown Publishing, 2018.

Beschloss, Michael. Presidential Courage, Simon & Schuster, 2007.

Bierle, Sarah Kay. Grant's Cincinnati The General's Horse, Gazzette665, January 27, 2017.

Bierman, Noah. and Stokols, Eli. Trump, trailing in race, fires his campaign manager, Los Angeles Times. July 15, 2020.

Biggerstaff, Lee. Cicero, David C. Puckett, Andy. Is Your Firm Underperforming? Your CEO Might Be Golfing Too Much, Harvard Business Review, November 30, 2016.

Block, Melissa. LBJ Carrier Poor Texas Town With Him in Civil Rights Fight, NPR.ORG, April 11, 2014.

Blumenthal, Sidney. The Political Life of Abraham Lincoln, A Self Made Man, Simon and Schuster, 2016.

Blumenthal, Sidney. Trump's Increasingly Weird Attempts To Compare Himself to Lincoln, The New Yorker, October 24, 2019.

Boles, John B. Jefferson Architect of American Liberty, Basic Books/Perseus Books, 2017.

Booth, William. Betty Ford's Tabled Resolution, Smithsonian Magazine, June 2008.

Bradley, James. The Imperial Cruise, Little Brown, November 2009.

Brenner, Marie. How Donald Trump and Roy Cohn's Ruthless Symbiosis Changed America, Vanity Fair, June 28, 2017.

Branch, Taylor. The Clinton Tapes Wrestling History With The President, Simon and Schuster, 2009.

Bremer, David H. Playing in Peoria, NYTimes, Nov 3,1985.

Brinkley, Douglas. American Moonshot John F. Kennedy and the Great Space Race, Harper, 2019.

Brodie, Fawn M. Thomas Jefferson, An Intimate History, W.W. Norton Company, 1974.Brooks, David. A ridiculously optimistic look at the next decade, The New York Times, Jan 2, 2020.

Bulman, May. Donald Trump has dangerous mental illness, say psychiatry experts at Yale Conference. www.independent co.uk., April 21, 2017.

Bump, Philip. Donald trump's father was arrested at KKK riot in New York in 1927, records reveal, www.Independent.co.uk, August 13, 2017.

Burke, Daniel. Jerry Falwell Jr.'s fatal miscalculation, cnn.com, August 30, 2020.

Bush, George H. W. All The Best, Scribner, 1999.

Bush, George H.W. January 5, 1993: Address at West Point, Presidential Speeches, UVA, Miller Center.

Bush, George W. Decision Points, Crown Publishers, 2010.

Carnegie, Dean. The Man in the Bottle http://www.themagicdetective.com/2011/05/man-in-bottle.html May 22, 2011.

Carter, Brandon. Baldwin trolls Trump after Twitter attack. Thehill.com, March 2, 2018.

Cassellman, Ben. Virus Wipes Out 5 Years of Economic Growth, The New York Times, July 31, 2020.

Center for Disease Control. Older Adults, June 25, 2020.

Chait, Jonathan. Republicans Keep Admitting Everything They Said About Obama Was a Lie, Fox News Sunday interview between Chris Wallace and Mick Mulvaney. NYMAG, Feb. 11, 2019.

Choi, David. Trump refuses to acknowledge John Lewis' achievements and claims He's done more for Black Americans, Business Insider, Aug 4, 2020.

Choi, Matthew. Mitch McConnel Campaign Tweets Image of Tombstone With Opponent's Name, www.politico.com, August 05, 2019.

Cillizza, Chris. Donald Trump lies more often than you wash your hands every day, cnn.com, June 10, 2019.

Chotiner, Isaac. Why Stuart Stevens Wants to Defeat Donald Trump, The New Yorker, August 03, 2020.

Cillizza, Chris. The 36 wackiest lines from Donald Trump's totally bizare Cabinet meeting, cnn.com, January 3, 2019

Cillizza, Chris. Donald Trump's 199 wildest lines of 2019, cnn.com, December 23, 2019.

Clark, Lesley. Congress' NRA Loyalist Say New Gun Laws Won't Ease Shooting Sprees, newsobserver.com, February 15, 2018.

Clinton, Bill. January 19, 1999: State of the Union Address, Presidential Speeches, UVA, Miller Center.

Clinton, Bill, My Life, Alfred A. Knoph, 2004.

CNBS, Trump and company could be under investigation for bank and insurance fraud, Manhattan DA Vance reveals, August 3, 2020.

Cobb, Andrienne. Tracking turnover in the Trump administration: Year three, forsensicnews.net, January 27, 2020.

Cobler, Nicolle. Austin American – Statesman, Texas Lt. Gov. Dan Patrick done listening to Dr. Anthony Fauci, USA Today, July 2, 2020.

Cohen, Michael. House Testimony/Marketing Campaigns, February 27, 2018.

Cochrane, Emily. Fuchs, Hailey. Vogel, Kenneth. Greenberg, Jessica Silver. Postal Service Suspends Changes After Outcry Over Delivery Slowdown, The New York Times, Aug. 18, 2020.

Cohen, Richard. Spiro Agnew was Trump before Trump, The Washington Post, September 3,2018.

Cohen, Roger. Trump's Plague, The New York Times, September 5, 2020.

Collins, Michael. Fritze, John. Collins, Eliza. Trump to Democrats: No deals on infrastructure, drug prices until they drop investigations, USA Today, May 22, 2019.

Collinson, Stephen. Trump ignores science at dangerous indoor rally, CNN Politics, September 14, 2020.

Collman, Ashley. Like Trump, Clinton also launched an Iraq airstrike as his impeachment inquiry was heating up, Business Insider, Jan 3, 2020.

Colvin, Jill. What did Jeffrey Epstein's famous friends know and see?, apnew.com, July 9, 2019.

Cook, Nancy. An unshackled Trump finally gets the presidency he always wanted, Politico.com, 9/19/2019.

Coolidge, Calvin. December 4, 1928: Sixth Annual Message, Coolidge Presidential Speeches, UVA, Miller Center.

Cooper, John Milton Jr. Woodrow Wilson, Alfred A. Knopf, 2009.

Coppins, McKay, The Man Who Broke Politics, The Atlantic, November 2018 issue.

Cotter, Daniel A. The Chief Justices, Twelve Table Press, 2019.

Crowley, Michael and Haberman, Maggie. Trump Condemns White Supremacy but Stops Short on Major Gun Control, NYTimes, Aug 5, 2019.

Cummings, William. Read the full text of Fiona Hill's opening statement in impeachment hearing, USA Today, November 21, 2019.

Date, S. V. Trump Golf Costs Top $110 Million – More Than Estimate For All of Obama's Travel, Huffpost, Aug 3, 2019.

Davis, Susan. A New Biden Administration Would Face Old Problems With Congress, npr.org, August 20, 2020.

Diamond, Jeremy. FDA commissioner refuses to defend Trump claim that 99% of Covid – 19 cases are harmless, cnn.com, July 5, 2020.

Dias, Elizabeth and Peters, Jeremy W. Evangelical Leaders Close Ranks With Trump After Scathing Editorial, The New York Times, Dec 20, 2019.

Dickson, Peter W. Reagan's Bargain/Charlie Wilson's War, Consortium News, 2008.

Doherty, Jennifer. Four-Star U.S. Army General Slams Trump's Behavior in Navy Seal Controversy: If He Was A General, We'd Fire Him, Newsweek, December 28, 2019.

Doubek, James. A Houston Doctor On His Hospital's Deadliest Week So Far, npr.org, July 31, 2020.

Douglas, Michael. Unbreaking America, Divided We Fall, America Has Been Hijacked, @represent.us, December 20, 2019.

Driftwood, Jimmy (writer) and Horton, Johnny (singer). The Battle of New Orleans, Columbia label,1959.

Duffey. Michael. George H.W. Bush Accomplished Much More as President Than He Ever Got Credit For, Time Magazine, December 1, 2018.

Ebbs, Stephanie. FDA revokes permission to treat Covid – 19 with hydroxychloroquine drug previously touted by Trump, abcnews.go.com, June 15, 2020.

Edmondson, Catie. Chief Defends Park Police In Clearing of Square in June, The New York Times, July 9, 2020.

Eisenhower, Dwight D. January 17,1961: Farewell Address, Presidential Speeches, UVA, Miller Center.

Elving, Ron. How Trump Breaks With Clinton and Nixon on Governing While Under Investigation, npr.org, May 23, 2019. Emerson, Bo. When Jimmy Carter Lusted In His Heart, The Atlanta Journal-Constitution, Sept 28, 2017.

Facher, Lev. As Trump claims credit for decline in opioid deaths, others see signs of danger ahead, www.statnews.com, July12, 2019.

Fahrenhoid, David, Reinhard, Beth. Kindy, Kimberly. Trump called Epstein a terrific guy who enjoyed younger women before denying relationship with him, The Washinton Post, July 8, 2019.

Feinberg, Ayal, Branton, Regina, and Martinez-Ebers, Valeri. Counties That Hosted a 2016 Trump Rally Saw A 226 Percent Increase In Hate Crimes, The Washington Post, March 22, 2019.

Fleishman, Glenn. The People vs. Donald Trump: Every Major Lawsuit and Investigation the President Faces, fortune.com, September 21, 2018.

Flexner, James Thomas. Washington The Indispensable Man, Little Brown, and Company,1974.

Ford, Gerald. A Time To Heal, Harper and Row and The Readers Digest Association Inc. 1979.

Ford, Gerald. Speech on Taking Office, August 9, 1974, Presidential Speeches, UVA, Miller Center.

Ford, Gerald. January 12, 1977: State of the Union Address, Presidential Speeches, UVA, Miller Center.

Forster, Katie. Mental health professionals warn Trump is incapable of being president, www.independent.com.uk, February 14, 2017.

Friedman, Thomas L. Overrated Warrior, Times Digest, January 5, 2020.

Friedman, Thomas L. Did Trump and Iran Just Bury the Hatchet, or the Future, The New York Times, Jan 8, 2020.

Galli, Mark. Trump Should Be Removed from Office, Christianity Today, December 19, 2019.

Garland, Hamlin. Ulysses S. Grant His life and character. New York Double Day & McClure Co, 1898.

Gartner, John. Trump's cognitive deficits seem worse. We need to know if he has dementia, USA Today, Apr 9, 2019.

Gershwin, George and Gershwin, Ira. Book by George S. Kaufman and Morrie Ryskind, Of Thee I Sing, Gershwin.com.

Gittleson, Ben. Study finds earlier coronavirus restrictions in US could have saved 36,000 lives, Trump calls it a 'political hit job,' abcnews.go.com, May 21, 2020.

Glass, Andrew. President Truman fires Gen. MacArthur: April 11, 1951, politico.com, April 10, 2017.

Goldberg, Jeffrey. Trump: Americans Who Died in War Are 'Losers and Suckers,' theatlantic.com, September 3, 2020.

Goodwin, Doris Kearns. The Bully Pulpit, Simon & Schuster, 2013.

Grant, Ulysses S. March 4,1869 First Inaugural Address, UVA Miller Center, Presidential Speeches.

Grant, Ulysses S. Message on Presidential Powers and Obligations Speech, May 4, 1876 to the House of Representatives, UVA, Miller Center.

Grant, Ulysses S. Memoirs and Selected Letters, The Library of America, 1990.

Greene David. Bond, Shannon. Twitter, Facebook Remove Trump Post Over False Claim About Children and Covid-19. npr.org, August 5, 2020.

Griffiths, James. As US and China force consulates to close, the risk of missteps and spiraling tensions rises, CNN, July, 24. 2020.

Gynne, S.C. Hymns of the Republic, Scribner, 2019. Also Gynne, S.C. The year D.C. trembled, danced behind barricades, Houston Chronicle Book Excerpt, November 3, 2019.

Haines, Tim. Rally Crowd Cheers Trump's Promise to Deregulate Energy Efficient Dishwashers, Showers, Sinks, realclearpolitics. com, January 15, 2020.

Hallum, Mark. Presidents Who Have Personally Killed People, History News Network, August 15, 2015.

Haltiwanger, John. Trump suggests the US should form a state-run, global news network to counter CNN's 'unfair' coverage, Business Insider, Nov 26, 2018.

Hamilton, E.L. President Theodore Roosevelt Acquired A New Pet From A 12 Year Old, www.thevintagenews,com, May 1, 2018.

Handover, Deborah. Confessions of a Trump Supporter's Daughter, gen.medium.com, Jun, 2020.

Hannon, Hannon. Trump Administration Is Discontinuing the Census Count a Month Early. But Why? slate.com, Aug 04,2020.

Hardesty, Robert L. The LBJ the Nation Seldom Saw, LBJ Presidential Library.

Harry S.Truman Presidential Library & Museum, https://www. trumanlibrary.org/kids/piano.htm.

Hayhoe, Katharine. Professor of Political Science at Texas Tech University, Ph.D in Atmospheric Science, Christians, Climate,

And Our Culture in the U.S., lecture at the Lanier Theological Library, September 28, 2019.

Hendricks, Sara. Trump Should Be Worried About These White House Ghosts Coming Out To Haunt Him, refinery 29.com, October 21, 2018.

Hansler, Jennifer. Pompeo breaks silence on poisoning of Russia opposition leader, cnn.com, August 25, 2020.

Herb, Jeremy. Cohen, Marshall. Polantz, Katelyn. Bipartisan Senate report details Trump campain contacts with Russia in 2016, adding to Mueller Findings, cnn.com, August 18, 2020.

Hinsdale, Mary Louise. A History of the President's Cabinet, Ann Arbor, MI: G. Wahr., 1911.

Hisson, Amy. Now Defend Yourself, You Damned Rascal, www.amyhisson.com, Nov 3, 2005.

History.com Editors. Ulysses S. Grant, https://www.history.com/topics/us-presidents/ulysses-s-grant-, August 21, 2018.

History.com. Editors, https://www.history.com/topics/us-presidents/woodrow-wilson, October 18, 2018.

History.com. Editors, George W. Bush First and Second Presidential Terms, June 7, 2019.

History.com. Editors, This Day in History, President Andrew Johnson Impeached, July 29, 2019.

History.com. Editors, Why Was It Called the 'Spanish Flu?' Mar 27, 2020.

Holt Rinehart Winston,1971.

Hulse, Carl. Pressure on Senate Leader to Secure Elections, New York Times, July 31, 2019.

Ingersoll, Robert Green. Selections from His Oratory and Writings (re: power Abraham Lincoln), 1888, bartleby.com.

Jacobs, Jennifer. Trump Says He May Ask for Resignation of Cabinet if Re-Elected. Bloomberg, August 15, 2020.

Jacobson, Louis. Is Texas one of the nation's most gerrymanders states, as Bet O'Rourke said? POLITIFACT, Aug 16, 2018.

Jakes, Lara. As protests in South America surged, so did Russian trolls on Twitter, U.S. finds, The New York Times, Jan 19, 2020.

Jervis, Rick. Voting rights: Texas voter purge is latest effort to target minority voters, USA Today, February 7, 2019.

Johnson, Alex. Navy Secretary Forced To Resign Amid Seal Controversary, nbcnews.com, Nov. 24, 2019.

Johnson, David W. Then and Now: What Woodrow Wilson's 1918 Pandemic Failure Can Teach Us Today, www.4sighthealth,com, April 23, 2020.

Johnson, Lyndon Baines. The Vantage Point Perspectives of The Presidency 1963-1969, Holt, Rinehart and Watson, 1971.

Johnson, Ted. Barack Obama, In Democratic Convention Speech, Will Say Trump Has Turned Presidency Into "One More Reality Show,: news.yahoo.com, August 19, 2020.

Jones, Brian Adam. The 8 Presidents With The Most Badass Military Records, https://taskandpurpose.com/8-presidents-badass-military-records, July 02, 2014.

Jones, Chuck. Trump's Golf Trips Could Cost Taxpayers over $340 million, Forbes, July 10, 2019.

Jones, Lora, Theatre Royal Haymarket, @lorajoneswriter (Instagram).

Jones, Sarah, E. Jean Carroll Trump Attacked Me in the Dressing Room of Bergdorf Goodman, nymag.com, June 21, 2019.

Joung, Madeleine. Trump Has Now Had More Cabinet Turnover Than, Reagan, Obama, and the Two Bushes, time.com, July 12, 2019.

Kannon-Youngs, Zolan. Olmos, Sergio. Baker, Mike. Goldman, Adam. At Start, F.B.I. Saw Protesters As Threatening, The New York Times, July 29, 2020.

Kaplan, Michael. Two Tributes to Andrew Jackson the Embodiment of the American Spirit, the New Jacksonian Blog, March 6, 2011.

Katz, Mark. Calvin Coolidge's Bone-Dry Humor Is a Lesson in Laugh for Candidates, thedailybeast.com, February 13, 2017.

Kearns, Doris Goodwin, The Divided Legacy of Lyndon B. Johnson, The Atlantic, Sep 7, 2018.

Keith, Tamara. White House Staff Turnover Was Already Record-Setting, NPR, March 7, 2018.

Kelly, Martin. 10 Things to Know About Andrew Jackson, www.thoughtco.com, September 10, 2018.

Kennedy, John F. May 25, 1961: The Goal of Sending a Man to the Moon, Presidential Speeches, UVA, Miller Center.

Kennedy, Lesley. 7 Contentious Trade Wars in U.S. History, History.com/news, Oct 2, 2018.

Kershaw, Ian. How Democracy Produce A Monster, The New York Times, February 3, 2008.

Kertscher, Tom. PolitiFact: Is Black Lives Mater a Marxist movement, Tampa Bay Times, July 22, 2020.

Kessler, Ronald. The Trump White House Changing The Rules Of The Game. Crown Forum, 2018.

Kessler, Glenn. A recent Supreme Court appointment in an election an election year without controversy, The Washington Post, Feb 24, 2016.

Kinzer, Stephen. The Brothers, John Foster Dulles, Allen Dulles, and Their Secret World War, St. Martins Griffin, 2013.

Klein, Betsy. Trump spend 1 of every 5 days in 2019 at a golf club, cnn.com, December 31, 2019.

Klein, Betsy. And Liptak, Kevin. White House refuses to denounce Confederate flag as Trump bemoans NASCAR's ban, CNN politics, July 6, 2020.

Klein, Christopher. How Blackbeard Lost His Head in a Bloody, Sword-Swinging Battle, History.com, November 20, 2018.

Kosinski, Michelle. Elwazer, Schams. Collinson, Stephen. Cable from UK's ambassador to the US blast Trump as inept, incompetent, CNN, July 8, 2019.

Krieg, Gregory. Newly released documents detail allegations of fraud in 2016 by GOP operative in North Carolina, amp.cnn.com. December 19, 2018.

Krugman, Paul. Australia's wildfires show us the road to hell, Houston Chronicle, January 13, 2020.

Krugman, Paul. Trump Can't Handle the Truth, New York Times, March 9, 2020.

Lamansky, Katrina, Trump-Clinton nasty? Not compared to these campaigns from the old days, CNN and WQAD8, September 23, 2016.

Lambrecht, Bill. Texas lawmakers warn against aid cuts, Houston Chronicle, April 20, 2019.

Landler, Mark. Jakes, Lara. Haberman, Maggie. Trump's Request of an Ambassador: Get the British Open for Me, ntimes.com, July 22, 2020.

Landry, Alysa. Theodore Roosevelt: The Only Good Indians Are the Dead Indians, indiancountrytoday.com. Jun 28, 2016.

Latson, Jennifer. Rudenesss, and kindness, trickle down from above, Houston Chronicle, March 6, 2020.

Lattman, Peter. Who Bought Magna Carta, The Wall Street Journal, Dec. 20, 2007.

Lehrer, Jim. Character Above All, PBS Broadcast Transcripts Parts 1-5, https://www.pbs.org/newshour/spc/character/transcript/trans1.html, May 29, 1996.

Lehman Institute. Mr. Lincoln and Friends, www.mrlincolnandfriends.org.Leonnig, Carol D. and Rucker, Phillip. You're a bunch of dopes and babies: Inside Trumps stunning tirade against generals, Washington Post, Jan. 17, 2020.

Lowe, Jacqueline. A Dialogue Between Amity Shlaes and Paul Vocker, former chairman of the Federal Reserve Bank, Bushcenter.org, February 1, 2013. (regarding Calvin Coolidge)

Maddow, Rachel. Trump dismantling of Obama era disease response leaves U.S. exposed (an interview with Laurie Garret, science journalist and healthy policy analyst) MSNBC, February 26, 2020.

Maddow, Rachel. Trump engaged in 'jury tampering on a mass, national scale,' MSNBC, Feb 24,2020.

Magnier, Mark. Phase one trade deal gives Donald Trump bragging rights but phase two is likely a mirage, analysts say, South China Morning Post, Jan. 14, 2020.

Mandel, Kyla. Expect to pay at least $400 billion over next 20 years to protect U.S. from rising seas, thinkprogress.org, Jun 20, 2019.

Manga, Dan and Breuninger, Kevin. Trump slams Roger Stone Juror before she testifies at retrial hearing, CNBC, February 25, 2020.

Manjoo, Farhad. Coronvairus is what you get when you ignore science, New York Times, March 4, 2020.

Margo, Del. El Paso mayor: Despite Trump's State of the Union Claim our relations with Mexico Thrive, www.usatoday.com/story/opinion/voices/2019/02/10/.

Mark, David. Trump's Iran attack distracts from impeachment - but can still hurt him politically, nbcnews.com, Jan 5, 2020.

Marshall, Robert. President Coolidge Adopted by the Sioux, http://readingthroughhistory.com/2014/06/23/coolidge-adopted-by-the-sioux/, June 23, 2014.

Maurer, Daniel. Motherless Brooklyn: Robert Moses, Miles Davis, and Donald Trump Walk into a Film, bedfordandbowery.com, Oct 11, 2019.

Maza, Cristina. Sanctioned Russian Oligarch's Company to Invest Millions in New Aluminum Plant In Mitch McConnell's State, Newsweek, April 15, 2019.

Mazza, Ed, Trump Moans Nobody Likes Me, And Twitter Critics Quickly Remind Him Why, www.huffpost.com, July 29, 2020.

McCormack, John. The Election Came Down to 77,744 Votes in Pennsylvania, Wisconsin, and Michigan, washingtonexaminer.com, November 10, 2016.

McKean, David and Sloan, Cliff. The Great Decision: Jefferson, Adams, Marshall, and the Battle for the Supreme Court. Public Affairs, 2009.

McPherson, James M. Tried By War Abraham Lincoln As Commander in Chief, The Penguin Press, 2008.

Meacham, Jon. Soul of America: The Battle For Our Better Angels. Random House., 2018.

Meacham, Jon. Thomas Jefferson The Art of Power. Random House, 2012.Metcalf, Allan. Is Donald Trump the Andrew Jackson of Our Time? The Chronicle of Higher Education, November 6, 2018.

Mezzeofiore, Gianluca. These Americas share what it feels like to be told: Go back to where they came from, CNN, July 15, 2019.

Millard, Candace. Destiny of the Republic, Anchor Books, January 2012.

Miller, Zeke. Book takes a swing at Trump on the links, Houston Chronicle, A2.

Miller, Zeke. Trump pattern is to create a crisis, retreat, claim victory, move on, Associated Press, July 14, 2019.

Montanaro, Domenico. 7 Takeways From The Republican National Convention, NPR, August 28, 2020.

Mooney, Michael J. Trump's Apostle, Texas Monthly, Jul 23, 2019.

Moran, Lee. Fox News Host: I Don't know Where To Begin Debunking Donald Trump's Latest Lie, Huffpost, August 3, 2019.

Mueller, Robert S. Special Counsel, Report On The Investigation Into Russian Interference In The 2016 Presidential Election, Volume I and II, March 2019.

Murdock, Sebastian. NRA Could Lose Tax-Exempt Status Over Shady Business Practices, huffpost.com, 04/19/2019.

Nakamura, David and Wagner, John. Trump mocks 16-year-old Greta Thunberg, Washington Post, December 12, 2019.NBC News, Trump retweets Epstein conspiracy theory, claiming Clinton connection, August 11, 2019.

NBC News, Trump's India trip ignored the New Delhi riots. But his silence isn't the most damning, Feb.28, 2020.

NCC Staff, Andrew Johnson: The most criticized president ever? Constitution Daily, National Constitution Center, July 31, 2019.

Neumann, Sean. Fox News Mistakenly Cropped President Trump from Photo with Jeffrey Epstein and Ghislaine Maxwell, people.com, July 7, m2020.

unfounded conspiracy theories that I was somehow involved in his death while he was locked up in a Federal jail under your jurisdiction: Trump retweets Epstein conspiracy theory, claiming Clinton connection, NBC New, August 11, 2019.

Newton, Jim. Eisenhower The White House Years, Doubleday, 2011.

Nixon, Richard M. August 9, 1974: Remarks on Departure from the White House, Presidential Speeches, UVA, Miller Center.

Nye, Logan. We are THE MIGHTY, https://www.wearethemighty. com/history/marshall-eisenhower-modern-military-leadershi p?rebelltitem=4#rebelltitem4, March 18, 2019.

Papenfuss, Mary. Trump Has Already Lost His Pricey China Trade War, Paul Krugman Warns, huffpost.com, Dec 16, 2019.

Parloff, Roger. Why U.S. Law Makes It Easy for Donald Trump To Stiff Contractors, fortune.com, September 30, 2016.

Pearl, Mike. All the Evidence We Could Find About Fred Trump's Alleged Involvement with the KKK, The Vice Guide to the 2016 Election, Mar 10, 2016.

Pearson, Natalie Obiko. Trump's Family Fortune Originated in a Canadian Gold-Rush Brother, Bloomberg, October 26, 2016.

Penzenstadler, Nick and Page, Susan. Exclusive: Trump's 3,500 lawsuits unprecedented for a presidential nominee, USA Today, June 1, 2016.

Perrett, Conner. Trump suggests he would 'negotiate' a 3rd term as president because he is probably entitled to it, Businessinsider. com, September 13, 2020.

Peters, Jeremy W. Trump Sets the 2020 tone: Like 2016, Only This Time 'the Squad' Is Here, New York Times, July 17, 2017.

Philipps, Dave. Trump Clears Three Service Members in War Crimes Case, New York Times, Nov. 15, 2019. Anguished Seals Recall Chief as Evil, New York Times, December 27, 2019.

Phillips, Kristine. Michael Cohen was sent back to prison as a retaliatory act over tell-all book about Trump, federal judge rules, www.usatoday.com. July 23, 2020.

Pierre, Joe, MD. Why Has America Become So Divided? Psychology Today, Sept 05, 2018.

Pohanka, Brian C. Fort Wagner and the 54th Massachusetts Volunteer Infantry, https://www.battlefields.org/learn/articles/fort-wagner-and-54th-massachusetts-volunteer-infantry.

PoltiFact. Trumps statements were awarded PolitiFact's 2015 and 2017 Lie of the Year, politifact.com.

Pontefract, Dan. What's Good For Our Country Was Good For General Motors, Forbes, Nov 26, 2018.

Porter, Tom. 350 health professionals sign a letter to Congress claiming Trump's mental health is deteriorating dangerously amid impeachment proceedings, Business Insider, December 5, 2019.

Price, Greg. Why is Paul Ryan Retiring? Five Reasons House Speaker Won't Seek Reelection, Newsweek, April 11, 2018.

Pruitt, Sarah. Lincoln's Peoria Speech, 160 Years later, Oct 16,2014, www.history.com.

Rappeport, Alan. Postal Service Pick With Ties to Trump Raises Concerns Ahead of 2020 Election, www.nytimes.com, May 7, 2020.

Reagan, Ronald. January 11, 1989: Farewell Address, Presidential Speeches, UVA, Miller Center.

Reagan, Ronald. Freedom Speech, www.reagan.com

Reilly, Rick. Commander in Cheat, Hachette Book Group, 2019.

Robb, Greg. Fed study finds Trump tariffs backfired, marketwatch.com, December 28, 2019.

Roberts, Andrew. Churchill, Viking, 2018.

Rogers, Katie. Trump Weighs In on the Death of John Lewis, One of His Most Vocal Critics, nyties.com. July 18, 2020.

Rogers, Katie. Bryson Taylor, Derrick. Murphy, Heather. Trump Adds Roger Stone to His List of Pardons and Commutations, nytimes.com, July 11, 2020.

Rosane, Olivia. Green Snow Raises Pollution Concerns in Russian City, https://www.ecowatch.com/green-snow-russia-pollution-2630056657.html, Feb 26, 2019.

Rosenfeld, Megan. French, Mary Ann and others. At my last White House Correspondent's dinner I played a farewell faux video: And On Tenor Sax, It's President Bill, The Washington Post, Jan 13, 1993.

Ross, Jim. Trump Called His Generals a "Bunch of Dopes and Babies in A Fit of Range, Book Claims, the dailybeast.com, January 17, 2020.

Roosevelt, Theodore. December 9,1908 Eighth Annual Message to the Senate and House of Representatives, UVA, Miller Center.

Roosevelt, Franklin. January 20, 1945: Fourth Inaugural Address, UVA, Miller Center.

Rothman, Lily. I am Not a Crook. The Nixon Tax Story Rachel Maddow Just Compared to Trump's, Time Magazine, March 15, 2017.

Rubenstein, David. Clinton and Bush, Peer to Peer Conversations the David Rubenstein Show, Bloomberg, Aug 9, 2017.

Rubenstein, David. May 4 2019 keynote speech Sinews of History at the 50th Anniversary, The National Churchill Museum, Westminster College, Fulton, MO.

Rucker, Philip and Leonnig, Carol. A Very Stable Genius, Penguin Publishing Group, 2020, 7-8 (Prologue).

Ruwitch, John. As China Imposes New Hong Kong Law, U.S. And Allies Take Steps To Retaliate, npr.org, July 2, 2020.

Sandburg, Carl. Lincoln Collector, Harcourt, Brace and Company, 1949.

Sarson, Steven. Barack Obama: American Historian, Bloomsbury Academic, 2018, 294.

Saul, Stephanie. Schmidt, Michael S. Steve Bannon Is Charged With Fraud in We Build the Wall Campaign, The New York Times, August 20, 2020.

Savage, Charlie. Barr's handling of Mueller report "distorted": New York Times, March 5, 2020.

Saxon, Reed. Bill Clinton pays the sax, Iconic presidential campaign moments, CBS News (AP).

Sciutto, Jjm. Trump advisers hesitated to give military options and warned adversaries over fears he might start a war, August 6, 2020.

Schultz, Colin. Nixon Prolonged Vietnam War for Political Gain...Unclassified Tapes Suggest, Smithsonian. Com, March 18, 2013.

Shear, Michael. Fuchs, Hailey. Vogel, Kenneth. Mail Delays Fuel Concern Trump Is Undercutting Postal System Ahead of Voting, The New York Times, July 31, 2020.

Shribman, David M. Did misguided US foreign policy lead to WWII?, The Boston Globe, May 10, 2010.

Schultz, Colin. George Washington Didn't Have Wooden Teeth – They Were Ivory, Smithsonian Magazine, November 7, 2014.

Schuman, Michael. China Built A Big Beautiful Wall, Too – And It Failed. The Houston Chronicle, January 23, 2019.

Selk, Avi. Trump says he's a genius. A study found these other presidents actually were, The Washington Post, Jan 7, 2018.

Senior, Jennifer. Trump's Napalm Politics? They Began With Newt, The New York Times, June 28, 2020.

Sheth, Sonam. Trump's campaign channeled nearly $400,000 to his private business in 2 days, Business Insider and www.msn.com, July 17, 2020.

Shakespeare, William. The Tempest, 1610-1611.

Sherman, Gabriel. He's Definitely Melting Down Over This: Trump, Germaphobe in Chief, Struggles to Control the Covid-19 Story, Vanity Fair, March 9, 2020.

Shlaes, Amity. Coolidge, Harper, February 12, 2013.

Shipler, David K. Robert McNamara and the Ghosts of Vietnam, The New York Times Magazine, August 10, 1997.

Simon, Scott. Remembering A Congressman Who Bucked His Party On An Impeachment, NPR, January 23, 2020.

Sloan, Cliff. and McKeen, David. The Great Decision: Jefferson, Adams, Marshall, and the Battle for the Supreme Court, Loc 23 of 4293.

Soergel, Andrew and Tolson, Jay. The 10 Worst Presidents, US News and World Report, March 29, 2014.Spalding, Matthew. https://www.heritage.org/commentary/the-man-who-would-not-be-king February 5, The Heritage Foundation, 2007.

Sprunt, Barbara. Trump Opposes Postal Service Funding But Says He'd Sign Bill Including it, NPR August 13, 2020.

Starr, Barbara. and Browne, Ryan. Esper Says Trump ordered him to allow Gallagher to keep his Trident Pin and remain a Seal, cnn.com, November 25, 2019.

Steinhauer, Jennifer. Amy McGrath Opens Campaign to Oust Mitch McConnell in Kentucky, New York Times, July 9, 2019.

Stevenson, Freeman. Top Scandals and Controversies of Each United States President, Deseret News U.S. & World, May 20, 2013.

Stieb, Matt. Even the Trump Transition Team Knew Some Appointees Were Bad Hires, New York Intelligencer, June 24, 2019.

Stieb, Matt. Dan Patrick of Texas on State Reopening: There Are More Important Things Than Living, nymag,com, Apr 21, 2020.

Stokols, Eli. Trump White House Saw Record Number of First-Year Staff Departures, The Wall Street Journal, Dec 28, 2017.

Sullivan, Eileen and Shear, Michael D. Horseface, Lowlife, Fat, Ugly: How the President Demeans Women, The New York Times, Oct 16, 2018.

Sutherland, David. George Washington, The Man Who Wouldn't Be King. PBS American Experience, DVD, Director and Producer David Sutherland, David Sutherland Productions, May 17, 2011.

Telford, Taylor. Mandate for use of U.S. steel unlikely to improve fortunes, Washington Post, July 17, 2019.Tepas, Kathyrn Dunn. President Trump's A Team Turnover is 74%, Brooking, EDU, July 2019.

Times Digest, After Storm, Smashed Glass and Vagrant Boats, The New York Times, August 28, 2020.

Tomlinson, Chris. Americans are fat, dumb, and dying from bad nutritional choices, Houston's Business Insider, TexasInc., November 25, 2019.

Tomlinson, Chris. Trade war is a suicide vest threatening global economy, Houston Chronicle, Aug 28, 2019.

Toobin, Jeffrey. Trump's Miss Universe Gambit, The New Yorker, February 19, 2018.

Trevizo, Perla. Trump Rolls Back Clean Water Rules, Houston Chronicle, January 24, 2019.

Truman, Harry S. January 15, 1953: Farewell Address, Presidential Speeches, UVA, Miller Center.

Trump, Donald J. No President has ever done what I have done for Evangelicals, or religion itself. It's not even close! Dec 20, 2019 Tweet and Dec 20, 2019 Tweet.

Trump, Mary. Too Much and Never Enough, Simon & Schuster, 2020.

Tumin, Remy and Walker, Elijah. Roger Stone promised to remain loyal to President Trump, The New York Time The Morning, July 12, 2020.

Underwood, Alexia. The controversial US Jerusalem embassy opening, explained, vox.com, May 16, 2018.

Updegrove, Mark J. Building A Better World, Parade Magazine, Feb18, 2018.

Vanden Brook, Tom. Qasem Soleimani: The Pentagon has tracked Iranian general for many years before he was killed, USA Today, January 4, 2020.

Volz, Dustin. Strobel, Warren P. Senate Panel's Probe Found Counterintelligence Risks In Trump's 2016 Campaign, The Wall Street Journal, Aug 18, 2020.

Von Drehle, David. Honor and Effort: What President Obama Achieve in Eight Years, Time.com, December 22, 2016.

Wagner, John. Itkowitz, Colby. Brice-Sadler, Michael. Trump says Democrats looked like fools during public hearings, The Washington Post, November 22, 2019.

Wagner, Kurt. Frier, Sarah. Facebook Removes Hundreds of QAnon Groups, Limits Thousands More, Bloomberg, August 19,2020.

Walsh, Joe. Trump Needs a Primary Challenge, Opinion Column The New York Times, August 14, 2019.

Wan, William and Bever, Lindsey. Studies: Trump may be making Latinos sick, Washington Post, July 20, 2019.

Wang, Jansi Lo. Census Door Knocking Cut A Month Short Amid Pressure To Finish Count: NPR, July 30, 2020.

Washington, George. March 15, 1783. http://www.historyplace.com/speeches/washington.htm

Wasserman, David. How Trump could lose by 5 million votes and still win in 2020, July 19, 2019, https://www.nbcnews.com/politics/2020-election/how-trump-could-lose-5-million-votes-still-win-2020-n1031601.

Whaples, Robert. Were Andrew Jackson's Policies Good for the Economy? The Independent Review, v. 18, n. 4, Spring 2014.

Wilents, Sean. Andrew Jackson, Times Books/Henry Holt and Company, 2005.

Wiles, Richard. Cost to address rising sea levels will touch everyone, Houston Chronicle, July 10, 2019.

Wilson, James Mikel. Churchill and Roosevelt: The Big Sleepover At The White House (Christmas 1941 – New Year 1942), Gate Keeper Press, 2015.

Wilson, Woodrow. Eighth Annual Message, December 7, 1920, UVA, Miller Center, https://millercenter.org/the-presidency/presidential-speeches

Wise, Alana. Trump Defends Kenosha Shooting Suspect, NPR, August 31, 2020.

Wolff, Michael. Siege Trump Under Fire, Henry Holt and Company, 2019.

Wong Edward. Jakes, Lara. Myers, Steven Lee. U.S. Orders China to Close Houston Consulate, Citing Efforts to Steal Trade Secrets, The New York Times, July 22, 2020.

Wong, Wilson. Siemaszko, Corky. Weeks after Sturgis motocycle rally, first Covid-19 death reported as cases accelerate in Midwest, nbcnew.com, Sept. 2, 2020.

Wood, Gordon S. Empire of Liberty: A history of the Early Republic, 1789 – 1815. Oxford University Press, 2009.

Woodard, Bob. The Last of the President's Men, Simon and Schuster, 2015.

Woodward, Bob. Rage, Simon & Schuster, 2020.

Wright, Lawrence. Camp David, Alley Theatre, February-March 2020.

Wu, Nicholas. This Is The Gun Control Legislation Mitch McConnell Won't Allow Senators to Vote On, USA Today, Aug 5, 2019.

Wuench, Robert. Freelance Writer, Author (Ashes on His Boot, Civil Sword, and Maid of Morgan's Point), and retired

Caterpillar executive. His five steps are a reflection of having done business in Africa, the Middle East, and Latin America as well as personal observations of eight dictators.

www.medicalnewstoday.com. The foliage and berries: Belladonna: Uses and Risks, July 1, 2017.

www.nytimes.com, Playing In Peoria, Nov 3, 1985.

https://www.history.com/topics/american-civil-war/draft-riots, The New York Riot Drafts, August 21, 2009.

https://en.m.wikipedia.org/wiki/Grant_administration_scandals#Books53.

https://www.aaap.org/president-trumps-first-budget-commits-significant-resources-fight-opioid-epidemic/ and https://www.drugabuse.gov/drugs-abuse/opioids/opioid-overdose-crisis.

Young, Stephen. 8 Times pastor Robert Jeffress Was a Stooge for Donald Trump, dallasobserver.com, June 17, 2019.

Youssef, Nancy A. In Generational Shift, Army Uses a New System to Promote Hundreds of Officers, Wall Street Journal, March 4, 2020.

Zhaq, Christina. Shepard Smith and other Fox News Hosts Criticize Trump's Go BackTweet: Xenophobic Eruption of Distraction, Newsweek, July 15, 2019.

SOURCE NOTES

Preface

Nothing discloses real character like the use of power: Robert Green Ingersoll, Selections from His Oratory and Writings (re: power Abraham Lincoln),1888, bartleby.com.

President Truman believed ghosts of past presidents occupied the White House: Sara Hendricks, Trump Should Be Worried About These White House Ghosts Coming Out To Haunt Him, refinery29.com, October 21, 2018.

If one were to accept that the White House is haunted by spirits, real or imagined, some of them may not be very pleased about the disturbances: Ibid.

Even though we lack the security clearance to march right up to these ghosts: Ibid.

From the foundation onward, controversy, scandal, civil rights issues, and outright incompetency have haunted the nation's capital: Freeman Stevenson, Top Scandals and Controversies of Each United States President, Deseret News U.S. & World, May 20, 2013.

Pierre submits that "many of us feel that the nation has never been so split have only been politically conscious for a few decades: Joe Pierre, Why Has America Become So Divided? Psychology Today. Sept 05, 2018.

As Shakespeare wrote, "What's past is prologue.": William Shakespeare, The Tempest, 1610-1611.

Acknowledgments

Spotswood was the Lieutenant Governor of the colony of Virginia: Christopher Klein, How Blackbeard Lost His Head in a Bloody, Sword-Swinging Battle, History.com, November 20, 2018.

In Jon Meacham's book Soul of America: The Battle For Our Better Angels: 267.

He pointed to Jane Addams: Ibid.

It is not only important but mentally invigorating to discuss political matters with people whose opinions differ radically from one's own: Ibid.

Meacham stated "If Mrs. Roosevelt were writing today: Ibid.

He added "wisdom generally comes from a free exchange of ideas: Ibid.

Introduction

each view the world in black and white terms: Yoni Appelbaum, How America Ends, The Atlantic, December 2019.

They believe if they don't win, they lose everything sacred to them and it's the end of democracy: Ibid.

Partisans have drifted further apart both in geography and ideology: Ibid.

At the fringes, distrust has become so fanatical that right-wing activists in Texas and left-wing activist in California have revived talk of secession: Ibid.

Other people believe the real playbook for all the political acrimony began with Newt Gingrich: Jennifer Senior, Trump's Napalm Politics? They Began With Newt, The New York Times, June 28, 2020. And McKay Coppins, The Man Who Broke Politics, The Atlantic, November 2018 issue.

Daniel Hand and former speaker share many characteristics, Ibid.

The primary tool employed by both extremes is not objective
   fact or legal justification: Deborah Handover, Confessions of
   a Trump Supporter's Daughter, gen.medium.com, Jun, 2020.
Social scientists would say that Free Ticket and Neti Pot people
   have internalized their political views: Ibid.
Senator Harry Reid, the democratic leader of that era first deployed
   the so-called "nuclear option" to squelch filibusters of President
   Obama's nominees for various political appointments: Daniel
   A. Cotter, The Chief Justices, 412- 415.
moral deficiencies damage the institution of the presidency,
   the reputation of the country, and the spirit and future of its
   people: Mark Galli, Trump Should Be Removed from Office,
   Christianity Today, December 19, 2019.
under a leader of such grossly immoral character, Ibid.

White House- Day One

U.K.'s ambassador to the U.S. had just called him inept, shallow,
   and ill-suited for office: Michelle Kosinski, Schams Elwazer,
   and Stephen Collinson. Cable from UK's ambassador to the
   US blast Trump as inept, incompetent, CNN, July 8, 2019.
"I have never met anyone crazier than POTUS:" Michael Wolfe,
   Siege, XIII.
He opened up Mivkys, an infamous hotel, bar, brothel and
   restaurant in New Orleans: Natalie Obiko Pearson, Trump's
   Family Fortune Originated in a Canadian Gold-Rush Brother,
   Bloomberg, October 26, 2016.
POTUS framed his election as a clash of civilizations: Jeremy W.
   Peters, Trump Sets the 2020 tone: Like 2016, Only This Time
   'the Squad' Is Here, New York Times, NBS News, July 17, 2017.
Even more confounding was that while he lost the popular vote
   by five million: David Wasserman, How Trump could lose by
   5 million votes and still win in 2020, July 19, 2019.

no generation in his family had ever fought in any war or served in any branch of the military: Marian Alfaro, Donald Trump Avoided the Military Draft 5 Times, Business Insider, Dec. 26, 2018. Trump and Military Service: A 100 Year Family History, nowaytrump.com, June 6, 2016

Days Two and Three – Back Swamp, LA Belladonna Winter Retreat

Daniel Hands hosted a private golf: many years ago, an event similar to this happened at Tour Eighteen in Houston and the local news had a field day.

The foliage and berries: Belladonna: Uses and Risks, Medical News, www.medicalnewstoday.com July 1, 2017.

Upon her discovering her husband's infidelity: a situation similar to this actually happened to a couple almost thirty years ago. But, it was the wives who ran off with one another. In full view of the neighbors, the husband tossed all her belonging on the front yard!

The Temple of Virtue - George Washington's Ghost #1

Known as the Hudson Highlands: James Thomas Flexner, Washington The Indispensable Man, 149.

Washington's trusty ghost dog, Sweet Lips, an American Foxhound sniffed the trail ahead for intruders: AKC Staff, 14 Presidents and Their Pups, akc.org.

a combination of animal and human teeth: Colin Schultz, George Washington Didn't Have Wooden Teeth – They Were Ivory, Smithsonian Magazine, November 7, 2014.

The Temple of Virtue: https://scholarworks.gvsu.edu/washington_temple_of_virtue/

Perhaps the most important gathering ever in the United States: Washington The Indispensable Man, 174.

Our weak and fragile Congress has asked the thirteen Colonies to help remunerate: Ibid., 166-169.

confident that the new government will in the end act responsibly: Ibid., 174.

Ask yourselves if General Yates were successful in seizing control of the Continental: Ibid., 170-172.

service of my country I have not only grown gray but almost blind: Ibid.

must not abandon that what we have achieved, a free and just nation page: Ibid. and http://www.historyplace.com/speeches/washington.htm

hardened soldiers begin to weep: Washington The Indispensable Man, 175.

Jefferson declared that the moderation and virtue of a single character: Ibid.

Following our victory, many wanted a monarchy which I refused: PBS American Experience, DVD, Director and Producer David Sutherland, David Sutherland Productions. George Washington, The Man Who Wouldn't Be King, https://www.heritage.org/commentary/the-man-who-would-not-be-king

After turning over four national security advisers, three chiefs of staffs, three directors of oval office operations, five communications directors, and numerous cabinet members: Nancy Cook, An unshackled Trump finally gets the presidency he always wanted, Politico.com, Sept 19, 2019.

Mount Vernon's dependency on slave labor as a misfortune: Washington The Indispensable Man, 387.

I left the house slaves who served me behind: Ibid., 390.

The National Archives - Thomas Jefferson's Ghost #3

Your uncanny and ruthless instincts help you understand that perception: Ronald Kessler, The Trump White House Changing the Rules of the Game, 270.

Federalists harbored a lot of acrimony: John B. Boles, Jefferson Architect of American Liberty, 316-320.

accused me of atheism or deism: Ibid, 314.

perverted every word which fell from my lips: Thomas Jefferson The Art of Power, XVIII.

according to one clergyman: Jefferson Architect of American Liberty, 314.

gleaming, white, marble, temple-like structure: Cliff Sloan and David McKeen, The Great Decision: Jefferson, Adams, Marshall, and the Battle for the Supreme Court, Loc 23 of 4293.

my biggest philosophical error: Ibid., 183.

real enmity and acrimony split the Senate and the House: Ibid., loc 56 of 429.

Marbury vs. Madison can be viewed as me vs. John Marshall: Ibid.

On the eve of the Marbury case: Ibid., 190-191.

we are all republicans, we are all federalists: Ibid.

We are people governed by the rule of law: Ibid.

established that federal law was superior to state law: Ibid., 184.

Supreme Court will be the final arbiter of the Constitution: Ibid.

establish the principal that judges cannot be impeached due to political disagreements: Ibid.

exercise temperance, patience, and love: Thomas Jefferson The Art of Power, 756-757.

always sought common ground: Jefferson Architect of American Liberty, 453.

President John Adams chose to honor the same day with our death: Fawn M. Brodie, Thomas Jefferson, An Intimate History, 468.

Just six month ago they filled the last vacancy on the Supreme Court. Rarely in our history have all judges on the court been of the same political persuasion: Daniel A. Cotter, The Chief Justices, 385,406.408, 411.

This move effectively gives these two leaders unprecedented power over our judicial system. In conjunction with the judges, the decisions they make will affect the nation for several generations: Ibid.

Protesting what they contend to be dominance of partisan politics in the Supreme Court, Ibid.

Battle of New Orleans - Andrew Jackson's Ghost #7

The Battle of New Orleans, sung by Johnny Horton: Written by Jimmy Driftwood, Columbia label,1959.

Can you believe I'm a politician? I can't even: https://www.cnn.com/2019/12/16/politics/trump-top-lines-2019/index.html

Modestly, if I do say so myself, I ran a great campaign: Ibid.

conflict essentially ended the War of 1812: Sean Wilents, Andrew Jackson, 32-34.

exacted our revenge on the British army, and their Indian and Spanish friends: Ibid.

The legend lived on after I survived the first attempted assassination of an American president: Brian Adam Jones, The 8 Presidents With The Most Badass Military Records, https://taskandpurpose.com/8-presidents-badass-military-records, July 02, 2014.

You gutted the authority of the general who supported jail time for that villain and disparaged his platoon who courageously called him out: Dave Philipps, Trump Clears Three Service Members in War Crimes Case, New York Times, Nov. 15, 2019. Anguished Seals Recall Chief as Evil, New York Times, December 27, 2019.

fun and honor and profit: Jon Meacham, Thomas Jefferson The Art of Power, page XIX. Gordon S. Wood, Empire of Liberty: A history of the Early Republic, 1789 – 1815, 280.

After leaving government, Burr headed to the Louisiana Territory: Thomas Jefferson The Art of Power, 630-635.

engaged the British in a dialogue: Jefferson Architect of American Liberty, 401.

Burr was tried for treason: Jefferson Architect of American Liberty, 400-408.

I inspired either love or hatred: Andrew Jackson, 2-12.

He slashed me with his saber: Ibid., 17.

I signed a trade agreement with my former enemy: Anirudh, 10 Major Accomplishments by Andrew Jackson and Whaples, Robert, Were Andrew Jackson's Policies Good for the Economy? 556.

I dwelled in a brutish time as America spread its frontiers: Michael Kaplan, Two Tributes to Andrew Jackson the Embodiment of the American Spirit, the New Jacksonian Blog, March 6, 2011 and Allan Metcalf, Is Donald Trump the Andrew Jackson of Our Time? The Chronicle of Higher Education, November 6, 2018.

I confess that I did have a volatile personality: Andrew Jackson, 153.

privileged political insiders: Ibid., 48-49.

attend Adams's inauguration: Ibid.

My dearest companions used to say I fought so many that on horseback that I rattled like a bag of marbles: Mark Hallum, Presidents Who Have Personally Killed People, History News Network, August 15, 2015.

fought a duel with Thomas Hart Benton: Amy Hisson, Now Defend Yourself, You Damned Rascal, www.amyhisson.com, Nov 3, 2005.

Samuel Swartwout, a "New York City fixer,": Andrew Jackson, 58-61.

Balanced the budget and paid off the national debt: Ibid., 70.

Supreme Court's ruling in Worchester v. Georgia (1832) that decided that Native Americans: Martin Kelly, 10 Things to Know About Andrew Jackson, www.thoughtco.com

Peoria Courthouse - Abraham Lincoln's Ghost #16

he had compared himself to Lincoln, boasting that his poll numbers were better than #16: Sidney Blumenthal, Trump's Increasingly Weird Attempts To Compare Himself to Lincoln, The New Yorker, October 24, 2019.

lasted three hours and history records it exceeded 17,000 words: Sarah Pruitt, Lincoln's Peoria Speech, 160 Years later, Oct 16, 2014, www.history.com

shepherded the bill: NYTimes, Playing in Peoria, Nov 3, 1985.

decide among themselves whether…free or slave states: Sidney Blumenthal, The Political Life of Abraham Lincoln, A Self Made Man, 3-5.

eventually led to the Civil War: Ibid.

It roused me as I had never been before on the issue: Sarah Pruitt, Lincoln's Peoria Speech, 160 Years later, Oct 16,2014, www. history.com.

I had won the popular vote: Lincoln-Douglas Debates, A&E Television Networks, August 21, 2018, https://www.history. com/topics/19th-century/lincoln-douglas-debates

In fact, Douglas and I respected, Ibid.

I once told an audience that he and I are about the best friends: The Lehman Institute, Mr. Lincoln and Friends, www. mrlincolnandfriends.org

I wish you to do nothing in life merely for revenge but that what you may do, shall be solely done with reference to the security of the future: Carl Sandburg, Lincoln Collector, 188.

Nor, did I punish the friends of my opponents: Ibid.

After Richmond fell to Union soldiers: Ibid.

you've crossed a line that even President Richard Nixon dared not cross in the depths of the Watergate scandal': Remy Tumin and Elijah Walker, Roger Stone promised to remain loyal to President Trump, The New York Time The Morning, July 12, 2020.

In the final year of the Civil War, I was widely hated by Republicans and Democrats alike: S.C. Gwynne, Hymns of the Republic: The Story of the Final Year of the American Civil War, 325.

With a "furious, defeated South and with death threats all around: Michael Beschloss, Presidents of War, 238.

hard drinking, impulsive, and ill-tempered Johnson be next in line to succeed me: Ibid.

The U.S. is a country for white men, and by God, as long as I am President, it shall be a government for white men: NCC Staff, Andrew Johnson: The most criticized president ever? Constitution Daily, National Constitution Center, July 31, 2019.

Fort Wagner - Ulysses Grant's Ghost #18

The animal was a gift from a wealthy businessman: Sarah Kay Bierle, Grant's Cincinnati The General's Horse, Gazzette665, January 27, 2017.

Grant was a superb horseman: Ibid.

Fourteen cannons bellowed: Brian C. Pohanka, Fort Wagner and the 54th Massachusetts Volunteer Infantry, https://www.battlefields.org/learn/articles/fort-wagner-and-54th-massachusetts-volunteer-infantry.

Can you see that all but one of these men are black soldiers?: Ibid.

By the conclusion of our great domestic struggle, 180,000 blacks served: Hymns of the Republic, 325.

And, I want you to know whilst they were dying for their country: James M. McPherson, Tried By War Abraham Lincoln As Commander in Chief, 201-203.

"contrasted the heroes of the 54th with the cowardly white murders: Ibid.

the blacks sure seemed willing to fight: Michael Beschloss, Presidents of War, 218-219.

I gave my whole-hearted support for arming the negroes: Ulysses S. Grant, Memoirs and Selected Letters, 1031–1032.

In the early stages of the Civil War, New Yorkers resented losing the South: New York Draft Riots, https://www.history.com/ topics/american-civil-war/draft-riots, August 21, 2009.

kept warning the working-class white citizens that emancipation would result in their replacement in the labor force: New York Riot Drafts.

"The New York Draft Riots remain the deadliest riots in U.S. history: Ibid.

Using every resource available to me: History.com Editors, Ulysses S. Grant, https://www.history.com/topics/us-presidents/ ulysses-s-grant-, August 21, 2018.

The Klan re-emerged in the first half of the 20th century: Ibid.

foster a peaceful reconciliation between the North and South: Ibid.

A great debt has been contracted in securing to us and our posterity the Union: Ulysses S. Grant, March 4,1869 First Inaugural Address, UVA Miller Center, Presidential Speeches.

some of the worst still exists: Louis Jacobson, Is Texas one of the nation's most gerrymanders states, as Bet O'Rourke said? POLITIFACT, Aug 16, 2018. Joseph Ax and Andrew Chung, Electoral map bias may worsen as U.S. gerrymandering battle shifts to states, Reuters, June 29, 2019. And David Meyers, The 12 worst House Districts: Experts label gerrymandering's dirty dozen, The Fulcrum, Nov 7, 2019.

In one of my last writings: Ulysses S. Grant, Memoirs and Selected Letters, 1119-1120.

incapable of recognizing some of my trusted: Hamlin *Garland, Ulysses S. Grant His life and character,* 440. and https://en.m.wikipedia. org/wiki/Grant_administration_scandals#Books53.

I was also too autocratic: Ibid.

However, I earnestly endeavored to respect the several trusts and duties and powers of the coordinate branches of government: Ulysses S. Grant, Message on Presidential Powers and Obligations Speech, May 4, 1876 to the House of Representatives, UVA, Miller Center.

corruption would be discovered in seven federal departments: Mary Louise *Hinsdale,* A History of the President's Cabinet. pp.207, 212–213 and https://en.m.wikipedia.org/wiki/ Grant_administration_scandals#Books53.

I trust my colleagues and their family employed here.: https:// www.thedailybeast.com/cheats/2017/03/06/trump-hires-rudy-giuliani-s-son https://www.huffpost.com/entry/william-barr-son-in-law-white-house_n_5c6bd826e4b0b9cc790012ce https://www.cnn.com/2019/05/08/politics/john-kelly-trump-family-ivanka-jared-kushner/index.html https://www.scmp. com/news/world/united-states-canada/article/2148195/ china-approves-13-new-ivanka-trump-trademarks-3.

He's the son of Lexington: Sarah Kay Bierle, Grant's Cincinnati, The General's Horse.

A Visit to a Deathbed – James Garfield's Ghost #20

The perpetrator, like many assassins, was delusional. He failed as lawyer and an evangelist. Sadly, just like in your times, he found it easy to find a cheap gun: Candace Millard, Destiny of the Republic. And Kevin Baker, The Doctors Who Killed a President, New York Times, Oct 2, 2011.

For almost 90 days I have endured every torture that medical care and knowledge of the time could inflict, Ibid.

He and his assistants continue to stick their ungloved fingers inside me to probe where the bullet has lodged: Ibid.

a new imaging device that Alexander Graham Bell has been racing to create to specifically locate metal concealed in my flesh: Ibid.

The physician who treats me ignores what modern medicine of the time offers: Ibid.

Dr. Joseph Lister, a British surgeon and a pioneer of antiseptic surgery, had already proven that washing hands and instruments could prevent infection and save lives: Ibid.

you suggest people should use hydroxychloroquine to prevent Covid: Stephanie Ebbs, FDA revokes permission to treat Covid – 19 with hydroxychloroquine drug previously touted by Trump, abcnews.go.com, June 15, 2020.

Then you falsely claim that 99% of Covid -19 cases are totally harmless: Jeremy Diamond, FDA commissioner refuses to defend Trump claim that 99% of Covid – 19 cases are harmless, cnn.com, July 5, 2020. And Dan Patrick, says there is something more important than living: Matt Stieb, Dan Patrick of Texas on State Reopening: There Are More Important Things Than Living, nymag.com, Apr 21, 2020.

he is tired of listening to Fauci: Nicole Cobler, Austin American – Statesman, Texas Lt. Gov. Dan Patrick done listening to Dr. Anthony Fauci, USA Today, July 2, 2020.

Did either of you or the Lt. Governor ever stop to think that about 80% of Covid related deaths in the U.S. are people over 65 years old: Center for Disease Conrol, Older Adults, Jun 25, 2020.

Last, I regret my brief infidelity: Ibid.

Why even NASCAR, a bunch of good old boys who play hard and run fast, supports the ban: Betsy Klein and Kevin Liptak, White House refuses to denounce Confederate flag as Trump bemoans NASCAR's ban, CNN politics, July 6, 2020.

A Trip On The Elysian - Teddy Roosevelt's Ghost #26

I set out on the longest train ride: Hamilton, E.L. President Theodore Roosevelt Acquired A New Pet From A 12 Year Old, www.thevintagenews,com, May 1, 2018.

70 feet of paneled virgin forested mahogany, equipped with the finest leather and velvet chairs: Ibid.

Without provocation, Roosevelt's Bull Terrier, Pete: AKC Staff, 14 Presidents and Their Pups.

marketing campaign to test my concept of a Square Deal: Doris Kearns Goodwin, The Bully Pulpit, 349-350.

you know about marketing campaigns: Michael Cohen, House Testimony, February 27, 2018.

took along the famous naturalist John Burroughs and camped with John Muir: The Bully Pulpit, 351.

In Indiana, they loved it when I said speak softly and carry a big stick: Ibid., 350.

a man who keeps his word and never promises: Ibid.

In Oregon, they cheered when I said do not like hardness of heart: Ibid.

In Arizona, I spoke of the Indians in my regiment from Texas: Ibid.

'I don't go as far as to think that the only good Indians are dead Indians, but I believe nine out of ten are: Alysa Landry, Theodore Landry, Theodore Roosevelt: The Only Good Indians Are the Dead Indians, indiancountrytoday.com. Jun 28, 2016.

When I reached Yellowstone and Yosemite, I stepped up my campaign to preserve America from exploitation: Ibid., 351.

When I arrived at the Grand Canyon: Ibid.

I urged with the sturdiest of rigor that our countrymen to leave as it is for children and generations to come: Ibid.

Upon entering the San Lorenzo Valley, I admired the majestic beauty of giant sequoias: Ibid., 352.

connection between forests and water conservation: Ibid.

prevent America's forests and waters from coming into the hands of a few men of great wealth: Ibid., 352.

"I'm going to deregulate energy-efficient dishwashers, showers, toilets and sinks: Tim Haines, Rally Crowd Cheers Trump's Promise to Deregulate Energy Efficient Dishwashers, Showers, Sinks, realclearpolitics.com, January 15, 2020.

I'm rolling back Obama Department of Energy efficiency standards so that you can actually wash and rinse your dishes: Ibid.

Our forefathers faced certain perils which we have outgrown: Theodore Roosevelt. December 9,1908 Eighth Annual Message to the Senate and House of Representatives, UVA, Miller Center.

We have increased instances of black rain and snow: Olivis Rosane, Green Snow Raises Pollution Concerns in Russan City, www.ecowatch, February 26, 2019.

There are over 26,000 indicators of global warning on this planet: Katharine Hayhoe, Professor of Political Science at Texas Tech University, Ph.D in Atmospheric Science, Christians, Climate, And Our Culture in the U.S., lecture at the Lanier Theological Library, September 28, 2019.

They warned President Johnson of the impending disaster and every president since him: Ibid.

fundamentalists who have paid scientists to deny climate change and claim it's a liberal concoction: Ibid.

thirty-eight of their studies were analyzed from scratch: Ibid.

Let's take your flawed, dastardly logic about natural cycles: Ibid.

you too are a creature of God. Caring about God's creation-the earth and people and other living thing is a genuine expression of faith: Ibid.

They are shutting down coal plants as quickly as they can and
investing billions of dollars to replace them: Ibid.

It is well to keep in mind that exactly as the anarchist is the
worst enemy of liberty and the reactionary the worst enemy of
order: Theodore Roosevelt. December 9,1908 Eighth Annual
Message to the Senate and House of Representatives, UVA,
Miller Center.

encouraged the Japanese to embrace a Monroe Doctrine: David
M. Shribman, Did misguided US foreign policy lead to WWII?,
The Boston Globe, May 10, 2010.

Washington National Cathedral - Woodrow Wilson's Ghost #28

History shows that I'm the only President ever entombed
here: History.com Editors, https://www.history.com/topics/
us-presidents/woodrow-wilson, October 18, 2018.

He hoped that the Cathedral would become the American version
of Westminster Abbey: J. Arthur Bloom, Why the National
Cathedral must exhume Woodrow Wilson, miltrailleuse.net,
2015.

I graduated from Princeton, earned a doctorate in political
science from John Hopkins, and once served as President of
Princeton: John Milton Cooper, Jr., Woodrow Wilson, 3, 8.

As the nation's president, I owed much of my success to the study
of politics: Woodrow Wilson, 10.

With great government went may deep secrets which we too long
delayed to look into and scrutinize with candid, fearless eyes:
Woodrow Wilson, Eighth Annual Message, December 7, 1920,
UVA, Miller Center.

There has been something crude and heartless and unfeeling in
our haste to succeed and be grea: Ibid.

strongly believe that anybody who presumes to know God's will is blasphemy: Ibid., 4-5.

As a result, I governed in a manner that separated church and state and religion and society: Ibid.

I do not feel that the religious views of religious tribes should be forced upon others...especially by government: Ibid.

counted Jews and Catholics among my closest political associates: Ibid.

became the first president to visit the Vatican and appoint the first Jew to the Supreme Court, Louis D. Brandeis. Ibid.

I abhor people who say they are doing certain things because God told them to: Ibid.

War isn't declared in the name of God; it is a human affair entirely: Ibid.

When I took the nation into World War I, it wasn't because our homeland had been attacked: Ibid.

I called my vision for the world "Peace Without Victory: Ibid., 6-7, 370-371.

left sore winners and unrepentant losers: Ibid., 7.

Isolationist minded Republicans in Congress: History.com Editors, https://www.history.com/topics/us-presidents/woodrow-wilson, October 18, 2018.

Tens of thousands were indeed eligible voters: Rick Jervis, Voting rights: Texas voter purge is latest effort to target minority voters, USA Today, February 7, 2019.

That decision shortened World War I: John Milton Cooper, Woodrow Wilson, 7.

Unfortunately, it came at a high price: David W. Johnson, Then and Now: What Woodrow Wilson's 1918 Pandemic Failure Can Teach Us Today, www.4sighthealth,com, April 23, 2020.

the most consequential mistake I made was to ignore the Spanish Flu epidemic, Ibid.

Both Allied and Central power nations censored reports of it to avoid affecting morale: Editors, History Channel, Why Was It Called the 'Spanish Flu?', www.history.com, Mar 27, 2020.

More of our troops died of the flu than the war: Ibid.

I suffered a debilitating case of the Spanish Flu: Ibid.

why the U.S., with only four percent of the world's population, has twenty-five percent of its coronavirus cases: Scottie Andrew, The US has 4% of the world's population but 25% of its coronavirus cases, CNNhealth, www.cnn.com , June 30, 2020.

The women were very instrumental in helping Republican Warren Harding: History.com Editors, https://www.history.com/topics/us-presidents/woodrow-wilson, October 18, 2018. And John Milton Cooper, Jr., Woodrow Wilson. 571-572.

The United States is of necessity the sample democracy of the world, and the triumph of Democracy depends upon its success: Woodrow Wilson, Eighth Annual Message, December 7, 1920.

It was my belief that he should be the representative of no constituency, but of the whole people: Jon Meacham, The Soul of America: The Battle for the Republic, 36.

"I have one other major regret, which in the light of history: John Milton Cooper, Woodrow Wilson, 11-12, 170-171.

Most of my cabinet members, like me, were born in the south and nearly all the congressional leadership: Ibid., 204, 205, 510.

Standing Rock - Calvin Coolidge's Ghost #30

Chauncy Yellow Robe, a prominent Lakota activist and teacher: Cecile R. Ganteaume, https://www.whatitmeanstobeamerican.org/encounters/what-calvin-coolidge-didnt-understand-about-native-americans/ November 30, 2017.

The headdress was a potent symbol of Lakota culture: Ibid.

the Lakotas gave Coolidge the name Wanbi Tokahe, meaning Leading Eagle: Ibid.

When my staff arranged for me to visit the Black Hills: Robert Marshall, President Coolidge Adopted by the Sioux, http:// readingthroughhistory.com/2014/06/23/coolidge-adopted-by-the-sioux/, June 23, 2014.

adopted me a mere forty years after U.S. troops massacred 153: Ibid.

triggered public outrage, with most Americans feeling: Ibid.

usher in the Indian Citizen Act of 1924 which automatically gave full U.S. citizenship to American Indians: Ibid.

acted as a strong proponent of tribal rights: Ibid.

I expressed regret at their poverty: Ibid.

They were systematically being placed in federally funded boarding schools: Ibid.

I remained popular throughout my presidency: History.com Editors https://www.history.com/topics/us-presidents/calvin-coolidge, September 12, 2018.

The people appreciated that I had a dry sense of humor: Mark Katz, Calvin Coolidge's Bone-Dry Humor Is a Lesson in Laugh for Candidates, thedailybeast.com, February 13, 2017.

The Roaring Twenties was a time of fast-paced social, cultural and technology changes: Ibid.

many Americans spent lavishly: Ibid.

I provided a stabilizing influence through all this rapid change: Ibid.

appointed a special council to investigate the Teapot Dome oil-lease scandal: Ibid.

my secretary of state to jail for accepting bribes to lease federal oil reserves without competitive bidding: Ibid.

cleaned up a lot of corruption that occurred under the Republican Harding administration: Ibid.

I was an honest guy, lived frugally, and did my best to restore
   public trust in government: Amity Shlaes, Coolidge, Harper,
   February 12, 2013, and Jacquelin Lowe, A Dialogue Between
   Amity Shlaes and Paul Vocker, former chairman of the Federal
   Reserve Bank, Bushcenter.org, February 1, 2013.

We cannot permit ourselves to be narrowed and dwarfed: Calvin
   Coolidge, Sixth Annual Message, December 4, 1928, UVA
   Miller Center Presidential Speeches.

In 1749 there was an ad in a London newspaper: Dean Carnegie,
   The Man in the Bottle http://www.themagicdetective.com/
   2011/05/man-in-bottle.htmlMay 22, 2011 and Lora Jones,
   Theatre Royal Haymarket, @lorajoneswriter (Instagram).

The ad promised that ticket holders would witness magic never
   seen before: Ibid.

On the evening of January 16th, the theatre was sold out: with a
   large crowd waiting outside still hoping to see the performance:
   Ibid.

One man looked on in amusement: Ibid.

The Manure Pile – Herbert Hoover's Ghost #31

Federal Reserve studies showed that tariffs led to relative
   reductions in manufacturing and increases in producer
   prices: Greg Robb, Fed study finds Trump tariffs backfired,
   marketwatch.com, December 28, 2019.

the chief business of the American people is business: I remained
   popular throughout my presidency: History.com Editors
   https://www.history.com/topics/us-presidents/calvin-
   coolidge, September 12, 2018.

I set high tariffs on imported goods to protect American industry:
   Ibid

expressions of the so-called New Deal my opponent, Franklin
   Roosevelt, espoused, would destroy the very foundations of

our American system: Herbert Hoover, Campaign Speech in Madison Square Garden, October 21, 1932, millercenter.org Presidential Speeches.

President Trump's tariffs on steel cost U.S. consumers and businesses more than $900,000 a year for every job created: Taylor Telford, Mandate for use of U.S. steel unlikely to improve fortunes, Washington Post, July 17, 2019.

Jobs in steel using industries outnumbered those in steel production by about 80 to 1: Ibid.

hit hard by Trump's tariffs, steel users were forced to absorb costs or pass them onto consumers: Ibid.

very few steel producing jobs were added because modern mills don't require more manpower: Ibid.

"Here were our most significant trade wars to date: Lesley Kennedy, 7 Contentious Trade Wars in U.S. History, History. com/news, Oct 2, 2018.

How dare they broadcast that his trade war looked increasingly like a suicide vest: Chris Tomlinson, Trade war is a suicide vest threatening global economy, Houston Chronicle, Aug 28, 2019.

He found it particularly insulting that the economist described him as an 18th century self-proclaimed Tariff man: Ibid.

fired your campaign manager because your brand's reputation in the political polls is mired in the mud too: Noah Bierman and Eli Stokols, Trump, trailing in race, fires his campaign manager, Los Angeles Times. July 15, 2020.

Oval Office - Franklin D. Roosevelt's Ghost #32

POTUS eclipsed all records of time spent by a president at golf resorts: Besty Klein, Trump spend 1 of every 5 days in 2019 at a golf club, cnn.com, December 31, 2019.

Few CEOs ever spared this much time away from the business without losing touch with their businesses or getting sacked:

Is Your Firm Underperforming?: Lee Biggerstaff, David C. Cicero, Andy Puckett Your CEO Might Be Golfing Too Much, Harvard Business Review, November 30, 2016.

But as a yardstick, a Forbes reporter estimates that at the rate Forty-five was going: Chuck Jones, Trump's Golf Trips Could Cost Taxpayers over $340 million, Forbes, July 10, 2019.

I stew over how our generals and admirals could allow this to happen: James Mikel Wilson, Churchill and Roosevelt: The Big Sleepover At The White House (Christmas 1941 – New Year 1942), 43-44.

Fala, a Scottish Terrier who receives more fan mail than I do: AKC Staff, 14 Presidents and Their Pups.

Then, I realize my own culpability in imposing trade sanctions and embargos on Japan: Ibid.

We provided Japan over 70% of their scrap, 80% of their oil, and over 90% of their copper: Ibid.

I pour Edward R. Murrow, the top reporter for CBS: Ibid.

We may make mistakes …but they must never be mistakes which result from faintness of heart: Franklin Roosevelt, January 20, 1945: Fourth Inaugural Address, millercenter.org

There he is in the White House Press room standing on a chair: Ibid., 68.

no one can know the truth…and even if we did know the truth it wouldn't be worth risking our financial relationship: Chris Cillizza, The 36 wackiest lines from Donald Trump's totally bizzare Cabinet meeting, cnn.com, January 3, 2019.

The Gymnasium - Harry Truman's Ghost #33

When I played this piece, Stalin signed the Potsdam Agreement: Harry S. Truman Presidential Library & Museum, https://www.trumanlibrary.org/kids/piano.htm

Truman whispered in POTUS's ear, "I know you've never heard this speech or read it: Andrew Roberts, Churchill and Roosevelt, 894-896, 902, 912, 968.

I fired MacArthur before another nuclear war happened: Andrew Glass, President Truman fires Gen. MacArthur: April 11, 1951, politico.com, April 10, 2017.

In Churchill's words about the adolescent United Nations while speaking at Fulton, MO: Ibid, 894.

to demonstrate to our citizens how simply and peacefully our American system could transfer the presidency from my hands to his: President Harry S. Truman, January 15, 1953: Farewell Address, Presidential Speeches, UVA, Miller Center.

Until this brief dreamy moment of regret, POTUS had never expressed remorse: Too Much and Never Enough, pages 24, 43. 207-209.

Congressional CC - Dwight Eisenhower's Ghost #34

Clearly, POTUS had fictionalized and understated his handicap to look like a big shot: Zeke Miller, Book takes a swing at Trump on the links, Houston Chronicle, A2. Rick Reilly, Commander in Cheat.

The only thing I see that you have accomplished are five bankruptcies and hidden behind tax scandals to line your pockets: Mary Trump, Too Much and Never Enough, 9, 11, 132, 136, 143, 197.

They were alarmed by your take on history, particularly the key alliances: Jim Ross, Trump Called His Generals a "Bunch of Dopes and Babies in A Fit of Range, Book Claims, the dailybeast.com, January 17, 2020 and Carol Leonnig and Philip Rucker, A Very Stable Genius, Penguin Random House, Jan 21, 2020.

you called the Chief of Staffs all a bunch of dopes and babies. Losers to be exact: Ibid.

Pentagon advisers now hesitate to give you any military options because you might select the most extreme response: Jim Sciutto, Trump advisers hesitated to give military options and warned adversaries over fears he might start a war, August 6, 2020.

I fear that you lack the capability to continue to grow, learn, or evolve in this job: Too Much and Never Enough, 197.

You can't control your emotions, moderate your responses, or absorb and synthesize information given to you: Ibid.

I'm just about the smartest man I know: Avi Selk, Trump says he's a genius. A study found these other presidents actually were, The Washington Post, Jan 7, 2018.

So, you paid a friend to take the test for you: Too Much and Never Enough, 72.

charge the countries where we have troops to pay our government for their services: Ibid.

no small coincidence that China has chosen 2020 as a perfect year to suppress Hong Kong's democratic tendencies: John Ruwitch, As China Imposes New Hong Kong Law, U.S. And Allies Take Steps To Retaliate, npr.org, July 2, 2020.

Belarus dictator in Eastern Europe has just tightened his iron-grip having mysteriously won over 80% of the popular vote: BBC, Belarus election: Opposition leader Tikhanovskaya fled for sake of her children, bbc.com, Aug 12, 2020.

Let me tell you about a real leader in my life: Jim Newton, Eisenhower The White House Years, 37 - 40.

Congress and my administration took a joint approach to the most vital issues: President Dwight D. Eisenhower, January 17,1961: Farewell Address, millercenter.org.

During the Korean War, General MacArthur and my Secretary of State, John Foster Dulles, tried to persuade me to push our military forces through North Korea: Eisenhower The White House Years, 77-84.

if they didn't back off in Korea, I may have to drop another nuclear bomb: Presidents of War, 487.

Stalin had told Mao to drag out the Korean war to damage the reputation of the Great Britain and the United States: Ibid.

Unrestrained, McCarthy "grilled, harassed, and defamed Americans: The White House Years, 153-155.

Truman denounced McCarthy for besmirching the loyalty of General Marshall and to trying to destroy Dean Acheson: Presidents of War, 477-478.

listened to the ultra-religious Hawks in my government: Stephen Kinzer, The Brothers John Foster Dulles Allen Dulles, and Their Secret World War, 3, 323 - 325.

Upon laying this daunting task on my shoulders, Marshall with cold, penetrating blue eyes: Logan Nye, We are THE MIGHTY, https://www.wearethemighty.com/history/marshall-eisenhower-modern-military-leadership?rebelltitem=4#rebelltitem4

Their persuasive influence launched violent campaigns against foreign leaders: The Brothers: 312 - 325.

"I thought what was good for the country was good for General Motors, and vice versa: Dan Pontefract, What's Good For Our Country Was Good For General Motors, Forbes, Nov 26, 2018.

Allen Dulles put in play the Bay of Pigs invasion of Cuba: Ibid.

History shows the Dulles as really bad boys who only saw the world in black and white, good and evil: Ibid.

The brothers ignored Winston Churchill's advice in the mid 1950's that Ho Chi Minh was unbeatable: Ibid.

When Stalin died, they ignored his successor's periodic overtures for peaceful coexistence: Ibid.

The Dulles boys helped install dictators friendly to America: Ibid.

Other than your egotistical compulsion to flaunt your power and satisfy your outsized ego: Alex Johnson, Navy Secretary Forced To Resign Amid Seal Controversary, nbcnews.com,

Nov. 24, 2019 and Barbara Starr and Ryan Browne, Esper Says Trump ordered him to allow Gallagher to keep his Trident Pin and remain a Seal, cnn.com. November 25, 2019.

the future will be blessed with peace and prosperity for all: President Dwight D. Eisenhower, January 17,1961: Farewell Address, Presidential Speeches, UVA, Miller Center.

If you were in charge of high-profile court martials: Jennifer Doherty, Four-Star U.S. Army General Slams Trump's Behavior in Navy Seal Controversy: If He Was A General, We'd Fire Him, Newsweek, December, 28, 2019.

One who uses his enormous power and America's great resources in the best interests of world peace and human betterment: Ibid.

Kennedy Space Center - John F. Kennedy's Ghost #35

The monstrous 363-feet tall, 3,100 ton Saturn V: Douglas Brinkley, American Moonshot, 296, 298-290, 432-446.

Shortly after winning the presidency, I decided that America's dillydallying: Ibid., XX-XXV.

a lavish financial investment in space would unite government, industry, academia, and the media in a grand project: Ibid.

the cost to the taxpayers swelled to over $25 billion: Ibid.

the quest yielded the technology-based economy the United States enjoys today: Ibid.

When the naysayers asked why go to the moon? I put my whole political career on the line: Ibid.

Kennedy's favorite ghost dog, Pushinka, who raised his leg and squirted POTUS's shoes: AKC Staff, 14 Presidents and Their Pups.

Many of them 'originated with Twitter accounts linked to the Russians: Lara Jakes, As protests in South America surged, so did Russian trolls on Twitter, U.S. finds, The New York Times, Jan 19, 2020.

in Ecuador, Peru, Bolivia, Colombia and Chile over one 30-day period the Russians posted similar' inflammatory messages within minutes of one another: Ibid.

Not only have the Russians under Putin perfected poisoning the internet traffic, they have also literally poisoned prominent opposition to the Kremlin: Jennifer Hansler, Pompeo breaks silence on poisoning of Russia opposition leader, cnn.com, August 25, 2020.

Eisenhower sometimes appointed liberal judges because they were better qualified: Eisenhower the White House Years, 356-357.

Lyndon Johnson once commented about the primary difference between Democrats and Republicans: Robert L. Hardesty, The LBJ the Nation Seldom Saw, LBJ Presidential Library.

Our collective experiences teach that no one nation has the powah or wisdom to solve all the problems of the world: President John F. Kennedy, May 25, 1961: The Goal of Sending a Man to the Moon, Presidential Speeches, UVA, Miller Center.

At the Ranch - Lyndon B. Johnson's Ghost #36

Throughout his life always in a hurry: Robert L. Hardesty, The LBJ the Nation Seldom Saw.

Johnson shouted "dang, the brakes don't work: Corey Adwar, Lyndon Johnson Liked Taking His Advisors Out For Joyrides That Ended With This Terrifying Prank, Business Insider, August 27, 2014.

like to think that I got far more out of Congress than he would have gotten: Kent Germany, Lyndon. B. Johnson: Impact and Legacy, UVA Miller Center and Doris Kearns Goodwin, The Divided Legacy of Lyndon B. Johnson, The Atlantic, Sep 7, 2018.

I passed unprecedented legislation to protect the land, air, water, wilderness and quality of life: Ibid.

quite proud that I extended Roosevelt's New Deal, including aid
  to education, Headstart, Medicare and Medicaid: Ibid.
During my presidency, It became my dream to make life better
  for more people: Ibid.
I ripped the glittering cellophane off our society and forced the
  nation to look at what lay underneath: The LBJ the Nation
  Seldom Saw.
My zealous initiatives for arts, the environment, poverty, racial
  justice and the workplace safety angered: Ibid.
I inherited that damn old crazy Asian war from Eisenhower
  and Kennedy: Kat Eschner, How Robert McNamara Came
  to Regret the War He Escalated, Smithsonian Magazine,
  November 29, 2016.
I trusted the wrong Generals and advisers: Lyndon Baines
  Johnson, The Vantage Point Perspectives of The Presidency
  1963-1969, 148-153.
Secretary of Defense Robert McNamara took a statistical
  approach to measuring success: David K. Shipler, Robert
  McNamara and the Ghosts of Vietnam, the New York Times
  Magazine, August 10, 1997.
kept asking for more troops, Ibid.,144-146.
If I walked on water, they'd say it was because I couldn't swim:
  Presidential Courage, 325.
I want to show you what we called the Mexican school I taught
  in for a year over in Cotulla, Texas: Melissa Block, LBJ Carrier
  Poor Texas Town With Him in Civil Rights Fight, NPR.ORG,
  April 11, 2014.
The children of Mexican-Americans had been taught that the
  end of life was a beet row, or a spinach field, or a cotton patch:
  Ibid.
Damn you for cuttin' that three-billion-dollar aid package to
  Central American countries which Congress and the United

Nations approved: Bill Lambrecht, Texas lawmakers warn against aid cuts, Houston Chronicle, April 20, 2019.

It's one more low water benchmark in your administration that amid an outpourin' of bipartisan tributes to the Congressmen's advancement of civil rights that you have said so little: Katie Rogers, Trump Weighs In on the Death of John Lewis, One of His Most Vocal Critics, nyties.com. July 18, 2020.

Déjà vu - Richard Nixon's Ghost #37

My former White House counsel John Dean testified: Bob Woodard, The Last of the President's Men, 136-137.

Before I knew it, Congressman Tom Railsback, a moderate Republican, broke with his party and helped draw up the articles of impeachment against me: Scott Simon, Remembering A Congressman Who Bucked His Party On An Impeachment, NPR, January 23, 2020.

I am not a crook! I said that not in response to Watergate: Lily Rothman, I am Not a Crook. The Nixon Tax Story Rachel Maddow Just Compared to Trump's, Time Magazine, March 15, 2017.

You know President Johnson was very close to ending the Viet Nam war: Presidents of War, 570-571 and Colin Schultz, Nixon Prolonged Vietnam War for Political Gain: Unclassified Tapes Suggest, Smithsonian. Com, March 18, 2013.

At least your Vice President hasn't gone to jail yet: Richard Cohen, Spiro Agnew was Trump before Trump, The Washington Post, September 3, 2018.

As the former governor of Maryland, he got greedy: Ibid.

Watergate was a bit of mess for me: The Last of the Presidents Men, 174-175.

He dared to go where I would never…jury and sentence tampering: Dan Manga and Kevin Breuninger, Trump slams

Roger Stone Juror before she testifies at retrial hearing, CNBC, February 25, 2020.

And it sends a frightening message that people who might serve as a juror on future cases near and dear to forty-five could be personally confronted and sullied: Rachel Maddow, Trump engaged in 'jury tampering on a mass, national scale,' MSNBC, Feb 24,2020.

My finest hour as President was certainly establishing relations with the Chinese Communists: Ibid., 92-92.

Always remember, some people may hate you, but they don't win unless you hate them back and act on that hatred. Nixon message to White House staff upon departure.

Words to describe others like stupid, loser, moron, fake news, zero talent, enemies of the people: President Trump's Favorite Words, Dictionary.com Everything after Z. Also Eileen Sullivan and Michael D. Shear, Horseface, Lowlife, Fat, Ugly: How the President Demeans Women, The New York Times, Oct 16, 2018.

With pride, I can tell you that during the five and a half years I sat in the Oval Office no man or woman entered my administration and left with more of this world's goods than when she or he arrived: President Richard M. Nixon, August 9, 1974: Remarks on Departure from the White House, Presidential Speeches, UVA, Miller Center.

Whacking the Ball - Gerald Ford's Ghost #38

After dinner, Nelson and his two boys joined me: Gerald Ford, A Time To Heal, 440-441.

As Nixon's Vice President, I got to observe the man up front and personal: The Last of the President's Men, 91.

For example, Nixon sent a memo to his Attorney General Mitchell that he wanted to go after the government's own witness: Ibid., 92-93.

My most important task upon inheriting the office, was to heal the nation: President Gerald Ford, Speech on Taking Office, August 9, 1974, Presidential Speeches, UVA, Miller Center.

First Lady Betty for dancing barefoot on the polished cabinet room table: William Booth, Betty Ford's Tabled Resolution, Smithsonian Magazine, June 2008.

I left a more perfect union than when my stewardship began: President Gerald Ford, January 12, 1977: State of the Union Address, Presidential Speeches, UVA, Miller Center.

Habitat for Humanity - Jimmy Carter's Phantom #39

slapped your hand rather than to vote to remove a criminal without a conscience from office: Mary Trump, Two Much and Never Enough, 14.

He never took criticism lightly, admitted mistakes, or backed down. He learned as a child to perfect the art of obfuscation: Ibid, 11, 12,13, 43, 44.

I did a Playboy Magazine interview during the run up to my election in 1976: Bo Emerson, When Jimmy Carter Lusted In His Heart, The Atlanta Journal-Constitution, Sept 28, 2017.

shocked the electorate and cost you the election: Mark Galli, Trump Should Be Removed from Office, Christianity Today.

Even that fanatical Baptist minister in Louisiana publicly defends you: Michael J. Mooney, Trump's Apostle, Texas Monthly, Jul 23, 2019. And Stephen Young, 8 Times pastor Robert Jeffress Was a Stooge for Donald Trump, dallasobserver.com, June 17, 2019.

my candid confession probably gave Gerald Ford a few more votes: When Jimmy Carter Lusted In His Heart, The Atlanta Journal-Constitution.

Jimmy who continued working on Habitat for Humanity projects well into his 90's: Mark J. Updegrove, Building A Better World, Parade Magazine, Feb18, 2018, 19-20.

It was stupid of Iran to escalate efforts to become a Mideast Imperial power following the nuclear treaty: Thomas L. Friedman, Overrated Warrior, TimesDigest, January 5, 2020.

Instead, he ordered the assignation on Iraqi soil of Qasem Soleimani, Iran's top military leader and second: Trump's Choice of Killing Stunned Defense Officials, TimesDigest, January 5, 2020.

Past presidents and military leaders believed the risk was greater than the value: Tom Vanden Brook, Qasem Soleimani: The Pentagon has tracked Iranian general for many years before he was killed, USA Today, January 4, 2020.

They realized that we could not afford to assassinate every bad guy who crosses us: Thomas L. Friedman, Did Trump and Iran Just Bury the Hatchet, or the Future, The New York Times, Jan 8, 2020.

Soleimani was a stupid man who wasted the lifting of sanctions that was part of the deal with Obama: Ibid.

his gains you nothing if you aren't smart enough to press hard now for a new nuclear deal while the iron is hot: Ibid.

Your critics question your motivation for approving the assassination: David Mark, Trump's Iran attack distracts from impeachment - but can still hurt him politically, nbcnews.com, Jan 5, 2020.

Worse yet, you've moved the American Embassy to Jerusalem, officially recognizing it as the capital of Israel during a particular tumultuous time for the region: Alexia Underwood, The controversial US Jerusalem embassy opening, explained, vox.com, May 16, 2018.

your toxic presidency may be making people sick: William Wan and Lindsey Bever, Studies: Trump may be making Latinos sick, Washington Post, July 20, 2019.

became the first president to receive the Nobel Peace Prize for orchestrating a long-lasting peace agreement between Egypt and Israel: Lawrence Wright, Camp David, Alley Theatre, February-March 2020.

I monitored 107 elections in 39 countries: Ibid.

Frankly, you and I couldn't be further apart: Ibid.

in North Carolina where the State Board of Elections released hundreds of pages of documents showing evidence of ballot fraud: Gregory Krieg, Newly released documents detail allegations of fraud in 2016 by GOP operative in North Carolina, amp.cnn.com. December 19, 2018.

Is it true what your sister said that the only time you ever go to church is when the cameras are there: Too Much and Never Enough, 9.

And that you have no principles? Ibid.

He has admitted to immoral actions in business and his relationship with women: Ibid.

Berlin Wall - Ronald's Reagan's Ghost #40

I shout Mr. Gorbachev, if you seek peace, if you seek prosperity for the Soviet Union and Eastern Europe: Michael Beschloss, Presidential Courage, 315-316.

Nobody since President Kennedy had talked so tough to the Russians: Ibid., 283.

When Nixon occupied the White House he thought I was a lightweight: Ibid., 282.

I took the Bible literally and felt that we were approaching Armageddon: Ibid., 285-86, 298, 299.

Gorbachev expected that I owned a palace like your Belladonna estate: Ibid., 323.

you've told too many lies, screwed too many people and made too many mistakes: Too Much and Never Enough, reoccurring themes throughout the book.

Nobody wants or can work long for you before discovering how pompous, artificial and insincere you are: Ibid.

Washington was the most heavily defended city on earth: S.C. Gynne, Hymns of the Republic, Scribner, 2019, 2.

A little story about a big ship, a young sailor, and a refugee: President Ronald Reagan, January 11, 1989: Farewell Address, Presidential Speeches, UVA, Miller Center.

Because that's what it was like to be an American in the 1980: Ibid.

We were among the first Presidents to get divorced: Ibid., 296.

As fellow Irish men, we very much enjoyed each other's humor and company: Ibid., 284.

During my time in office I won a nickname, 'The Great Communicator': President Ronald Reagan, January 11, 1989: Farewell Address.

Thanks to Congressman Charlie Wilson and my tacit support: Peter W. Dickson, Reagan's Bargain/Charlie Wilson's War, Consortium News, 2008.

signed the Intermediate-Range Nuclear Forces Treaty...a step in the right direction that brought sighs of relief around the world: William Cummings, Read the full text of Fiona Hill's opening statement in impeachment hearing, USA Today, November 21, 2019.

Our ambassadors aren't paid by the American taxpayers to ask personal financial favors for their presidents. It's also against the Emoluments Clause of the U.S. Constitution: Mark Landler, Lara Jakes, and Maggie Haberman, Trump's Request of an Ambassador: Get the British Open for Me, ntimes.com, July 22, 2020.

signed an open letter saying that your mental state makes you incapable of serving safely as president: Katie Forster, Mental health professionals warn Trump is incapable of being president, www.independent.com.uk, February 14, 2017. May Bulman, Donald Trump has dangerous mental illness, say psychiatry experts at Yale Conference. www.independent

co.uk., April 21, 2017. Tom Porter, 350 health professionals sign a letter to Congress claiming Trump's mental health is deteriorating dangerously amid impeachment proceedings, Business Insider, December 5, 2019.

And seven months later your own niece expressed the same fears for the country in her new book. She has a PHD in Psychology: Mary Trump, Too Much and Never Enough, 23- 26, 209, 210.

George H.W. Bush's Ghost #41

Bush, who had served as Ambassador to China: George H.W. Bush, All The Best, 199.

immigration spiked to unprecedented levels: Alan Bersin, Nate Bruggeman, and Ben Rohrbaugh, Yes There's a Crisis on the Border. And It's Trump's Fault, PoliticoMagazine, April 05, 2019.

Feel the wall is unnecessary, including the Mayor of El Paso: Del Margo, El Paso mayor: Despite Trump's State of the Union Claim our relations with Mexico Thrive, www.usatoday.com/story/opinion/voices/2019/02/10/

I just loved that game and was pretty good at it: Michael Duffy, George H.W. Bush Accomplished Much More as President Than He Ever Got Credit For, Time Magazine, December 1, 2018.

When they made a ringer, the Chinese got to tell me what they needed from us. And when I made a ringer, I told them what we expected: Although Bush enjoyed horseshoes there is no evidence that he traded horseshoes for foreign policy. *The author just imagined this.*

even if you reach agreement with those countries you pushed into a trade war: Mark Magnier, Phase one trade deal gives Donald Trump bragging rights but phase two is likely a mirage, analysts say, South China Morning Post, Jan. 14, 2020.

many members on both sides of Congress—didn't want the script to play out the way it has: Mary Papenfuss, Trump Has Already Lost His Pricey China Trade War, Paul Krugman Warns, huffpost.com, Dec 16, 2019.

How can you possibly call that a victory: Ibid.

your trade war has hurt the American farmers to the tune of almost $35 billion: Ibid.

caught them red handed trying to steal our technology and medical research: Edward Wong, Lara Jakes, Seven Lee Myers, U.S. Orders China to Close Houston Consulate, Citing Efforts to Steal Trade Secrets, The New York Times, July 22, 2020.

They've pledged to increase exchanges at all levels, cooperate on finding a cure for Covid-19, and strengthen coordination on major internal and regional affairs: James Griffiths, As US and China force consulates to close, the risk of missteps and spiraling tensions rises, CNN, July 24. 2020.

'since you've come into office, the US and China have spent the past three years ripping out the software of their relationship. Now we are literally ripping out the hardware: Ibid.

They have become very wise to your "five-chapter playbook: Mark Magnier, Phase one trade deal gives Donald Trump bragging rights but phase two is likely a mirage, analysts say, South China Morning Post, Jan. 14, 2020.

Why didn't you react with the same swiftness and sense of urgency: All The Best, 476-81, 483-86.

Little Big Hands, as president you have several obligations: President George H.W. Bush, January 5, 1993 Address at West Point, Presidential Speeches, UVA, Miller Center.

when we travel in a motorcade no more sirens: Michael Duffy, Time Magazine.

A few like James Buchanan, Warren Harding, Andrew Johnson: Andrew Soergel and Jay Tolson, The 10 Worst Presidents, US News and World Report, March 29, 2014.

You moaned 'Nobody likes Me' and then answered the root cause, PERSONALITY: Ed Mazza, Trump Moans Nobody Likes Me, And Twitter Critics Quickly Remind Him Why, www.huffpost.com, July 29, 2020.

My TV show: Mary Trump, observations about The Apprentice and Donald's image and myth as the brash, self- made dealmaker, Too Much and Never Enough, 11.

Heartbreak Hotel - Bill Clinton's Phantom #42

Clinton belted out an impressive version of Heartbreak Hotel: Reed Saxon, Bill Clinton pays the sax, Iconic presidential campaign moments, CBS News (AP).

As a matter of routine, you underpay them and dispute and litigate their services: Alexandra Berzon, Donald Trump's Business Plan Left a Trail of Unpaid Bills, wsj.com, June 9, 2016. And Roger Parloff, Why U.S. Law Makes It Easy for Donald Trump To Stiff Contractors, fortune.com, September 30, 2016.

Investors have discovered that your business model screws others, and your profits are built on a shaky—no, shady—foundation: Mary Trump, Too Much and Never Enough, 141-142.

Your number of lawsuits was unmatched when you began campaigning for office: Glenn Fleishman, The People vs. Donald Trump: Every Major Lawsuit and Investigation the President Faces, fortune.com, September 21, 2018. And Nick Penzenstadler and Susan Page, Exclusive: Trump's 3,500 lawsuits unprecedented for a presidential nominee, USA Today, June 1, 2016.

smoking doesn't kill, condoms don't protect, and the best way to curb an epidemic is through prayer: Farhad Manjoo, Coronvairus is what you get when you ignore science, New York Times, March 4, 2020.

Here we are at the 2013 Moscow Miss Universe Pageant: Jeffrey Toobin, Trump's Miss Universe Gambit, The New Yorker, February 19, 2018.

None of these girls had to possess talent to participate in Miss Universe: Ibid.

One of your great joys in life was flirting and circulating among the contestants while they rehearsed a day or two before the pageant began: Ibid.

Although I retained a cadre of qualified judges, you reserved the right to pick nine of the top fifteen finalists out of the original eighty-six contestants: Ibid.

Each of my businesses mutually reinforced and complemented all the other Belladonna products—from hotels to steak, vodka, women, clothing, and golf resorts: Ibid.

Even though American viewers fell from twelve million when I bought the pageant to fewer than four million by the time of the Moscow event, I had a grander and more profitable goal in mind: Ibid.

But I regret that my brother, Bubba, told that golf sportswriter that we don't rely on American banks. We have all the funding we need out of Russia: Ibid.

You famously called him a 'terrific guy' and I praised his 'intellect and philanthropic efforts: Jill Colvin, What did Jeffrey Epstein's famous friends know and see?, apnew.com, July 9, 2019.

Fox News had to apologize for inadvertently cropping you out of a photo with Epstein: Sean Neumann, Fox News Mistakenly Cropped President Trump from Photo with Jeffrey Epstein and Ghislaine Maxwell, people.com, July 7, 2020.

And, you sure have made a mess of the North American Free Trade Agreement: American Experience, Legacy of the Clinton Administration, 2012.

At my last White House Correspondent's dinner I played a farewell faux video: Megan Rosenfeld, Mary Ann French, Mary Ann and others, And On Tenor Sax, It's President Bill, The Washington Post, Jan 13, 1993.

you wouldn't work with Congress on fixing infrastructure, or anything else of substance: Ron Elving, How Trump Breaks With Clinton and Nixon on Governing While Under Investigation, npr.org, May 23, 2019.

I feel I never really had a honeymoon with the press: Taylor Branch, The Clinton Tapes Wrestling History With The President, 11.

I am quite proud of my service to my country: Ibid.

I intervened to end the civil war and ethnic conflict: Bill Clinton, My Life, 868, 892, 924, 935, 945.

this sordid political action group continues to shoot themselves in the foot: Sebastian Murdock, NRA Could Lose Tax-Exempt Status Over Shady Business Practices, huffpost.com, April 4, 2019.

I warned that our 'most fateful new challenge will come from global warming: President Bill Clinton, January 19, 1999: State of the Union Address, Presidential Speeches, UVA, Miller Center.

Two years ago, thirty-five mental health professionals signed an open letter saying that your mental state makes you incapable of serving safely as president.

wildfires show the planet the road to hell: Paul Krugman, Australia's wildfires show us the road to hell, Houston Chronicle, January 13, 2020.

The Interview - George W. Bush's Phantom #43

And, then as part of Presidential privilege, he sent a follow up letter that probibited: Grace Ashford, Michael Cohen Says Trump Told Him to Threaten Schools not to Release Grades, The New York Times, Feb 27, 2019.

a large crowd gathered to watch David Rubenstein interview on stage Bill Clinton and George W. Bush: David Rubenstein,

Clinton and Bush, Peer to Peer Conversations the David Rubenstein Show, Bloomberg, Aug 9, 2017.

Rubenstein had cofounded the Carlyle Fund, one of the largest private equity funds in the world. More importantly he was also a world class philanthropist: Ibid.

Having paid the winning bid of $21.5 million at a Sotheby's auction: Peter Lattman, Who Bought Magna Carta, The Wall Street Journal, Dec. 20, 2007.

Rubenstein felt deeply disturbed that many Americans could not name the three branches of government: David Rubenstein, from a keynote speech at the National Churchill Museums 50th Anniversary, May 4, 2019.

Having discovered that many in Congress also lacked a firm grasp of the country's history and guiding principles: Ibid.

So here is the gist of it and I'm goin' to ad lib a bit for the sake of relevance: David Rubenstein, Clinton and Bush, Peer to Peer Conversations the David Rubenstein Show.

"Freedom is never more than one generation away from extinction: Ronald Reagan Freedom Speech, www.reagan.com

How else can you explain your suggestion that the November presidential election be postponed: Donald Trump suggests delay to 2020 US presidential election, BBC News, July 30, 2020.

"Without an invitation and often unannounced, how about the way you've sent masked, camaouflaged federal law enforcersinto states and cities run by liberal governments: Zolan Kannon-Youngs, Sergio Olmos, Mike Baker, and Adam Goldman, At Start, F.B.I. Saw Protesters As Threatening, The New York Times, July 29, 2020.

Or, clearing Lafayette Square of peaceful demonstrators for a photo op of you holding a bible in your hand at St. John's Episcopal Church: Catie, Edmondson, Chief Defends Park Police In Clearing of Square in June, The New York Times, July 9, 2020.

"How do you explain overridin' the rule of law by pardoning conflicted felons: Katie Rogers, Derrick Bryson Taylor, and Heather Murphy, Trump Adds Roger Stone to His List of Pardons and Commutations, nytimes.com, July 11, 2020.

Then to prevent your personal attorney from writing a book about you, you kept him under lock and key: Kristine Phillips, Michael Cohen was sent back to prison as a retaliatory act over tell-all book about Trump, federal judge rules, www.usatoday.com. July 23, 2020.

What about feathering your own nest by channeling campaign money to your private businesses…restaurants, hotels, and golf courses: Sonam Sheth, Trump's campaign channeled nearly $400,000 to his private business in 2 days, Business Insider and www.msn.com, July 17, 2020.

Shamelessly, you have promoted your own businesses even though it's a conflict of interest while president: Ibid.

You hand-pick a political ally to take charge of the postal system on the pretense of expense control: Alan Rappeport, Postal Service Pick With Ties to Trump Raises Concerns Ahead of 2020 Election, www.nytimes.com, May 7, 2020.

Your real motive…interfere with and limit the voting by mail: Michael Shear, Hailey Fuchs, Kenneth Vogel, Mail Delays Fuel Concern Trump Is Undercutting Postal System Ahead of Voting, The New York Times, July 31, 2020

you speculate that there will be massive voter fraud in the coming election: Ibid.

further add to the toxic mix when you claim Black Lives Matter are communists: Tom Kertscher, PolitiFact: Is Black Lives Mater a Marxist movement, Tampa Bay Times, July 22, 2020.

He orchestrated a sedition law, makin' it illegal to criticize his government: Katrina Lamansky, Trump-Clinton nasty? Not compared to these campaigns from the old days, CNN and WQAD8, September 23, 2016.

Some of the things I'm most proud of are my response to terrorism
committed on the World Trade Center and the Pentagon:
George W. Bush First and Second Presidential Terms, By
History.com editors, June 7, 2019.

you insinuate that my Dad was a 'loser' for getting shot down in
World War II and then inferrin' that he and I were 'suckers:
Jeffrey Goldberg, Trump: Americans Who Died in War Are
'Losers and Suckers,' theatlantic.com, September 3, 2020.

But the enormous cost of fighting two wars, broad tax cuts, and
America's worst financial crisis since the Great Depression:
Ibid.

As president, I had the honor of eulogizing Gerald Ford and
Ronald Reagan: George W. Bush, Decision Points, 473-477.

Quittin' drinking was one of the toughest decisions I ever made:
Ibid., 1-3.

Lies, and Damn Lies - Barack Obama's Phantom #44

It's catastrophic for the American people that you fell under Roy
Cohn's influence. Marie Brenner, How Donald Trump and
Roy Cohn's Ruthless Symbiosis Changed America, Vanity Fair,
June 28, 2017.

Joe McCarthy's right-hand man during the early 1950's when
they trumped up all kinds of false charges about the enemy
within: Ibid.

Cohn became the premier practitioner of hardball deal-making
and inside fixes: Ibid.

That's the man who taught you to scare potential adversaries
with hollow threats and spurious lawsuits: Ibid.

Wouldn't Roy love to see this moment? Boy do we miss him: Ibid.

it's fair to say that 77,000 votes out of more than 136 million
cast decided the election and 'trumped" the popular vote: John
McCormack, The Election Came Down to 77,744 Votes in

Pennsylvania, Wisconsin, and Michigan, washingtonexaminer. com, November 10, 2016.

made a joke during your last campaign about being paid by Russian President Vladimir Putin: Jake Sherman, Why Ryan called it quits, politico.com, April 11, 2018.

said in an interview that he was 'an old Jack Kemp guy who believed strongly in inclusive, aspirational politics that brought people together rather than divided them: Ibid.

The resulting polarization had made it harder to achieve political goodwill in America: Ibid.

the production served up a biting satire on American politics and the public attitude toward them: George and Ira Gerschwin. Book by George S. Kaufma and Morrie Ryskind, Of Thee I Sing, Gershwin.com

Wintergreen, the star of the musical, was elected President on a campaign of nonsense: Ibid.

two songs that are relevant yet today! One about impeachment and another about a woman wronged who makes her case public: Ibid.

White House chief of staff Mick Mulvaney confessed to Fox News that the Republican Congress never wanted to pass laws: Jonathan Chait, Republicans Keep Admitting Everything They Said About Obama Was a Lie, Fox News Sunday interview between Chris Wallace and Mick Mulvaney. NYMAG, Feb. 11, 2019.

the last thing they were interested in was giving me any legislative successes...particularly Mitch McConnell: Ibid.

He even boasted that he pressured Republicans to refuse to compromise: Ibid.

told Democratic leaders that he wouldn't work with them on shared priorities such as bringing down the cost of prescription drugs unless they stopped investigating him: Michael Collins, John Fritze, and Eliza Collins, Trump to Democrats: No deals on infrastructure, drug prices until they drop investigations, USA Today, May 22, 2019.

More than 1,000 former federal prosecutors have signed a statement: Ben Berwick and Kristy Parker, President Trump argues he Is above the law. A thousand prosecutors say he's wrong, Los Angeles Times, May 30, 2019.

On the 2050 PolitiFact scorecard, 70% of your statements were rated patently false: PoltiFact,Trumps statements were awarded PolitiFact's 2015 and 2017 Lie of the Year, politifact.com

Although in his first 869 days as president your hero said 10,796 things that were either misleading or outright false: Chris Cillizza, Donald Trump lies more often than you wash your hands every day, cnn.com, June 10, 2019.

Your frequent lies, distortions, and disclaimers make me wonder if you might have hardening of the arteries, Alzheimers, or some other form of dementia? Some certainly suspected that your presidential hero did: John Gartner, Trump's cognitive deficits seem worse. We need to know if he has dementia, USA Today, Apr 9, 2019.

Other politicians have some shame in dissembling, misrepresenting, spinning, prevaricating and masking the truth: Michael Wolff, Siege Trump Under Fire, 75-79.

when you began trying to defund the Center for Disease Control and Prevention: Liz Alesse, Did Trump try to cut the CDC's budget as Democrats claim? Analysis, abcnew.go.com, February 28, 2020 and Rachel Maddow, Trump dismantling of Obama era disease response leaves U.S. exposed (an interview with Laurie Garret, science journalist and healthy policy analyst), MSNBC, February 26, 2020

down-played its seriousness: Paul Krugman, Trump Can't Handle the Truth, New York Times, March 9, 2020

governor of South Dakota who refused to cancel the 80th Annual Sturgis Motorcyle Rally in Sturgies, S.D.: Wilson Wong and

Corky Siemaszko, Weeks after Sturgis motocycle rally, first Covid-19 death reported as cases accelerate in Midwest, nbcnew.com, Sept. 2, 2020.

'last week he signed more death certificates than in his entire life almost all put together: James Doubek, A Houston Doctor On His Hospital's Deadliest Week So Far, npr.org, July 31, 2020.

It's the worst three month collapse in our nation's history: Ben Cassellman, Virus Wipes Out 5 Years of Economic Growth, The New York Times, July 31, 2020.

By rebuffing the truths that science reveals about our planet and diseases, you've accelerated the collapse of the economy: Farhad Manjoo, Coronvairus is what you get when you ignore science, New York Times, March 4, 2020.

your days of feeling of believing that you can do whatever you want and not one can stop you: Daniel Maurer, Motherless Brooklyn: Robert Moses, Miles Davis, and Donald Trump Walk into a Film, bedfordandbowery.com, Oct 11, 2019.

Epstein, whom you called a really a terrific guy: David Fahrenhoid, Beth Reinhard, Kimberly Kindy, Trump called Epstein a terrific guy who enjoyed younger women before denying relationship with him, The Washinton Post, July 8, 2019.

Personally, I am proud of the Paris Climate Agreement, the Affordable Care Act, my election as the first black president, disposing of Osama bin Laden, and setting the nation on a path to economic recovery: David Von Drehle, Honor and Effort: What President Obama Achieve in Eight Years, Time. com, December 22, 2016.

My assessment is that you haven't grown in your capacity as president because you can't: Ted Johnson, Barack Obama, In Democratic Convention Speech, Will Say Trump Has Turned Presidency Into "One More Reality Show,: news.yahoo.com, August 19, 2020.

turned your presidency into one more sad reality show: Ibid.

The arc of the moral universe is long, but it bends toward justice: Steven Sarson, Barack Obama: American Historian, 294.

President #oo: Daniel Hands

A Final Reckoning - Two Scenarios

subpoenaed by Congress for tax evasion and falsified documents: CNBS, Trump and company could be under investigation for bank and insurance fraud, Manhattan DA Vance reveals, August 3, 2020.

Not since my hero Andrew Jackson swept the election back in the 1800's, when he did a great job, has anyone run a campaign like mine: Chris Cillizza, Donald Trump's 199 wildest lines of 2019, cnn.com, Dec 23, 2019.

On the side, I quietly hedged my bets and continued to work on my plan to build a classy Belladonna Hotel in Moscow Square: BBC, Four questions about Trump's tower in Moscow that never was, bbc.com, January 18, 2019.

I will get Putin on this program and we will get Hands elected: Ibid.

I was a little new to the job, a little new to the profession: Donald Trump's 199 wildest lines of 2019.

People that should have stepped up did not step up: Eli Stokols, Trump White House Saw Record Number of First-Year Staff Departures, The Wall Street Journal, Dec 28, 2017.

in my first 1,095 days in office, 489 top officials have left their positions: Adrienne Cobb, Tracking turnover in the Trump administration: Year three, forsensicnews.net, January 27, 2020.

I've heard as high as $275 billion we lose on illegal immigration: Chris Cillizza, The 36 wackiest lines from Donald Trump's totally bizarre Cabinet meeting, cnn.com, January 3, 2019.

created the President's Commission on Combating Drug Addiction and the Opioid Crisis: Lev Facher, As Trump claims credit for decline in opioid deaths, others see signs of danger ahead, www.statnews.com, July12, 2019. And, https://www. aaap.org/president-trumps-first-budget-commits-significant-resources-fight-opioid-epidemic/ and https://www.drugabuse. gov/drugs-abuse/opioids/opioid-overdose-crisis

had I acted sooner, over 30,000 lives could have been saved: Ben Gittleson, Study finds earlier coronavirus restrictions in US could have saved 36,000 lives, Trump calls it a 'political hit job,' abcnews.go.com, May 21, 2020.

That's why I gave the American people the greatest tax cuts ever. The deductible is so high: Ibid.

Much, much bigger, much better than anybody: Donald Trump's 199 wildest lines of 2019.

My tax action should preserve some congressional seats and Electoral College votes for my friends: Jansi Lo Wang, Census Door Knocking Cut A Month Short Amid Pressure To Finish Count: NPR, July 30, 2020.

No President has ever done what I have done for Evangelicals, or religion itself. It's not even close!: Donald J. Trump, @ realDonaldTrump 12:18 PM Dec 20, 2019 Tweet and 6:12 AM Dec 20, 2019 Tweet.

the former Texas governor told me that I was the Chosen One: Elizabeth Dias and Jeremy W. Peters, Evangelical Leaders Close Ranks With Trump After Scathing Editorial, The New York Times, Dec 20, 2019.

And I will be remembered as a professional at technology: Donald Trump's 199 wildest lines of 2019.

Census drag on it would have counted more of the estimated 40% who have yet to respond or be contacted: Elliot Hannon, Trump Administration Is Discontinuing the Census Count a Month Early. But Why? slate.com, Aug 04, 2020.

done more for black Americans than me: David Choi, Trump refuses to acknowledge John Lewis' achievements and claims

He's done more for Black Americans, businessinsider, Aug 4, 2020.

On the same weekend as the El Paso shooting, my good buddy Billy tweeted an image of a tombstone: Matthew Choi, Mitch McConnel Campaign Tweets Image of Tombstone With Opponent's Name, www.politico.com, August 05, 2019.

How was I to know they would spend $55 million on the 2016 elections, including $30 million to support me: Lesley Clark, Congress' NRA Loyalist Say New Gun Laws Won't Ease Shooting Sprees, newsobserver.com, February 15, 2018.

had the audacity to report that I made false claims about the effect of the U.S. tariffs: Lee Moran, Fox News Host: I Don't know Where To Begin Debunking Donald Trump's Latest Lie, Huffpost, August 3, 2019.

After the anti-Hispanic online manifesto of a shooter in El Paso who killed twenty-two people: Michael Crowley and Maggie Haberman, Trump Condemns White Supremacy but Stops Short on Major Gun Control, NYTimes, Aug 5, 2019.

counties that hosted a 2016 Trump rally saw a 226 percent increase in hate crimes: Ayal Feinberg, Regina Branton, and Valeri Martinez-Ebers, Counties That Hosted a 2016 Rally Saw A 226 Percent Increase In Hate Crimes, The Washington Post, March 22, 2019.

Senate Majority Leader, who repeatedly blocked discussion of gun control legislation: Nicholas Wu, This Is The Gun Conrol Legislation Mitch McConnell Won't Allow Senators to Vote On, USA Today, Aug 5, 2019.

he singled out six new congressmen and women who he claimed were critical of America. Christina Zhaq, Shepard smith and other Fox News Hosts Criticize Trump's Go Back Tweet: Xenophobic Eruption of Distraction, Newsweek, July 15, 2019 and Gianluca Mezzeofiore, These Americas share what it feels like to be told: Go back to where they came from, CNN, July 15, 2019.

He had pressured and brokered a peace initiative between Israel and the United Arab Emirates: BBC NEWS, Israel and UAE strike historic deal to normalize relations, www.bbc.com, August 13, 2020.

startled the nation when he eliminated over-time work at the post office and announced his decision to hold back their resources: Barbara Sprunt, Trump Opposes Postal Service Funding But Says He'd Sign Bill Including it, NPR August 13, 2020.

Neither understood the intricacies of the federal post office nor that it was a public service that was never intended to make a profit: Michael Warren and Kristen Holmes, With slower mail and election concerns, Trump's postmaster general is in the hot seat, CNN, Aug 16, 2020.

I've examined my soul and repent the hateful rhetoric I've spewed in the past about President Daniel Hands' political opponents: Joe Walsh, Trump Needs a Primary Challenge, Opinion Column The New York Times, August 14, 2019.

POTUS is careless on fiscal matters: Ibid.

we require a candidate who can look Little Big Hands squarely in the eye: Ibid.

Scenario One

The leaders of the Neti Pot Wing used the same instruments of power mastered by dictators around the globe who clung to their office for years: Robert Wuench, Freelance Writer, Author (Ashes on His Boot and Civil Sword), and retired Caterpillar executive. His five steps are a reflection of having done business in Africa, the Middle East, and Latin America as well as personal observations of eight dictators. The author added a sixth.

he eliminated over-time work at the post office and announced his decision to hold back their resources: Emily Cochrane,

Hailey Fuchs, Kenneth Vogel, and Jessica Silver Greenberg, Postal Service Suspends Changes After Outcry Over Delivery Slowdown, The New York Times, Aug. 18, 2020.

In a blatant attempt to disenfranchise voters: Ibid.

called to testify before the House and Senate and twenty state attorneys general said they would file lawsuits; Ibid.

The timing of Jerry Falwell's suspension from the head of Liberty University, a Christian focused campus: Paul Bedard, Exclusive: Falwell says Fatal Attraction threat led to depression, Washington Examiner, August 23, 2020.

He also foolishly posted a video of himself with an arm around a woman with both of their shorts unzipped: an unheralded natural disaster occurred in the Gulf of Mexico: Times Digest, After Storm, Smashed Glass and Vagrant Boats, The New York Times, August 28, 2020.

He turned the people's house into a political house, a violation of the Hatch Act: Domenico Montanaro, 7 Takeaways From The Republican National Convention, NPR, August 28, 2020.

Scenario Two

Why Little Big Hands had remained popular with a lot of polite Southerners for so long defied convention: Isaac Chotiner, Why Stuart Stevens Wants to Defeat Donald Trump, The New Yorker, August 03, 2020.

The Lincoln Project, a group of dedicated Americans, who held accountable those who violated their oath to the Constitution.

if he got re-elected, he might replace his whole cabinet: Jennifer Jacobs, Trump Says He May Ask for Resignation of Cabinet if Re-Elected. Bloomberg, August 15, 2020.

He was accused in a scheme to use funds designated for construction for personal expenses: Stephanie Saul and Michael

S. Schmidt, Steve Bannon Is Charged With Fraud in We Build the Wall Campaign, The New York Times, August 20, 2020.

Facebook removed or restricted QAnon accounts and other far right groups from its main social network: Kurt Wagner and Sarah Frier, Facebook Removes Hundreds of QAnon Groups, Limits Thousands More, Bloomberg, August 19, 2020.

Judicial Watch, a conservative tax-exempt group, that POTUS's golf outings had topped $110 million thirty months into his presidency: S.V. Date, Trump Golf Costs Top $110 Million – More Than Estimate For All of Obama's Travel, Huffpost, Aug 3, 2019.

Twitter and Facebook removed his posts: David Greene and Shannon Bond, Twitter, Facebook Remove Trump Post Over False Claim About Children and Covid-19. npr.org, August 5, 2020.

report confirmed that personnel on Little Big Hand's 2016 campaign did have contacts with the Russians: Dustin Volz and Warren P. Strobel, Senate Panel's Probe Found Counterintelligence Risks In Trump's 2016 Campaign, The Wall Street Journal, Aug 18, 2020. And Jeremy Herb, Marshall Cohen, and Katelyn Polantz, Bipartisan Senate report details Trump campaign contacts with Russia in 2016, adding to Mueller Findings, cnn.com, August 18, 2020.

The cruelness factor got magnified when Little Big Hands called those who died in military action 'losers' and those who served 'suckers': Jeffrey Goldberg, Trump: Americans Who Died in War Are 'Losers and Suckers,'theatlantic.com, September 3, 2020.

He even wondered "Who were the good guys in this war?": Ibid.

an epidemic of myopic, partisan ignorance: Author Brandon Weber, Facebook post, August 20, 2019.

She pledged that she would not play Russian roulette with the Coronavirus like her adversary: Peter Baker and Annie

Karnie, Trump Accuses Democrats of Outbreak Hoax, New York Times, February 29, 2020.

She chastised him for entertaining a 'herd immunity' solution that could conceivably claim over two million lives: Yasmeen Abutaleb and Josh Dawsey, Trump advisor pushing 'herd immunity,' Houston Chronicle, September 1, 2020.

might be an action in self- defense: Alana Wise, Trump Defends Kenosha Shooting Suspect, NPR, August 31, 2020.

blamed all the bad news and resulting crash in the stock market on what he labeled "his nasty political enemies' rhetoric": Gabriel Sherman, He's Definitely Melting Down Over This: Trump, Germaphobe in Chief, Struggles to Control the Covid-19 Story, Vanity Fair, March 9, 2020.

everything wrong in Washington began with the Republican Senate Majority Leader from Kentucky, decades ago: Jennifer Steinhauer, Amy McGrath Opens Campaign to Oust Mitch McConnell in Kentucky, New York Times, July 9, 2019.

Drawing upon a quote from Winston Churchill about one of his own adversaries: Andrew Roberts, Churchill Walking With Destiny, 919.

President Little-Big Hands' rude hand practically annihilated the institution we know as the United States of America: Philip Rucker and Carol Leonnig, A Very Stable Genius, Penguin Publishing Group, 2020, 7-8 (Prologue).

Over the course of four years he almost pulled down what our forefather's prudence, deliberation and foresight took centuries to build: Ibid.

a cultural change blossomed in America called the 'Civic Renaissance: Ibid.

During her time in office Springer took every opportunity she could, by word and example, to remind those serving in her administration and Congress and the American people that rudeness and kindness trickle down from above: Jennifer Latson, Rudenesss, and kindness, trickle down from above, Houston Chronicle, March 6, 2020.

a Senate that had forgotten how to deliberate and legislate: Susan Davis, A New Biden Administration Would Face Old Problems With Congress, npr.org, August 20, 2020.

all they had done the previous four years was advance her list of preferred nominees for lifetime appointments on the federal bench: Ibid.

'swing back to the old days of more bipartisanship" Ibid.

There was plenty of work for them all to do: Ibid.

She contended that the situation is so bad that that only about 40% of Americans trust our elections: Michael Douglas, Unbreaking America, Divided We Fall, America Has Been Hijacked, @represent.us, December 20, 2019.

Springer, leading by example, joined the *Represent Us* movement (@represent.us) and advocated membership in this bi-partisan organization, or one like it: Ibid.

if real change in government were to ever occur, it would come by passing and implementing, state by state, The American Anti-Corruption Act, or something similar: Ibid.

Epilogue

George Washington was the first President to reward his voters: Paul Bedard, George Washington Plied Voters with Booze, U.S. New and World Report, Nov. 8, 2011.

When Lincoln became convinced that the entire democratic foundation was about to implode, he assumed unprecedented authority to wage war: Presidents of War, 236-237.

Declaring a true national emergency, he suspended habeas corpus, created military courts to try civilians, and used his sweeping powers: Tried by War, 269.

"Throughout the war, he made clear that his expansion of presidential authority was intended merely for the duration of the conflict: Presidents of War, 236-237.

He did not seek power for himself to satisfy any ego or clandestine purpose: Ibid.

Lincoln's leadership illustrates the overwhelming importance of political skill and preparation to hold the highest office in the land: Ibid.

while president, he applied his parliamentary skills to relate to congress and to consult members when strong differences of opinion emerged: Ibid.

Another important difference between the three men is that Lincoln did not try to trick or lie to Congress and the American people to suit his purposes: Ibid.

Jefferson feared that the America President yielded too much power and he resisted the temptation to magnify the pomp and power of the office of the President. Jefferson: Architect of American Liberty, 453.

Americans must not forget that German Chancellor Adolph Hitler and French statesman and military leader Napoleon Bonaparte a rose to power in a republic: Ian Kershaw, How Democracy Produce A Monster, The New York Times, February 3, 2008.

Alarmingly, a similar beat goes on in over fifty countries today run by dictators and autocrats: Dictatorship Countries 2019, World Population Review.

How much does character matter in the selection of a president and how do we define, measure and judge it: Jim Lehrer, Character Above All, PBS Broadcast Transcripts Parts 1-5, https://www.pbs.org/newshour/spc/character/transcript/trans1.html, May 29, 1996.

To get some answers, Jim Leher, an icon in the broadcasting world and host of twelve presidential debates, moderated a classic discussion Character Above All: Ibid.

Some of their measures included the company a person keeps, how truthful he is, how he treats others, a sense of fair play, and acceptance of personal responsibility and blame: Ibid.

Another way to get a glimpse of at character is reflected in a new survey the military began using in 2020 to promote officers to battalion commanders: Nancy A. Youssef, In Generational Shift, Army Uses a New System to Promote Hundreds of Officers, Wall Street Journal, March 4, 2020.

I have seen the great mass of ideologies grow and spread before my eyes: Roger Cohen, Trump's Plague, The New York Times, September 5, 2020.

"We weaken our greatness when we confuse our patriotism with tribal rivalries: Joe Pierre, M.D., Why Has America Become So Divided? Psychology Today, Sep 05, 2018.

GLOSSARY OF PERSONS, ENTITIES AND PLACES

Nonfictional

All the presidential visitors either ghosts (deceased) or phantoms (living). Listed in order and by the number of their presidency.

Spiro Agnew – Nixon's Vice President sent to jail
Winston Churchill – UK Prime Minister
Roy Cohn – Joseph McCarthy's disciple, a political fixer, and corrupt businessman
John Dean – Nixon's White House Counsel
Allen Dulles – US Director of the CIA
John Foster Dulles – US Secretary of State
HR Haldeman – Nixon's Chief of Staff
Herbert Humphrey – Democratic candidate for president opposing Nixon
Robert Kennedy – President Kennedy's advisor and eventual US Attorney General
Joseph McCarthy – A vicious and corrupt US Senator
Robert McNamara – Secretary of Defense
Edward R. Murrow – Top reporter for CBS
Aleksey Navalny – Russian activist and politician
Vladimir Putin – Russian President

Tom Railsback – Moderate US Congressman from the author's hometown

Dr. Joseph Varon – Chief of Critical Care at Houston's United Memorial Medical Center

Charley Wilson – General Motor's CEO

Fictional

Val Z. Antrom – U.S. Senate candidate for West Virginia

Back Swamp – Nearest Louisiana town to Belladonna estate

Belladonna – President Daniel Hands's mansion and estate in Back Swamp, LA

Sir Jamie Z. Baird – U.K. Ambassador to the U.S.

Tony Z. Bark – U.S Attorney General

Belladonna – President Hands's expansive and ostentatious estate

Willard Z.Bliss – Garfield's quack doctor

Joseph Z. Borsch – Russian born businessman with ties to the mob

Billy Z. Brickell – U.S. Senate Majority Leader

Jerome Z. Buster – Lt. Governor of Texas

Justin Z. Daniels – Supreme Court Judge

Shane Z. Dickens – Post Office General

Timothy Justin Fannon – Chief architect for POTUS's bid for president in 2016 and later White House Chief strategist

Free Ticket Wing – Extreme liberals

Ferret and Opossum News – An ultra-right-wing broadcast network

All Ghosts – Deceased Presidents

Josephine Z. Greensmith – Press secretary intern

Anthony Z. Hands – President Daniel Hands's father

Blair Hands – President Hands's first wife, divorced

Bubba Z. Hands – President Hands's younger brother

Charla Z. Hands – President Hands's niece

Daniel Z. Hands – President #00 aka Little Big Hands and POTUS

Jessica and Clyde Z. Hands – President Hands's children from first wife

Little Big Hands – President #00 aka Daniel Hands and POTUS

Natasha Z. Hands – President Hands's third wife, separated

Penelope Z. Hands – Presidents Hands's older sister

Andrey Z. Handtrov – President Hands's grandfather

Angelica Z. Hernandez – Dutiful cook

Sarah Z. Hernandez – The cook's young daughter attending medical school

Marjory Z. Hickenbottom – POTUS's part time caddy and club hostess

Jasper Z. Johnson – POTUS's grandfather on his mother's side

Ms. Lily Z. Knockwurst – A lady of the evening

Jamie Z. Leaks – Head of the EPA

Michael Z. Mickey – Chief of Staff

Craig Z. Millert – Special Counsel for U.S. Department of Justice

Paul Z. McCavity - Former POTUS campaign manager and felon

Governor Morebucks – aka Poppy Warbucks, U.S. Vice President and former governor of LA

All Phantoms – Living Presidents

Neti Pot Wing – Extreme conservatives

Henry Z. Noxolo – White House janitor

Timothy Z. Noxolo – Henry's brilliant teenage son

Roger Z. Oaks – Secretary of State

Spud Z. Oehler – Iowa farmer

Cliff Z. Parsons – Conservative political consultant, lobbyist and convicted felon

Charles Z. Pastor – POTUS's personal assistant

Art Z. Pigeon – Former governor of Texas

Nancy Z. Pilar – The Democrat Speaker of the U.S. House of Representatives from California

POTUS – President #00 aka President Daniel Hands and Little Big Hands

William Z. Rankles – Host of popular conservative talk show

Annie Oakley Remington – A prominent broadcaster for Ferret and Opossum News

Chauncey Yellow Robe – Prominent Lakota activist and teacher.

Wesley Z. Smith – The former Republican Speaker of the U.S. House of Representatives

Eileen Choy Z. Springer – Candidate for president opposing Daniel Hands

Dr. Stanley Z. Steward – Director of the National Institute of Allergy and Infectious Diseases

Dr. Wots Z. Themater – POTUS's physician

Madison Z. Treacher – President of Liberty U

Marcus Z. Valentini – Little Big Hand's personal lawyer and unofficial ambassador

Poppy Warbucks – Vice President and former governor of Louisiana aka Morebucks

Swisher Z. Wilson – Iowa farmer

Roger Z. Yikes – Little Big Hand's personal lawyer

Dominick Z. York – U.S Attorney for Southern District of New York

Breta Z. Youngburg – Sixteen-year-old climate activist from Sweden

ABOUT THE AUTHOR

James Mikel Wilson has either traveled, worked, or lived in over thirty countries and forty-seven states. This is his fourth book, a hybrid of political satire and historical fiction. He is the recipient of the Author Academy Award in historical fiction. One of his works has been converted to a stage play. Wilson collects Lionel trains, North American Indian artifacts, and books signed by U.S. Presidents and First Ladies. He and his wife have enjoyed the company of five dogs. He is a Son of the American Revolution and a war veteran.

Wilson's previous books are *Paw Tracks Here and Abroad: A Dog's Tale, Churchill and Roosevelt: The Big Sleepover at the White House, and Mr. Froggy's Dilemma.* The author is a member of The Authors Guild. To learn more about him go to www.jamesmikelwilson.com